Helen Toner and John Reynolds

Cambridge O Level

English Language

Coursebook

Second edition

CAMBRIDGE
UNIVERSITY PRESS

CAMBRIDGE
UNIVERSITY PRESS

University Printing House, Cambridge CB2 8BS, United Kingdom

One Liberty Plaza, 20th Floor, New York, NY 10006, USA

477 Williamstown Road, Port Melbourne, VIC 3207, Australia

4843/24, 2nd Floor, Ansari Road, Daryaganj, Delhi – 110002, India

79 Anson Road, #06–04/06, Singapore 079906

Cambridge University Press is part of the University of Cambridge.

It furthers the University's mission by disseminating knowledge in the pursuit of education, learning and research at the highest international levels of excellence.

www.cambridge.org
Information on this title: education.cambridge.org

© Cambridge University Press 2016

First published in 2008
Second edition 2016
20 19 18 17 16 15 14 13 12 11 10 9 8 7 6 5 4 3

Printed in Poland by Opolgraf

A catalogue record for this publication is available from the British Library

ISBN 978-1-107-61080-4 Paperback

Additional resources for this publication at education.cambridge.org

....

Contents

Preface

This book is written by two experienced teachers of GCE and O Level English and is intended specifically to help students following the Cambridge O Level English Language syllabus (1123) and their teachers.

The book is in two sections: Section 1 deals with the requirements of Directed Writing and Composition and Section 2, which deals with Reading for Ideas and Reading for Meaning. In both sections you will find information about key skills required for success, practice exercises, exemplar material for the different tasks and useful advice on how to improve your work. The book is designed to be used both as a textbook to support you throughout your English course and also as a study aid to help you to prepare for examinations.

The list of people from whom the authors have received advice and assistance is far too long for them all to be included here. However, we would, in particular, like to record our thanks to all the teachers with whom we have worked over the years and from whom we have learnt so much and, in particular, to the thousands of students whose various skills and limitations have provided the basis for much of the advice in this book.

Acknowledgements

The authors and publishers acknowledge the following sources of copyright material and are grateful for the permissions granted. While every effort has been made, it has not always been possible to identify the sources of all the material used, or to trace all copyright holders. If any omissions are brought to our notice, we will be happy to include the appropriate acknowledgements on reprinting.

Past exam paper questions throughout are reproduced by permission of Cambridge International Examinations

pp. 20, 31 *Himalaya* by Michael Palin, with permission from The Orion Publishing Group; p. 29 *A Goddess in the Stones: travels in India* by Norman Lewis, Picador; p. 30 From *Neither Here Nor There* by Bill Bryson, published by Doubleday, reprinted by permission of The Random House Group Limited, and Bill Bryson; p. 39 'Why homework is a bad idea' by Liz Elias, writing on Hub Pages as DzyMzLizzy; p. 43 *I Can't Stay Long* by Laurie Lee, reproduced with permission of Curtis Brown, Ltd, London on behalf of Laurie Lee, copyright © 1975; p. 47 *Sequins for a Ragged Hem* by Amryl Johnson; p. 52 *My Family and Other Animals* by Gerald Durrell, reproduced by permission of Curtis Brown, London; p. 60 'Coconuts' is used by kind permission of the author, David Iglehart; p. 82 excerpt from *Atonement* by Ian McEwan, published by Jonathan Cape, reproduced by permission of The Random House Group, Ltd., and with permission of Rogers Coleridge and White, and used by permission of Doubleday, an imprint of the Knopf Doubleday Publishing Group, a division of Penguin Random House LLC. All rights reserved © 2002 by Ian McEwan; p. 83 *Long Walk to Freedom* by Nelson Mandela, Little, Brown and Company; p. 90 excerpt from *Travels on my Elephant* by Mark Shand reprinted by permission of Eland Publishing Ltd © Mark Shand 1991; pp. 91, 133, 143 Extract from *Scottish Mysteries* by Donald M. Fraser is reproduced by permission of Mercat Press, an imprint of Birlinn Ltd; p. 94 excerpts adapted from *Disasters at Sea* by Captain Richard A Cahill, used by permission of The Nautical Institute; pp. 130, 131 *Miss Garnet's Angel* by Sally Vickers, reprinted by permission of HarperCollins Publishers Ltd © 2000 Sally Vickers; pp. 134, 152 *The Greenpeace Book of Coral Reefs* by Sue Wells and Nick Hanna, Sterling Publishing, 1992; pp. 136, 138, 145 *The God of Small Things* by Arundhati Roy, copyright © Arundhati Roy, 1997; p. 137 *World's Apart: An Explorer's Life* by Robin Hanbury-Tenison, Arrow Books with permission of the author; pp. 139, 145, 146 excerpts from *Animals on the Farm* by Judy Urquhart, used by kind permission of the author; p. 142 *The Power and the Glory* by Graham Greene, Viking Penguin, David Higham Associates; pp. 146, 152, 165 *The Death of Venice* by Stephen Fay & Philip Knightley, Andre Deutsch, 1976; p. 155 *The Millstone* by Margaret Drabble, 1965, Weidenfeld & Nicolson; pp. 166, 167 *Chocolat* by Joanne Harris, published by Doubleday, reprinted by permission of The Random House Group Limited.

Photos:
Cover debra millet/Alamy Stock Photo; p. 10 Darrin Henry/Fotolia; p. 14 schok-oladenseite/Fotolia; p. 17 mellsva/Fotolia; p. 19 RTimages/Shutterstock; p. 20 ElenaMirage/Fotolia; p. 24 Tyler Olson/Fotolia; p. 30 MasterLu/Fotolia; p. 35 JackF/Fotolia; p. 37 Monkey Business/Fotolia; p. 38 Jandrie Lombard/Fotolia; p. 41 Richard Rosser/REX Shutterstock; p. 45 NAN/Fotolia; p. 48 Prisma Bildagentur AG/Alamy Stock Photo; p. 49 M.studio/Fotolia; p. 52 mgkuijpers/Fotolia; p. 60 Harald Biebel/Fotolia; p. 66 rosinka79/Fotolia; p. 79 sergio34/Fotolia; p. 81 Monkey Business/Fotolia ; p. 82 nikonomad/Fotolia; p. 83 Richard Young/REX Shutterstock; p. 85 gornostaj/Fotolia; p. 87 Igor Mojzes/Fotolia; p. 90 Brad Pict/Fotolia; p. 91 huci/Fotolia; p. 92 Atmosphere1/Shutterstock; p. 93 milatas/Fotolia; p. 94 Michael Rosskothen/Fotolia; p. 95 photographicss/Fotolia; p. 95 Freesurf/Fotolia; p. 106 ChameleonsEye/Shutterstock; p. 107 zatletic/Fotolia; p. 111 moonrise/Fotolia; p. 112 borisoff/Fotolia; p.117 snaptitude/Fotolia; p. 117 gstockstudio/Fotolia; p. 117 liza5450/Fotolia; p. 121 Markus Mainka/Fotolia; p. 124 whim_dachs/Fotolia; p. 126 Sergey Peterman/Fotolia; p. 128 Halfpoint/Fotolia; p. 139 Hortigüela/Fotolia; p. 136 LeitnerR/Fotolia; p. 137 quickshooting/Fotolia; p. 139 ellemarien7/Fotolia; p. 144 jamocki/Fotolia; p. 147 ET1972/Fotolia; p. 149 Tim Gainey/Alamy Stock Photo; p. 154 lapas77/Fotolia; p. 157 daniel_kaesche/Fotolia; p. 159 Minerva Studio/Fotolia; p. 163 Yuri Bizgaimer/Fotolia; p. 167 xalanx/Fotolia; p. 168 Petr Malyshev/Fotolia

General Introduction

The Cambridge O Level English syllabus is divided into Writing and Reading and, in order to reflect that division, the textbook is divided into two main sections, one on Writing and the other on Reading. As you work with the textbook, you will find explanations of the skills you are required to learn which will help you prepare for your examinations. You will be given exercises to help you to build up these skills in a progressive manner.

The syllabus has been revised recently and the book takes this into consideration, outlining the changes as they occur. It is hoped that you will see that these changes are minimal in terms of the skills you need.

Each of the two main sections of the textbook, that on Writing and that on Reading, has a brief introduction in which the content of the section is described. Each introduction is followed by a number of chapters which are designed to take you through particular aspects of the syllabus, offering you explanations, exercises and links to the appropriate Assessment Objectives.

It would clearly not be desirable to study English without speaking it, even if your study is not geared towards an oral examination. Consequently, many of the exercises in this book are designed to be tackled with a partner or in a group. Your teacher will decide which of these exercises he or she wishes you to complete on your own, and which he or she wishes you to complete in pair or group discussion. Pair and group discussions are easy and enjoyable ways to learn to speak better English.

Disclaimer: *'The questions, example answers, marks awarded and/or comments that appear in this book were written by the author(s). In the examination, the way marks would be awarded to answers like these may be different.'*

Cambridge International Examinations bears no responsibility for the example answers to questions taken from its past question papers which are contained in this publication.

1 Introduction to Writing

Assessment of your writing skills comprises two parts in the Cambridge examinations, namely Directed Writing and Composition.

Being able to express yourself and your thoughts fluently and precisely in written English is a valuable skill that is fundamental to everyone's life and is one that you will need to practise in a wide range of contexts, such as writing letters to support applications for jobs or for university places, reports for information and discussion and even to fulfil your ambition to make your fortune by writing the best-selling novel that is deep inside you. Communicating your ideas in writing, as you are well aware, is also an integral requirement of many of the subjects that you are studying in school.

No matter what the purpose of your writing, it is important at all times to keep the audience for whom you are writing clearly in mind and to ask yourself questions such as, *'Will what I am writing be understood by the people who will be reading it?', 'Have I chosen the most suitable words to convey exactly what I mean?'* etc.etc.

The writing tasks in the Cambridge O Level English Language syllabus teach you skills on how well you can convey clearly to a reader your ideas on and understanding of a particular topic through careful choice of vocabulary, accuracy of spelling, punctuation and grammar and your ability to structure and organise your ideas by using paragraphs.

Paper 1 is the Writing Paper . It lasts for 1 hour and 30 minutes and in total is worth 60 marks. There are two parts to the paper and you must answer both of them.

1 **Directed Writing** requires you to respond to a task relevant to the world of study, work or the community and write, for example, a letter, speech, report or article. You are usually expected to write about 200–300 words. Teachers will assess your work in terms of its fitness for purpose and the quality of written expression.

2 **Composition** requires you to write an essay, both language (written expression) and content being of importance here. You should write about 350–500 words on one topic only. You are usually offered a choice of five narrative/ descriptive/argumentative essay titles.

These two writing tasks will test your ability to 'communicate accurately, appropriately and effectively in writing'. In order to demonstrate this, you will need to develop skills as defined in the following assessment objectives.

1. W1 Articulate experience and express what is thought, felt and imagined

2. W2 Sequence facts, ideas and opinions

3. W3 Use a range of appropriate vocabulary

4. W4 Use register appropriate to audience and context

5. W5 Make accurate use of spelling, punctuation and grammar

You are expected to articulate experience and express what is thought, felt and imagined.
This means that you should consciously choose words and use a range of sentence structures and types along with appropriate literary devices, such as similes and metaphors, that your readers can both understand and share your experiences, thoughts and feelings or those of a character which you have created as part of a story.

You are expected to communicate using a register appropriate to audience and context.
This means that you should adapt your language and the content of your writing to meet the requirements of the task you have been set and to appeal to the specific audience for whom you are writing.

You are expected to sequence facts, ideas and opinions.
This means that whatever type of essay you write you should ensure that the ideas it contains are structured to develop logically from one point to the next by the use of planned and linked paragraphs.

You are expected to communicate clearly, using a range of appropriate vocabulary.
This means that you should choose the words you use carefully in order to convey your meaning precisely; that you should structure your sentences logically and use a range of sentence types; that you should organise your work into paragraphs and that there should be a focused and consistent development of ideas from beginning to end.

You are expected to communicate accurately.
This will be assessed through how well you use correct Standard English spelling, grammar, punctuation and vocabulary in particular.

Time constraints

Suppose you are given 1 hour and 30 minutes in an examination. During this time you must plan and write two separate tasks. You should not have any serious problems with completing both tasks in the time available but keeping the following points in mind may help you to do so effectively.

- It is suggested that you write between 200–300 words for Directed Writing and between 350–500 words for Composition. You should certainly not exceed the upper word limit. By doing so, you will put yourself under unnecessary pressure. In practice, about 250 words for Directed Writing and 450 words for Composition should be adequate.

- Remember that the quality of your written English is more important than the quantity you write.

- In any examination, read through the question paper carefully before you start to write. Before entering the examination room you should already have some idea of the type of essay which you are most confident about writing well under examination conditions.

  Remember that you only have one chance in an examination – do not spoil it by deciding on a whim to attempt a type of essay with which you are not confident.

- Teachers often notice that many students choose to write on a topic about which they have very few ideas and for which they lack the imagination and vocabulary range required to write convincingly. This applies particularly to those students who mistakenly choose the narrative or argumentative topics and run out of ideas after the first two paragraphs.

- Once you have decided on the title on which you will write in Composition, make sure that you have a clear understanding of exactly what is required of you; many students limit their performance by only partially following the instructions of the title and writing an essay not on the given topic but on something only loosely connected with it.

  Before starting on Directed Writing, be sure that you have a good understanding of the topics for Composition; it is a good idea to know what the task involves so that you plan how best to apportion your time.

- Spend some time planning before you begin to write. However, do not take planning to extremes – there is absolutely no need to write your complete essay for Composition as a rough draft and then to re-write it more neatly; doing this just increases the pressure you are under. However, you should make a plan of the basic structure of your essay and organise this plan into paragraph topics.

  It is a good idea to make sure that you know how your essay will conclude before you start to write it.

- Remember the reader; you are writing something which may be read by someone who lives in another part of the world and almost certainly belongs to a different generation and culture from yours. The more you can engage and entertain that reader, the more successful your writing is likely to be.

  Think about the sort of information you need to give so that the reader can understand clearly what you are writing about; choose your words carefully to give as clear a picture of what you are describing as you can.

- You can best engage the reader by writing about something with which you are familiar; always try to set your essay within a context or background which is or could be within your own experience.

- Try to avoid relying too much on re-hashing other essays which you have done in preparing for your examinations as it is very difficult to make such material fit the particular topic on which you are writing.

Standard English

The syllabus aims require you to write in Standard English and also to employ different forms of writing to suit a range of purposes. Let us look at these requirements in greater detail.

It is easy to misinterpret what is meant by the phrase 'Standard English'. It is not an instruction to write in an unnecessarily formal and over-literary style.

However, it is important when you are producing a piece of Composition to keep in mind the fact that the person for whom you are writing will be of an older generation and living in a country several thousands of miles away. This is not to say that your readers will not be familiar with teenagers and their attitudes, but they may not be fully up-to-date with the colloquial or dialect terms which you might use as a matter of course when speaking to your own friends. **Standard English is the use of the accepted conventions of expression and grammatical structures which are common to speakers and writers of English of all ages throughout the world.**

Writing to suit a range of purposes

- You should adapt your writing to meet the requirements of the particular task you have chosen and use a tone and register which will be suitable for your chosen genre and the audience for whom you are writing. You might be asked to write a letter to a friend or to write a report of an incident for your Headteacher; the latter requires a different format from the former; it also requires a more formal tone in your writing as it is highly unlikely that you would write a formal report for your Headteacher in the same relaxed style that you would use when writing to a friend of your own age. Teachers are appreciative of students who show that they have read the question carefully to adopt a tone which is suitable for their purpose.

- While writing an essay, a letter, a speech, a report or anything else, you should always remember the teachers who will be reading your work. They are likely to appreciate your adoption of a suitable tone (for example, your use of an appropriate valediction at the end of a letter or your introduction of convincing personal references in the main body of the letter) but will be considerably less impressed if you use the abbreviations suitable for text messaging, as these are not Standard English usage.

- It is important that you adapt your tone to suit the requirements of the particular type of essay that you are writing. For example, you need to consider whether writing the essay in the first person ('I think that . . .') is preferable to adopting a more formal or impersonal tone ('People think that . . .'). Again, if you choose to write the narrative topic, what style of narrative are you going to produce and what typical features of that style will most effectively suit the tale you are going to tell? If you choose a descriptive essay, should you write a factual or impressionistic description? Whichever you choose, it is important that you use a vocabulary which is suitable to your chosen approach and that your approach stays consistent throughout your essay.

- Finally, remember to write legibly and present your finished work clearly and attractively. Although your teachers might not assess your work on the quality of your handwriting, it is important to ensure that they can easily read what you have written. Illegible words and phrases result in the reader having only a partial understanding of what you are trying to say and this is likely to result in your being less successful than would be the case if your answers were clearly written.

2 The different types of Composition tasks

Argumentative essays

An argumentative essay is one that requires you to put forward a point of view and to justify your reasons for holding it. You will be judged on how effectively you present your ideas through the ways in which they are structured and by the examples you use to support them. It is not usually necessary to try to consider in detail both sides of any argument but it is important that you develop your ideas logically in order to produce a convincing and persuasive conclusion. It is likely that you will write in a formal register although you should avoid sounding too pompous.

Descriptive essays

Descriptive essays may ask you to write about a place or to describe a person or an event. The title will almost certainly give you the opportunity to describe a place or a person that you know well or an event which happened to you. (It is worth keeping in mind that the readers of your essay are unlikely to have a close knowledge of the person or place that you are describing. So the more details you can give in your writing, the more interest there will be for the person reading it.) It is likely that you will use an informal or even colloquial approach when writing this type of essay.

Some students mistakenly think that the best way to approach this type of task is by making up the person or place which they are describing; this is not a particularly good idea as it increases the difficulty and pressure of the task. It is far better to spend your time thinking about choosing the most effective vocabulary and comparisons to bring alive the very special qualities of a place or person you know well, rather than spending this time in trying to imagine a place or a person who does not exist.

Discursive essays

Discursive essays allow you to explore your ideas about a particular topic. They differ from argumentative titles because you are not required to develop your ideas logically towards a particular conclusion but instead to consider different aspects of a particular idea or situation. Teachers usually look at how well you can consider the implications of the points you make and how skilfully you can relate them to the central topic about which you are writing. You may want to adopt a formal tone and an impartial approach to the topic but it is equally acceptable to write about it from your own personal standpoint.

Personal essays

Personal essays are a mixture of descriptive and discursive essays that require you to write about something which you have experienced personally. It may be something like your first day at school or a family occasion in which you have taken part. Teachers generally expect you to choose an actual occasion in your life and to give a true account of it. However, a successful personal essay depends very much on how skilfully the writer selects and organises details of the event being described; you may find that it is a good idea to re-order details in order to make them more interesting to your reader. Remember that although the situation you are writing about may be very familiar to you, it will be necessary to provide some context for the events so that your reader is not confused. Personal writing can produce some very enjoyable accounts but the best are always carefully structured to achieve maximum effect.

Narrative essays

Narrative essays require you to write a story and may either provide you with a sentence on which to base your writing or ask you to write a story based on a particular situation. Many students choose to write a narrative essay as they think that it is an easy choice but, in fact, it is very difficult to construct and write a convincing short story within a given period of time. If you choose this topic, it is important that you have a clear understanding of what the title requires before you begin to write and that you avoid creating too involved or too complicated a plot. Planning is very important with this type of essay as it is very easy to get caught up in the story which you are making up and then find that you have introduced so many interesting characters and so many twists and turns into the plot that you've actually got enough material for a three-volume novel and nowhere near enough time to write it in!

3 Key writing skills

In order to write English confidently and accurately, it is important that you have a sound understanding of the various technicalities of writing, such as the different parts of speech, punctuation, spelling, grammar and usage. In order to ensure your understanding of these, the following sections contain the main details that you should be familiar with. There are also some exercises to test your understanding.

Parts of speech

The different words in a sentence have different functions. In order to have a clear understanding of the mechanics of writing, it is important to know the names of the different parts of speech and to be aware of their features.

Nouns

> **Key terms**
>
> **Nouns** are naming words; they apply to the names given to persons, places or things.

The different types of nouns are as follows:

- **Common nouns**: A common noun is the name of any unspecified person, place or thing, for example girl, town, car.

- **Proper nouns**: A proper noun is the name given to a particular person, place or thing, for example Leena, Mumbai, Toyota.

- **Abstract nouns:** An abstract noun is the name given to something intangible like an idea, for example thought, love, happiness.

- **Collective nouns:** A collective noun is a single word, which describes a collection of things or people, for example flock, team, audience, queue. There is no hard and fast rule as to whether collective nouns should be considered grammatically as singular or plural. However, if the collection of things is functioning as a single unit then it should be expressed using the singular. If, however, the noun describes a collection of individuals functioning independently, then it could be expressed using the plural.

  Think of the difference between these two statements: *The team was playing well* and *The team were playing badly*.

Verbs

For example
i   The boy *kicked* the football.
ii   The tap *dripped*.
iii The caterpillar *became* a butterfly.

In each of these examples the verb is the word written in italics.

In the first example, the verb 'kicked' is followed by the noun 'football', which is referred to technically as the object of the verb. A verb which is followed by an object is called a **transitive verb**.

In the second example, there is no object in the sentence and a verb like 'dripped', which is not followed by an object is, therefore, called **an intransitive verb**.

Finally, the verb in the third example 'became' expresses a state of being and not an action. In this sentence, the subject of the verb 'caterpillar' and the word following it 'butterfly' refer to the same thing; the word following verbs like 'become' is referred to as the complement of the sentence.

A **finite or main verb** is a form of verb which expresses an action or state of being, which is complete in itself. It has tense (past, present or future) and number (singular or plural); for example: I walked along the road. He waits for me at the corner. It is a fine day. There are no clouds in the sky. Tomorrow will bring both sunshine and rain. All of these simple sentences make complete sense and it is the form of the verb which ensures that this is so.

Another feature of a finite verb is that it can be in either the active or the passive voice. In the former, the subject of the verb performs the action ('The dog bit the man') whereas in the latter, the subject suffers the action of the verb ('The man was bitten by the dog').

Not all forms of the verb, however, convey a complete meaning and, therefore, need to relate to something else in the sentence. Such forms of the verb are known **as non-finite**.

The most common non-finite parts of a verb are the infinitive (to laugh; to burn etc), the present participle (laughing; burning) and the past participle (laughed, burnt).

When used in sentences, the infinitive functions as a noun – He liked to laugh. The participles usually function as adjectives – The laughing man fell off his chair; The burnt wood was still smoking several hours after the fire started.

Pronouns

Key terms

A **pronoun** such as I, you, he, she, it, we, they, this, that, anyone, anybody etc. is a word used in place of a noun. Use of pronouns prevents unnecessary and clumsy repetitions of nouns.

For example

'Vijay and his sister went to the river to swim. When Vijay and his sister arrived there, Vijay and his sister found that the river was dried up.'

By using a pronoun the meaning would be more effectively expressed: 'Vijay and his sister went to the river to swim. When they arrived there, they found that it was dried up.'

Adjectives

Key terms

An **adjective** is a word used to describe a noun.

For example

The red house had a *huge* bedroom in which some very *naughty* children could be found.

Adverbs

Key terms

An **adverb** is a word which qualifies (that is, adds to the meaning of) a verb, an adjective or another adverb. Many, but not all, adverbs end in –ly.

For example

i   The boy finished his dinner *quickly*.
ii I had a *rather* small breakfast.
iii The sun was shining *very* brightly.

In the first example an **adverb** is used to qualify a verb, in the second the adverb qualifies an adjective and in the third, one adverb qualifies another.

Prepositions

Key terms

A **preposition** is a word used with a following noun or pronoun to show the connection between persons or things. Common prepositions include: about, above, across, against, along, around, at, before, behind, beneath, beside, between, by, down, during, except, for, from, near, off, on, over, round, since, till, towards, under, until, up, upon.

Articles

Key terms

The word 'the' is referred to as the definite **article**; the words 'a' and 'an' are known as indefinite articles.

Conjunctions and interjections

Key terms

A **conjunction** is a word used to connect words or groups of words.

For example

and, or, but, however

Key terms

An **interjection** is a word used to express a feeling such as joy or anger and is usually indicated by the use of an exclamation mark.

For example

What! Oh! Hurray!

Exercise 1

Read the following passage and then copy and complete the table provided by identifying the function of each word in it.

It was raining heavily. Amrit was sitting indoors, eating a cake and watching television. He was bored as the television programme was dull and uninteresting. Oh, how he wished the rain would stop! However, the weather did not seem to upset his younger sister, Rita; she was sitting happily on the floor and reading a book that was full of brightly coloured pictures.

Nouns	Verbs	Adjectives	Adverbs	Pronouns	Prepositions	Conjunctions	Interjections

Sentence types and structures

Some definitions

A **phrase** is a group of words which does not contain a finite verb. For example: 'The dog, *lazing in the sun*, seemed thoroughly content with life.' The words in italics together comprise a phrase beginning with a present participle and, in this case, they function together as an adjective describing the dog.

A clause is a group of words which does contain a finite verb. There are two types of clauses: **main clauses** and **subordinate clauses**. A main clause is a single unit of sense and can stand alone to make complete sense. For example: '*Salim ate his breakfast.*'

However, a subordinate clause does not make complete sense on its own; it is dependent on a main clause to which it relates; for example, '*Salim ate his breakfast which he had cooked all by himself*'. In this sentence, although the subordinate clause provides further information about Salim's breakfast, it does not make sense unless the reader knows the content of the preceding main clause. The word *which* is what is known as a relative pronoun (other common relative pronouns are *who* and *that*) and is used to join two clauses together.

A main clause, therefore, can, like the example above, function as a sentence. Such a sentence (consisting of just one main clause) is known as a **simple sentence**. A sentence which consists of two or more main clauses joined by a conjunction or conjunctions ('Salim ate his breakfast and then he left the house and walked to school.') is known as a **compound sentence**. Finally, a sentence which contains a mixture of main and subordinate clauses ('Salim ate his breakfast, which he had cooked all by himself, and then left the house to go to school which was on the other side of town.') is known as a **complex sentence**.

Just as it is important to demonstrate that you are in command of a varied vocabulary, it is equally important to show that you can use a range of sentence structures to add variety and interest to your writing. Try to include a balance of simple and complex sentences so that you avoid monotony; in general, the more involved your ideas are, the more you are likely to use lengthy sentences. However, short sentences are often a very effective way to add emphasis to your writing.

The type of sentence structures that you use will help to determine the tone of your writing. Consistently using complex sentences will create a formal tone which is suitable for argumentative essays whereas shorter sentences might well be more effective for a narrative essay. The ability to show control of complex sentences and structures in your writing, however, is one of the criteria that teachers usually look for in writing which is of very good standard.

Exercise 2

Combine each of the following pairs or groups of short sentences into one longer sentence. You can omit words and alter the wording where necessary. Do not rely too much on the use of simple conjunctions such as *and*.

1   One afternoon I went for a stroll. The town was strangely quiet. There were very few people on the streets. The sky was of an ominous grey colour.

2   The school is situated in the countryside. It is an old redbrick building. It is easily seen amidst the surrounding fields.

3   Jasmine's mother works very hard. She cooks for all the family. She goes to the market every day. She wishes she could afford to employ a maid.

4   We were lost. We had been walking in circles for the last three hours. Every tree in the jungle looked the same. Night was starting to fall. It was growing dark.

5   Nissar was late leaving home. He drove his car quickly. He had a long way to travel. He had to meet his friends at the club. He knew they would not wait there for long.

Exercise 3

Here is an episode of a story set out in note form. Tell the story in full using no more than three paragraphs and paying particular attention to sentence building. You may include additional details as appropriate.

Mr Patel has a bad memory – forgets important details – arranges special celebration for wife's birthday – invites many friends and family members – hires town hall for the party – employs two top quality chefs to prepare food – books a popular band to play music – no expense spared – guests due to arrive at 7.30 pm – Mr Patel and wife arrive 7.00 – no-one else there by 8.00 – Mr Patel and wife are a little worried – by 9.00 – no-one there apart from Mr and Mrs Patel, the chefs and the band – Mr Patel in despair – decides to phone people – realises he has left cell phone behind – goes home to fetch it – opens up desk to pick up phone – discovers bundle of invitations – he had forgotten to post them.

Accuracy of expression

Use correct grammar and punctuation

To produce a good piece of work in Composition, it is important that your writing is secure in the use of the main punctuation marks. Remember, the point of punctuation is to help the reader grasp the meaning of what you are writing; you cannot communicate clearly without using punctuation accurately.

The most important punctuation marks are as follows.

Full Stop (.)
The full stop is used to indicate a long pause and to mark the end of a sentence.

Comma (,)
The comma is used to indicate a short pause; it should never be used to mark the end of a sentence.

Semicolon (;)
The semicolon is used to indicate a longer pause than a comma and is also used to link two main clauses with a common subject.

Question Mark (?)

The question mark is used instead of a full stop at the end of a direct question.

Exclamation Mark (!)

The exclamation mark is used instead of a full stop at the end of a sentence after making an exclamation. It is also used after an interjection.

Apostrophe (')

The apostrophe is used either to show possession or to indicate the omission of a letter or letters.

Speech Marks (" ")

The speech marks are used to indicate direct speech.

Colon (:)

The colon is used to introduce a statement or quotation or to act as a pause or balancing point between two balanced statements.

When punctuating a sentence never put in a stop at any place unless a pause is required in the reading.

A guide to the use of the more complicated punctuation marks follows.

Full stops

A full stop is used to mark the end of a sentence. For example: *'It was a wet and cold morning in the middle of November. Padma, warm and comfortable beneath the covers, did not want to get out of bed.'* Here there are two separate statements, each containing a main verb and each with a different subject; it is, therefore, correct to indicate the pause between them by using a full stop.

A full stop is also used to indicate words that are abbreviated when the abbreviated form of the word ends with a different letter from the full form of the word. For example: '3rd Sept.'

Commas

The following are the main occasions when commas should be used; the first six are purely mechanical, the other two require a little more thought.

1 To separate words or phrases in a list or series (except for the last two which are usually joined by 'and'). For example: *'In the kitchen there were a large oven, pots, pans, bottles, glasses and a stand containing cutlery.'*

2 To mark off the name or title of a person being spoken to. For example: *'Padma, there's someone at the door to see you.'* or *'Excuse me, sir, you've just dropped your wallet.'*

3 To mark off words or phrases in apposition. For example: 'The restaurant owner, Mr. Miah, is a very rich man.' or 'Mr. Miah, the restaurant owner, is a very rich man.'

4 To mark off words and phrases such as 'however', 'therefore', 'by the way', 'nevertheless', 'moreover' etc. that have been interjected into a sentence. For example: *'At the same time, however, you should be very careful.'*

5 To mark off phrases beginning with a participle when a pause is required in the reading. For example*: 'My sister, seeing that I was upset, asked me what was the matter.'*

6 In conjunction with speech marks to indicate the beginning of a passage of direct speech: *'The teacher stood up and said, "……."*

7 To separate an adjectival clause beginning with 'who', 'whom' or 'which' from the rest of the sentence, when it is non-defining.

This is a particularly tricky use of the comma, but the following example will help to explain the point: *'The Queen ordered that all the birds, which were sitting on the wall, should be fed.'*

In the above sentence, the clause *which were sitting on the wall* must be non-defining and, therefore, implies that all the birds in existence happened to be sitting on the Queen's wall. However, if the commas were omitted, the sense would be that the Queen ordered that only the birds sitting on the wall were to be fed (those in the trees and on the grass were presumably to go hungry!).

8 To break up a sentence into smaller parts and to help the reader to grasp the meaning. **For example:** *Ajay, clumsy and awkward, stumbled into the room, knocked over a small table and then, before he could do any more damage, sank into the nearest chair.'*

Semicolons

A semicolon is used for two main purposes.

1 To separate two main clauses when a conjunction such as 'and' or 'but' is omitted. For example: *'Rita felt particularly tired that morning; she did not want to get out of bed.'*

2 To separate clauses or phrases in a list or series. For example: *'Salim jumped out of the chair; quickly walked out of the room; slammed the door behind him; searched for his bicycle in the garden and then rode off quickly to find his friends.'*

Colons

There are three main uses for the colon.

1 To separate two clauses where the second explains more fully the meaning of the first. For example: *'He was feeling very cheerful that morning: the sun was shining and it was the first day of the summer holidays.'*

2 To introduce a number of items in a list. For example: *'Before departure, please check that you have the following: passport, money, tickets, change of clothes and cell phones.'*

3 To introduce a speech or quotation. For example: *'Juliet: Romeo, Romeo, wherefore art thou Romeo?'*

Apostrophes

The apostrophe is used for two main purposes; the first one is quite straight-forward; the second is a little more complicated.

1 To indicate the omission of a letter or letters when a word or words have been contracted. For example: 'I didn't do that. It's not true. You weren't there.'

2 To indicate possession. In English, the possessive form of a noun is shown as following.

    a   In the singular, the possessive form is made by adding *–'s*

girl	the girl's book
boy	the boy's hat
house	the house's windows

    b   In the plural, when the plural is made by adding *–s* to the singular, the possessive is made by adding an apostrophe after the *–s (s')*

girls	the girls' books
boys	the boys' hats
houses	the houses' windows

Notes

1 When the plural of a noun is not made by adding *–s*, the possessive is made by adding *–'s*.

men	the men's office
children	the children's toys
women	the women's cars

2 The apostrophe is required in expressions like: a month's wait; a week's holiday; an hour's journey.

Speech marks and inverted commas

Speech marks (inverted commas) are used to enclose a passage of direct speech, that is the precise words which are said (or thought) by somebody. There are three patterns by which speech can be represented.

1 Anita's father said to her, "If it doesn't rain tomorrow, we'll visit the seaside."

2 "Please, Daddy," replied Anita, "can we go even if it does rain? I'm sure it will stop by the afternoon."

3 "I suppose we could," answered her father. "We ought to make the most of our holiday."

Dashes and hyphens

The dash has a variety of uses. Its main use is to indicate an interruption to the planned flow of a sentence, for example by an afterthought or interjection. A dash is placed before and after the words interjected into the sentence unless the interruption occurs at the end of a sentence when a full stop, question mark or exclamation mark replaces the second dash.

For example

"He showed me his new house – very nice it was too – that he had purchased from a famous celebrity."

"He showed me his new house that he had purchased from a famous celebrity – and very nice it was too!"

Another function of the dash is to indicate when a word or sentence is left incomplete.

For example

"The police made sure the identity of Mr S — was not revealed."

"Please, please don't — he begged, but it was too late!"

Finally, a dash can be used to indicate a sudden dramatic end to a sentence:

For example

"I'll tell you who the culprit was," said the detective. "It was — the Headteacher."

A hyphen is not a punctuation mark at all; it is simply a device for linking compound words together. For example, the phrase 'six-foot Guards' means that there are some guards who are six feet tall; on the other hand 'six Foot-Guards' means that altogether in number there are six Foot-Guards (soldiers belonging to the regiment of Foot-Guards).

The hyphen is also used to split a word into syllables when there is no room to fit the complete word into the space at the end of a line. In this case, the hyphen should always be placed between syllables, for example, 'walk-ing' but not 'walkin-g'.

The dash is distinguishable from the hyphen in appearance by being slightly longer.

Importance of punctuation

Using punctuation correctly is important in ensuring that you communicate clearly. For teachers to appreciate your work, you should be able to demonstrate secure control of full stops, commas and apostrophes; in particular you should be able to use full stops confidently to separate sentences.

One of the features of a high level writing performance is the ability of the writer to use punctuation devices such as semicolons and colons to shape meaning and to elicit particular responses from the reader.

Positive punctuation

What are your thoughts about the way these three statements have been punctuated?

1   When she awoke, the rain was pounding down heavily on the roof of the house, Sunita decided that it would be a good idea to go back to sleep.

2 When she awoke, the rain was pounding down heavily on the roof of the house. Sunita decided that it would be a good idea to go back to sleep.

3 When she awoke, the rain was pounding down heavily on the roof of the house; Sunita decided that it would be a good idea to go back to sleep.

There is clearly an error of punctuation in the first sentence as the comma is not a strong enough punctuation mark to separate the two main clauses.

The next two sentences, however, are correctly punctuated. In the second sentence, the full stop is used to make two independent sentences and to separate the two main clauses.

However, by using a semicolon between the clauses in the third sentence, the writer has succeeded in giving equal emphasis to each part of what is now one unified sentence which skilfully combines the two main ideas.

Exercise 4

Rewrite the following sentences using commas, full stops, semicolons, apostrophes and speech marks as required.

1 The journey can be made by road rail sea or air

2 If for instance you want to buy a television set the best place to go is the electrical shop you can find this in the centre of town

3 Sanjeevs books were lost somewhere in his fathers office

4 Excuse me sir can you tell me whats happened to my football?

5 Abraham Lincoln the President of the United States was assassinated while watching a play

6 According to the Fahrenheit scale as you know water boils at 212 degrees on the other hand according to the Centigrade scale it boils at 100 degrees

7 Many animals are renowned for their ferocity the tiger the lion the rhinoceros and the wolf are just a few of these

8 He had waited all day for his turn it was now six o'clock in the evening and he decided it was time to go home

9 We thank you very much for your hospitality said Rohit now we would like to wish you good night

10 Have we far to go now? asked my sister from the back seat of the car I'm getting very bored with this journey

11 The two teachers cars were damaged when the schools best batsman hit a huge boundary

12 The detective looked closely at the murder scene This looks like a good clue I have a good idea who was responsible he said triumphantly

Exercise 5

Provide the missing punctuation marks for the following piece of writing. Use capital letters wherever required.

They had been driving for hours the countryside was flat and uninteresting and jamals attention as he sat behind the wheel of the old battered toyota was beginning to wander ahead of him he could see a shape like a hill although it was difficult to distinguish things clearly because of the mist which was rising from the ground in his mind he thought it could be a great castle maybe it was where the wicked witch was keeping the beautiful princess prisoner watch out suddenly cried out ahmed be careful what youre doing you idiot you nearly drove us into the ditch just now sorry mumbled jamal I must have been daydreaming

Exercise 6

Now write some interesting sentences of your own illustrating all the different punctuation devices that have been explained in this section. You should try to show the different effects that can be achieved by being in control of punctuation.

Paragraphing

Paragraphing is one of the most important ways of structuring and organising your writing.

> ### Remember
> Teachers are impressed by essays which are clearly structured through connected and linked paragraphs.
>
> All paragraphs should contain a topic sentence, i.e. a sentence which contains the main point of the paragraph. You can vary the structure of your writing by varying the position in which you place the topic sentence in different paragraphs. A good way to plan your work is through noting the different topic paragraphs you will use throughout the essay.
>
> Once you have decided on your topic sentence, the rest of the paragraph should relate to it and develop from or towards it in a logical and coherent way.

When you are planning your essay, it is a good idea to plan your work by thinking about paragraphs and their topics.

An example of a well-constructed paragraph follows; the topic sentence is written in bold type.

There is a strict dress code for the Golden Temple. First of all the head must be covered at all times. Scarves of various colours are readily available for non-Sikhs, either from any one of the 17 young lads who converge on you as soon as you pull up outside, or more cheaply from one of the stalls inside the forecourt. Shoes and socks must be removed. Hands must then be washed at marble-lined public basins and bare feet passed through a trough of water at the bottom of the steps.

Source: from *Himalaya* by Michael Palin

In this paragraph, the first sentence is the topic sentence; it introduces the point about the dress code needed for a visit to the Golden Temple and the rest of the paragraph develops naturally from this point, with each subsequent sentence adding further details which provide the reader with further information.

Exercise 1

Here is another paragraph from the same book, only this time the sentences have been muddled up. Read through it and then re-write it in the correct order. You should start by identifying the topic sentence and then beginning with it.

One is entirely devoted to a chapatti production line.

When one side is done the chapattis are flipped over in quick, dexterous movements of a long thin implement with a half-moon end.

The piles are then removed and carried out to the refectory. The kitchen is spread through several buildings.

A rat skips nimbly out of the way as fresh sacks of flour are cut open and fed into the bowels of a slowly turning machine, which regurgitates the flour as dough.

When the flipper is satisfied both sides are right he gives an extra strong flick, which sends the chapatti flying off the hotplate to land neatly on a pile on the floor.

One group of helpers rolls the dough into balls, another flattens each ball out into a pancake, and another lays them out on hotplates the size of double beds, made from cast-iron sheets laid on bricks with gas fires underneath, and capable of taking a couple of hundred chapattis at a time.

Source: from *Himalaya* by Michael Palin

Exercise 2

Below are four topic sentences. Use each of them as the basis for a single paragraph of your own. Try to vary the position of the topic sentence by putting one at the start of a paragraph, one at the middle and one at the end. You could also write different paragraphs using the same topic sentence in different positions and consider the effects thus produced.

1   This is what I like best about my family home.

2   When it was all over, she quickly left the room.

3   This is the most memorable thing about the main street first thing in the morning.

4   When he woke up, it was the first thing he remembered.

Grammar and syntax

Grammar is the science of language and involves the rules of standard written and spoken expression. Syntax refers specifically to the grammatical structure of sentences.

English, as everyone who speaks and writes it knows, is a grammatically complex language which is continually developing. This is not the place to give a detailed account of the grammatical structures of English. But in order for your writing to convey its meaning clearly and unambiguously to the reader, it is important that you are thoroughly familiar with certain formalities of English syntax.

Remember

In one of his essays, George Orwell listed what he considered to be some basic rules of good writing. Perhaps the most important one of these was the final one in which he advised his readers to 'break any of these rules, rather than say anything outright barbarous'! It is important that you keep this advice in mind at all times. Rigid adherence to what are perceived to be the unfaltering laws of grammatical correctness can frequently produce writing which is stilted and unnecessarily pompous in tone. To take one simple example; some people believe that they should never use colloquial contractions (such as 'they're', 'you're', 'that's') in their writing.

Certainly, such contractions may be out of place in a particularly formal piece of writing. But if you are writing a letter to a friend (for example as a Directed Writing task, or an informal piece of description or narrative for Composition), not using such contractions would be likely to spoil the overall tone and register of your writing. The result will be that the reader would find it difficult to be fully engaged with what you are saying.

Errors of agreement

It is important that subjects and their verbs should agree in number (i.e. whether they are singular or plural). Sometimes, especially in a complex sentence, it is very easy to forget this. For example, in the following sentence, the writer has forgotten that the subject of the sentence ('storeroom') is singular because of the number of plural nouns which come between it and the verb ('were'):

'The storeroom, full of books, broken desks and chairs, buckets, brooms and vacuum cleaners were very much in need of tidying up.'

Consistency in tenses

One of the most common errors made by students in their writing is to fail to write consistently in the same tense. A simple example of this is shown in this sentence: *'I was feeling happy so I go to see my best friend.'*

In this example, the writer has started in the past tense (was) and has then changed to the present (go). This is incorrect and confuses the reader.

However, confusion with tenses is not always as straightforward as in this example. Look at the following passage and decide what is wrong with it.

It is a very warm day so I decided to visit my friend, Vijay. The idea would be a good one as Vijay would live in a house near the sea and I think that we should visit the beach.

The tenses in these sentences are very confused indeed. The writer begins in the present tense, then slips into the past before using two unnecessary conditional forms ('would' and 'should') before coming back to the present again with 'think'.

Re-write the above two sentences using first of all the present tense consistently and then the past tense. Which version do you prefer?

Other common errors

Wrongly used prepositions

Prepositions are words that are placed usually before nouns and pronouns to indicate some relation, for example in, on, to, at. Using these precisely is an essential requirement for expressing yourself accurately.

For example
'He fell by the telephone' has a different meaning from 'He fell on the telephone'.

Misunderstanding of singular nouns ending in –*s*

The items of clothing known as jeans and pants are grammatically plural forms and do not have singular forms; it is, therefore, incorrect to write '*He was wearing a pair of pant*' and '*She spilt drink on her jean*'.

Tautology

Tautology is saying exactly the same thing more than once, especially within the same sentence. For example, '*At the end of the outing the students returned back to school*' and '*The true facts of the accident are these*'. In these sentences the words *back* and *true* are unnecessary: *return* means to go back and *facts* are, by definition, true.

Spelling

As most students are fully aware, English spelling is difficult to learn because it is often irregular and, in particular, does not give a simple representation of the spoken sounds. The guidelines that follow, however, may sometimes help you to avoid making some of the more common spelling errors.

> **Notes**
>
> A prefix is a syllable added to the beginning of a word which modifies its meanings. Similarly, a suffix is a syllable added to the end of a word.
> - Words of one syllable ending in a single consonant following a single vowel double the consonant before a suffix starting with a vowel: *swim, swimmer, sad, sadden, bat, batting*.
> - The last consonant is also doubled in words of more than one syllable if that consonant follows a single vowel and if the accent is on the final syllable: *permit, permitted, refer, referring, begin, beginner*.
> - There is no doubling of the final consonant when (a) the consonant follows double vowels, or (b) when the accent is **not** on the final syllable: *conceal, concealed, proceed, proceeding, offer, offering, benefit, benefited*.
> - When adverbs are formed by adding —*ly* to adjectives ending in —*l*, there is always a double —l: *full, fully, helpful, helpfully*.
> - Words ending in a silent —*e* drop the —*e* before a suffix beginning with a vowel but retain it before one beginning with a consonant: *love, lovable*, lovely; e*xcite, exciting, e*xcitement. However, if there is a *c* or *g* before the silent *e*, the e is retained before a suffix beginning with a vowel: *notice, noticeable, courage, courageous*.
> - Words ending in —*y* following a consonant change the —*y* into —*i* before a suffix: *baby, babies, fry, fried*. However, if the —*y* follows a vowel the change to —*i* does not take place: *monkey, monkeys, chimney, chimneys*.
> - In words having the sound of 'ee', —*i* comes before —*e* except after c: *believe, receive, conceit*. (Exceptions to this rule are: *seize, counterfeit, weird*.)
> - When prefixes such as *un—, en—* or *in—* are added to words beginning with 'n', a double 'n' occurs: *necessary, unnecessary, named, unnamed, numerable, innumerable*.

Tone and register

Let us look more closely at two of the Assessment Objectives:

- use a range of appropriate vocabulary
- use register appropriate to audience and context.

These refer to the tone or register of your writing or, in other words, to those features of your writing which give it its individual quality or style. For example, your tone could be described as formal or informal, humorous or serious and should be very much suited to the type of writing that you are producing. What is especially important is that your tone stays consistent throughout your essay. The key features that go to making up a writer's tone are:

- writer's standpoint
- vocabulary
- sentence types and structures
- use of figures of speech.

Now we'll consider these features more closely.

Writer's standpoint

By this, we mean the attitude which, as a writer, you choose to adopt in order to present your ideas and character to the reader. The first decision to be made is whether you are going to use the first or third person to express yourself.

In general, if you choose to write in the first person ('I think …') you are likely to establish an informal tone as you are talking directly to the reader as an acquaintance. This informality of tone can be reinforced by the use of colloquial abbreviations ('I don't agree with this point of view' etc.).

If you choose to write in the third person ('It is thought that …' or 'People think …'), then your tone becomes more objective and impartial as you have removed the personal element. So, you are likely to produce a more formal piece of writing.

It should be remembered that if you are writing a story, then the choice of narrative standpoint is particularly important as the decision to use a first person approach means that your story can deal only with events which can be known to and experienced by the narrator; if you choose to write using a third person narrative, you are in a position of having a more complex overview of the events in your story.

Many students create significant problems for themselves when ending their stories by not thinking through the implications of their choice of narrative standpoint before they begin to write. Conclusions such as 'and then I died …' are seldom convincing!

Vocabulary

The proper words in the proper places – Jonathan Swift

Never use a long word where a short one will do – George Orwell

These two statements from two great writers of English remind us that having a wide enough vocabulary to be able to select exactly the word you need to convey a precise shade of meaning is an essential requirement for writing an impressive essay.

However, it should be noted that neither writer suggests that good writing depends on showing off a wide vocabulary simply for the sake of doing so. English is a language rich in synonyms and the ability to be able to select the most suitable words is a skill which all writers should aim to develop.

In your own writing you should always try to keep a clear picture in your mind of what you are writing about and then think carefully of the most effective words to convey what you are thinking about to your reader: in particular, well-chosen verbs and adverbs can be especially helpful for doing this.

Exercise 1

Now let's look at an exercise to test your awareness of the shades of meaning in different words, all used to describe something which you can smell. Use each of the following words in a different sentence in order to bring out its full meaning. You should use each word as a noun.

- smell
- odour
- perfume
- scent
- aroma
- stench
- stink

Exercise 2

Here is another exercise in choosing the best word to convey a precise meaning. This time you are required to look at adjectives and adverbs and should choose the most appropriate word from the different options you are given in order to produce a paragraph which describes a particular atmosphere.

The street swarmed with (fierce/frantic) people all rushing (carelessly/desperately) to reach their destinations. In the road, (angry/frustrated) motorists sat in their cars, (noisily/fiercely) sounding their horns in their hope to break up the (huge/unending) traffic jam. A policeman stood (bewilderedly/importantly) on a (small/rickety) platform surrounded by traffic, his signals being completely ignored by all concerned. On one side of the road, sitting under a (tattered/colourful) umbrella to shelter him from the (burning/relentless) sun, sat an (old/aged) man who was watching the scene with (detached/amused) interest.

Notes

None of these words is wrong; you are being asked to choose those you think describe the scene with most clarity. You should also aim to produce a description which is consistent in its tone.

Confusions

Many writers of English blur the communication of what they want to say by confusing words which either sound similar to another one or which have a similar but not exactly equivalent meaning.

Some of these words are listed below. Write sentences with each of them to make their meaning clear.

Notes

You may need to use a dictionary to check the meaning of some or all of them.

avoid/prevent _____

stay/live _____

bring/take _____

uninterested/disinterested _____

bored/boring _____

there/their/they're _____

your/you're _____

horde/hoard _____

principal/principle _____

affect/effect _____

Figures of speech

Another way to make your writing interesting is by making use of figures of speech such as similes and metaphors as these can add depth and detail to what you intend to say.

A **simile** is a comparison introduced by the words *like* or *as*, in which things, actions, people etc. are compared with other things, actions, ideas etc. of a totally different kind. For example: 'The teacher surged into the classroom *like a stately galleon in full sail*.'

A **metaphor** is a kind of concentrated simile in which a comparison is made by saying that one thing is actually another thing of a totally different kind; for example: '*The banner of smoke* flew proudly from the factory chimney.' Instead of saying that the smoke from the chimney looked like a large flag flying from it (which would be using a simile) the use of the metaphor makes the smoke and the banner one and the same thing, with the result that the comparison is more immediate in its effect.

It is important, however, that you use such figures of speech selectively and thoughtfully. Try to be original in your use of similes and avoid using clichéd comparisons such as *he ran like the wind*. However, you should also make sure that there are clear points of comparison between the two elements of your similes. It is also a good idea not to overdo the use of similes as too many will have the effect of clogging up your writing — remember, be selective and always think about what might be the effect on the reader of the stylistic choices you have made.

Your choice of similes and comparisons should give an indication of your personality as a writer and is, therefore, another way of establishing the individual tone of your writing.

4 Descriptive writing

Composition usually presents you with a selection of five titles from which you must choose one to write about. These titles cover a range of different types of writing. However, teachers expect you to write about your personal experiences or opinions; you do not have to pretend to be someone you are not in order to impress them.

When you are thinking about which topic you should choose to write about, try to keep the following points in mind:

- you only have a limited period of time to plan and write your essay

- planning is important but do not produce an over-elaborate plan

- choose a topic which does not require you to spend too long thinking about what you should write — as far as possible write about something which is closely familiar to you

- you should be aware of the type of writing you are best at; try to choose the topic which lets you write this type of essay

- remember that your work will be judged by teachers as much on how you express yourself as on the content. Using accurate grammatical structures and appropriate vocabulary is also equally important.

In general, Composition involves five different types of writing, namely descriptive writing, argumentative writing, discursive writing, personal account and narrative writing. All of these will allow you to present your own personal views and feelings. Sometimes, one title will cover more than one type of writing. Here is a selection of essay titles taken from or similar to those found in examination papers with the type of writing each requires indicated in brackets.

1   Describe an important person living in your community and say why you admire him/her. (Descriptive)

2   Write about an occasion when a special family meal produced unexpected results. (Personal Account)

    Cambridge O Level English Language 1120 Paper 1 Section A, June 2004

3   You once made a decision that caused problems for a friend. Write about what the decision was and what happened as a result of it. (Personal Account)

4   Should we worry so much about endangered species? What is your view? (Argumentative)

    Cambridge O Level English Language 1120 Paper 1 Section A, June 2004

5   Write a story which begins with the words, 'It was only when I arrived at the house that I realised I had forgotten …'. (Narrative)

As you can see, no matter what type of writing is required, at least four of these topics allow you to write from your direct personal experience.

Topic 5 provides the opportunity to make up a fictional narrative if you wish, but there's no reason why you could not write from personal experience, if that seems appropriate.

Now let us look at these different types of writing more closely.

Descriptive writing

The descriptive topic is in some ways meant for one of the more straightforward pieces of writing and allows you to write about something with which you are familiar. It is also likely to capture the interest of the person who is reading it.

There are different types of descriptive essay topics:

- a description of a place or a scene or a building

- a description of an event or an occasion

- a description of a person or an animal.

This is a fairly simple list and you can almost certainly think of other variations. However, the common factor is that in all of them you can write personally about your perception of what is being described.

When you are writing under time constraints, it is much better to write about something or someone that is familiar to you than to worry about having to make something up. For example, conjure up in your mind a clear picture of a place you know well to give you a basis for your description. Once you have done this, you can then add some extra details (which can, of course, be made up) to make it more interesting.

Exercise 1

Here are some examples of different types of descriptive writing. Read through each of them carefully and, in discussion with a partner, decide on the features that make them effective passages of descriptive writing. List examples of words and phrases and explain why they help to convey the scene or people being described to the readers. Try to describe and comment on the writers' tone of voice. Do not read the comments which follow until you have done this.

Passage: (a) Kundili

We arrived at Kundili after a four-hour drive to find a seething multitude, drawn from a number of tribes, gathered into a mile-wide dust bowl at the conjunction of the main road into Andhra Pradesh and a number of country byways leading down from the hills. Under the hard forthright midday sun it was a sight to guarantee eye-strain and eventual headaches. The sky was bleached white, with drifts in it of what appeared at first as red smoke blowing across, but which proved to be the blood-red dust, which lay a quarter-inch deep on every surface, caught up by the gusting wind. When the dust was blown across the sun it turned dark, swelled up and seemed to tremble. From all points of the market came the piercing glitter of metal articles for sale, from sheets of corrugated iron, pots and pans, and above all from the rows of polished aluminium receptacles for sale.

Source: from *A Goddess in the Stones* by Norman Lewis

Passage: (b) Istanbul

Sighing, I smeared a little of the brown water around my face, then went out to see Istanbul. It is the noisiest, dirtiest, busiest city I've ever seen. Everywhere there is noise—car horns tooting, sirens shrilling, people shouting, muezzins wailing, ferries on the Bosphorus sounding their booming horns. Everywhere, too, there is ceaseless activity—people pushing carts, carrying trays of food or coffee, humping huge and ungainly loads (I saw one guy with a sofa on his back), people every five feet selling something: lottery tickets, wrist-watches, cigarettes, replica perfumes.

Every few paces people come up to you wanting to shine your shoes, sell you postcards or guidebooks, lead you to their brother's carpet shop or otherwise induce you to part with some trifling sum of money.

Along the Galata Bridge, swarming with pedestrians, beggars and load bearers, amateur fishermen stood pulling the most poisoned-looking fish I ever hope to see from the oily waters below. At the end of the bridge two guys were crossing the street to Sirkeci Station, threading their way through the traffic leading brown bears on leashes. No one gave them a second glance. Istanbul is, in short, one of those great and exhilarating cities where almost anything seems possible.

The one truly unbearable thing in the city is the Turkish pop music. It is inescapable. It assaults you from every restaurant doorway, from every lemonade stand, from every passing cab. If you can imagine a man having an operation without anaesthetic to a background accompaniment of frantic sitar-playing, you will have some idea of what popular Turkish music is like.

I wandered around for a couple of hours, impressed by the tumult, amazed that in one place there could be so much activity. I walked past the Blue Mosque and Aya Sofia, peeling postcard salesmen from my sleeve as I went, and tried to go to Topkapi, but it was closed. I headed instead for what I thought was the national archaeological museum, but I somehow missed it and found myself presently at the entrance to a large, inviting and miraculously tranquil park, the Giilhane. It was full of cool shade and happy families. There was a free zoo, evidently much loved by children, and somewhere a cafe playing Turkish torture music, but softly enough to be tolerable.

At the bottom of a gently sloping central avenue, the park ended in a sudden and stunning view of the Bosphorus, glittery and blue. I took a seat at an open-air taverna, ordered a coke and gazed across the water to the white houses gleaming on the brown hillside of Uskiidar two miles across the strait. Distant cars glinted in the hot sunshine and ferries plied doggedly back and forth across the Bosphorus and on out to the distant Princes' Islands, adrift in a bluish haze. It was beautiful and a perfect place to stop.

Source: from *Neither Here Nor There: Travels in Europe* by Bill Bryson

Passage: (c) Train to Lahore

Porters cluster around us and a thin-faced ascetic old man with a Gandalf-like white beard grabs one of my cases, hoists the other onto his head and, a little disappointed that I choose to carry my own shoulder bag, marches off through the crowds.

Our driver nods approvingly. This old man is a great character, he says. He was carrying bags for British officers before independence. That was 55 years ago.

There are three classes on the train, two with air-con and one without.

We're in air-con, 2nd class and are made comfortable by an army of solicitous attendants marshalled by a man in a white suit, green peaked hat and a crimson arm band, grandly embroidered with the words Conductor Guard. A rich cast of characters, all with titles clearly inscribed on jackets or lapels, come through offering refreshment of various kinds. My favourite is the Iceman, a stocky, embattled figure in a frayed white jacket, whose bulbous eyes and droopy moustache remind me of a small-time crook in a French gangster movie. He hauls a huge bucket in which is a block of ice with bottles squeezed around it. There is a tired, emaciated Sweet Seller and various perkier, smartly turned-out young men described on their lapel badges as either Buttlers [sic] or Waiters. Waiter No. 14 brings chai, sweet milky tea, and Buttler No. 7 collects the money.

Source: from *Himalaya* by Michael Palin

All of these extracts describe either places or people and all of them are written in the first person and therefore record a personal response. Despite the differences of the characters of the writers which appear in the extracts, there are several similarities between the passages. All of them concentrate on focusing on precise details of the scene or characters they are describing.

In extract (a) the details are particularly concerned with the descriptions of the 'piercing glitter' of the articles which are on sale; extract (b) contains both detail and the writer's reactions to and feelings about the city he is describing; and in extract (c) the character of the Iceman is conveyed in particular through the details of his physical description with which we are provided.

Tools for descriptive writing

In order to bring a scene alive for the reader, it is a good idea to think about ways of describing how it appeals to the different senses such as smell and hearing. Effective descriptive writing makes use of certain linguistic devices which help to make clear what is being described. Among these devices are: similes, metaphors, adjectives.

Another way to ensure that your descriptions are as precise and effective as possible is to think carefully about your choice of verbs and the adverbs which describe them.

Examples of these devices and their effects in the printed extracts are:
- **Simile:** For example, a *Gandalf-like white beard* (Gandalf is a wizard in *The Lord of the Rings*)

- **Metaphor:** For example, *the sky was bleached white*

- **Adjectives:** For example, *the blood-red dust*

- **Verbs:** For example, *humping huge and ungainly loads*

- **Adverbs:** For example, *ferries plied doggedly*.

Exercise 2

Now re-read the three passages; from each one select two or three descriptions and explain carefully how the examples you have chosen use language to achieve the desired effects. In particular, you should consider the writers' vocabulary, the range and type of sentence structures they use, their tone of voice and the figures of speech they use.

Exercise 3

Here is a rather bland account. Rewrite it, by adding some additional details and information, using descriptive writing tools such as similes, metaphors, adjectives, carefully chosen verbs and adverbs, to create (i) a happy atmosphere and (ii) a threatening atmosphere.

> Anwar was walking beside the river. It was during the afternoon. The day had been hot but now the sun was no longer directly overhead. Anwar had been at school for the whole day. He was feeling tired and wanted to get home quickly. He was thinking about his dinner and seeing his family. Ahead of him he could see some figures. They were coming towards him. The sun's rays made it difficult to see them clearly. He could not recognise any of the figures. They came closer to him. They stopped in front of him and spoke to him.

Remember

Make sure that you use adjectives and similes sparingly; overuse of them can produce a rather static and overloaded piece of descriptive writing.

Exercise 4

Write a descriptive paragraph giving a clear and precise description of the following; remember to concentrate on describing and not writing a narrative. Try to make your description as interesting as possible:

The family car

A school classroom

An old person riding a bicycle

The view from your bedroom window early in the morning

A busy city street.

Preparing for a descriptive writing task

Here is a descriptive writing task with some suggestions on how to approach it and what could be included in it. Think about these points and then organise the notes into paragraph topics and write your own essay using them.

> **Notes**
>
> **Describe a busy local market**
>
> - Do I take a narrative approach or should I just focus on giving impressions?
> - Describe some of the stalls and the people who run them.
> - Describe some of the customers.
> - What time of day shall I choose?
> - What about the weather?
> - The location of the market.
> - The senses: sounds, sights, smells (taste and touch?).
> - Do I describe the market in a positive or negative way?
> - What is my attitude to the vendors — are they to be trusted?
> - What tone of voice do I use? Should I be humorous or should I just give a straight-forward account?
> - I must remember the reader. He or she won't be familiar with the market so I must make sure that my details are clear.

Finally, here is a selection of descriptive essay titles similar to those that you might be given in an examination. Choose one and write between 350 and 500 words.

1 Describe somewhere you go to when you want to be alone and say why this place is so special to you.

2 Describe the scene at a concert hall or sports ground before the main event begins.

3 Describe your favourite shop or market stall and some of the people who work there.

4 Describe a ceremony in which all your family took part.

5 Describe a place which you know well at two different times of the day.

Argumentative writing

An argumentative writing task requires you to construct a logically-developed argument. It is not necessary to attempt to give equal weight to opposing points of view, but what you write should be clear and rational and supported by appropriate examples and references. You should try to avoid becoming too emotional in your approach and/or filling your essay with personal comments and anecdotes which detract from your main line of argument.

Exercise 1

Here is an example of a piece of argumentative writing. Read it through carefully and list the features that you think make it an effective piece of argumentative writing. Do you think that there are any features of it which reduce its effectiveness? Do not read the commentary which follows until you have done this.

'You Can't Judge a Book by its Cover'

Do you agree with this statement?

I often hear people say things like, 'Wow! Look at that girl! I love her dress,' or, 'Oooh, see that boy! He's got a great physique!!' When saying these things, do we ever stop to think that we are only looking at the appearance of a person and not at their inner self and what they possess inside them?

Nowadays, people seem to concentrate too much on what they look like and what others think of them. It always seems to be about a person's appearance and not about that person's actual personality. This is a mistaken attitude to have, as we fail to see what people are really like and what they have inside them.

As humans, we tend to make judgements of people by looking only at their appearance. For instance, people might say, 'Look at the dress that girl is wearing! I'm sure she can't come from a very good family.' In saying this, we have automatically judged that girl only on the grounds of what she looks like and the clothes she is wearing.

We have failed to see what lies inside her and what she is really like. We do this all the time, often without realising that we are doing it. Is that what we really want?

A number of people may argue that it is a good thing to dress up and look good, not only for others but for ourselves as well. I definitely agree with this. However, it should not happen to the extent that this becomes everything a person cares about. Think about it; if all we cared about was what we looked like, nobody would see us for the people we really are, but rather for what we look like on the outside. If we continue with this attitude then we may well produce a future society which cares only about superficial appearance; is this what we really want? I don't think so. When watching television we automatically make comments about how good-looking or not certain presenters are and quite often comment on what they are wearing. In many cases, however, while we are doing this we fail to take any notice of what they are saying and the important messages they may be trying to communicate. This is what having too much interest in appearance is doing to us. It makes us miss out on some of the important things we should be paying attention to.

People, often teenagers, say things such as, 'There's no way I'd go out with that girl; she's so unattractive!' Such a comment shows that the person making it has been conditioned by the attitudes of the society of which he is a part. His friends tend to spend their time commenting on the appearance of people, and so he automatically judges the girl only by what she looks like—and the appreciation of beauty is a very subjective thing, anyway. I'm sure this is not the attitude we would want our children to have. We must stop paying too much attention to the physical appearance of people around us, and of ourselves.

Being too interested in appearance even leads to people being distracted from their studies. I'm sure parents have heard their children say things like, 'Mum, I can't study right now. I have to get ready and look good. I'm going out tonight!' This is exactly what happens when people care too much about their appearance. They usually tend to stop doing work only because they care so much about their appearance. It becomes a pointless distraction.

We, as individuals in our society, must make sure that we stop worrying too much about our appearance as this is what will lead to us becoming an egotistic and ignorant generation. Appearance is not everything.

Suppose this essay was written under time constraints and was appreciated by teachers. Here are some of the reasons that make it an effective piece of argumentative writing.

- The tone is confident, not overly formal and clearly conveys the attitude of the writer.

- There is a focused and direct opening which immediately engages the reader.

- The writer keeps the argument within the bounds of his/her own experience.

- There is a clear focus on the topic.

- The writer does not try to include more points than it is possible to handle within the limited time available.

- The essay is structured through logically connected paragraphs which help to further the writer's argument.

- There is a confident control of sentence structures and types with short sentences being used effectively to emphasise key points.

- The writer skilfully blends direct statements with direct questions which engage the reader and develop the argument.

- The essay develops from particular comments to more generalised concerns which widen the scope of the argument.

- There is a strong conclusion which powerfully sums up and re-emphasises the writer's point of view.

Planning points

A good argumentative essay should be based on a well-controlled structure which leads the reader clearly from a well-defined opening to a forceful conclusion. A good way to make a plan for such an essay is by writing down the topics of each paragraph and then organising them into their most effective order. Here is the paragraph plan for the essay given earlier.

- Introduction: Do we judge people only by their appearance? (Note that, for effect, the writer has made this point the topic of the opening two paragraphs.)

- It is a feature of human nature to do so.

- However, many people consider it important to look good.

- At some time or other we all comment on the appearance of other people.

- Our opinions of people's appearance are influenced by the views of those around us.

- But beauty is in the eye of the beholder.

- Conclusion: Appearance is not everything and a society which thinks it is will not be a pleasant one.

Exercise 2

Here is an example of a less successful attempt at writing an argumentative essay. This contains many errors of expression. It contains a number of relevant points but the structure of the essay and the linking between paragraphs have quite serious limitations. Read the essay carefully and then (i) re-write it, correcting all the errors of expression that you can identify and (ii) write your own response to the task, using the ideas contained in this essay, but re-organising and developing them to produce a more focused piece of work.

'Do you Consider Sport an Important part of Life?'

Sports means every physical and mental effort we make to use extra energy our body consume, for example energies like fat, that most of us consume regularly. Sport is the key to a healthier life.

Sport is an important part of our life. Through sport we can prevent us from getting diseases like cholesterol, cardiovascular diseases, diabetes. Doing sports activities will help us from getting these diseases. Nowday, campaigns are made by government to sensitise people about diseases like cholesterol, diabetes as this level of people carring diabetes is rising everyday.

With sport, specially football helps us to develop strategies either in playing football or in other part of our life, for example in making new business strategies, in business decision making. And also sports helps us to face problems in life and become more responsible, patient and face social matters more easily and become more dynamic.

Nowdays sport is not only becoming an activity better a job because many people are talent in many sport field like football, Athletics and many others, scientifically in is prove that when a person is doing sport, his/her organs are more developed than those who are not doing.

By doing sport the life expectancy of our organs tend to have a longer life than other citizens. Also with sport we help our body to re-inforce our muscles so as to be able to do work which needs efforts and in some ways helping others like encouraging friends or neighbours to do sport, by showing them how to do sports.

By giving elders and youngsters the example that we must do sport to have a good health, encourage future generations to have a good health by doing sports and naturally will sensitise people not only to have a good health but also to a good health we need a good environment, and also a good or clear place to do sports activities. By this it will carry down a reduction in pollution, of course it won't be an immediate change it will take years to come, but where there is a will there is a way.

Sports for me is not only important in some way or another it is vital. Because with sport we can bring many changes in our life either Physical, Health, or Attitudes and behaviours, with sport a person can be more discipline and responsible in life. Sports is the key to success.

Exercise 3: Structuring an Argument

Here is a collection of jumbled topic sentences which, when reorganised, will provide the skeleton for an argumentative essay on the subject, 'Life is so easy for teenagers today; it was so much harder when their parents were young.'

How far do you agree with this comment? Organise the sentences into what you consider to be the most effective order and then write your essay based on this plan.

- Advances in technology have made things a lot easier for teenagers nowadays.
- When I compare my life with that of my parents, I notice that there are many differences.
- Advances in the technology which is so readily available to nearly all teenagers, as well as making things easier, also produce their own problems.
- On the other hand, my friends and I face considerably more and different pressures.
- Taking all these points into consideration, it is possible to come to the following conclusion.
- Other changes in society have also meant that today's teenagers have an easier time than our parents did.
- These were certainly issues which did not bother our parents as the causes of them did not exist in their day.

Emotive vocabulary

In Chapter 2, we looked at how carefully chosen vocabulary allows a writer to convey precise shades of meaning. Having an awareness of the connotations associated with certain words and phrases and of their effect on a reader is particularly helpful when you are writing argumentatively and trying to encourage a reader to agree with your point of view. Consider these statements made by a politician:

'We should consider the possibility of raising taxes; however, our opponents in parliament will not be in favour of this.'

'We should consider the possibility of raising taxes; however, our enemies in parliament will not be in favour of this.'

'Opponent' is a neutral word; it simply refers to members of a different political party with different principles. 'Enemies', however, is an emotionally-charged word and implies that the people with different ideas (the same people who were described in the previous sentence as 'opponents') have some malicious purpose and want to cause harm to the speaker and his/her colleagues. The second sentence would be likely, therefore, to provoke an angrier response from the speaker's supporters.

Exercise 4: Emotive Language

Identify and explain the effects of the emotively-charged language in the following paragraph.

> Out in the vast and empty oceans, if we are lucky, we will be able to observe the whales—the noble, graceful and immensely powerful giants of the sea. They are peaceful creatures whose self-contained, gentle lives do not interfere with our land-based existence. We become aware of them when they burst awesomely from the depths, spouting water skywards as if in greeting to those who are watching.

> And yet, there are some people whose response to their nobility and innocent joy of living is a harsh and cruel one. To them, the whale is an object of sport which they must hunt and destroy in order to prove the pathetic superiority of their murderous technology. The factory ships are a dark stain on the wide seas.

Tools for argumentative writing

When you are writing to express your views on a particular topic, one of your main concerns is to convince your readers of your point of view and to persuade them to agree with you. There are certain writing techniques that you can use which will help you to be successful in this purpose. For example, with this type of writing, it is important that you adopt an appropriate tone (you should aim to be persuasive but not aggressive); you should pay close attention to the structure of your argument, particularly to introductory and concluding paragraphs and to the devices you use to link paragraphs as a way of furthering your argument.

Remember to try to use actual examples and, if appropriate, facts and statistics to support your arguments. You also need to think carefully about your vocabulary, especially whether to choose emotively-toned words.

Exercise 5

Here is an extract from an article entitled 'Why Homework is a Bad Idea' published in 'Hub Pages', an on-line magazine site. It is a good example of how an argument is constructed and expressed in such a way as to persuade the reader to share the writer's point of view.

Read the passage carefully. With a partner, make notes of the main points of the writer's argument and then identify and explain the key features of the writer's expression, in particular commenting on any use of emotively-toned language. Read the comments following the passage after you have done this.

Depending upon the school in question, children can be subjected to homework as early as kindergarten, and certainly this burden has been imposed on every child by the third grade.

At the elementary school level, especially, this is a bad idea because young children are known for having a very short attention span. They have already been forced to sit still for approximately 6 hours at school, with usually only 2 short recess breaks and lunch.

Any teacher can vouch for the restlessness that occurs by the end of the day. By the time school is out, the kids just want to go home, relax, and *be a kid*! It is the rare child who enjoys homework, and whose parents do not wage battles of one degree or another over the subject.

Typically, the child will arrive home, have a snack, possibly a short play break, and then be sat down to do their homework. I doubt there are many parents who will not agree that this can be a traumatic time. The child has already been exercising his or her brain all day at school. They need time to digest the material, not do busy work at home.

Busy work, you say? Yes, that is exactly what homework is. Especially the sort of homework that involves copying out questions already printed in the textbook. This is a waste of time, paper, and face it, a cause of frustration, extra tiredness and sloppy penmanship. Little hands tire and cramp up easily.

If you look at school as a child's 'job' and compare other jobs held by adults, you will soon realize that there are not very many jobs that require the employees to take work home and continue to work on their own time. The teaching profession is one of the exceptions, but they can reduce their own 'homework' load *by not assigning homework to their students*! Look at all the extra paperwork and 'correcting' that would eliminate!

There is another even more practical reason for eliminating homework. The common argument in favor is that the homework is intended to reinforce the day's lessons.

That's a nice theory, but it is something of a straw man defense. If the lesson was presented well, and the student understood it, they will remember it.

If the lesson was not understood, then what happens at homework time? The student is lost, has no idea of the concept, and will practice and reinforce errors instead. Now, extra time and work must be done to reverse this problem, the student will have suffered wasted time, some degree of mental trauma in having his/her work red-penciled, and depending upon thier personality, a possible blow to their self-esteem.

This is a good example of a piece of effective argumentative writing. The writer adopts a deliberately controversial stance; the tone of voice, however, is initially calm and reasoned, at times almost colloquial in its vocabulary ('be a kid') and use of personal pronouns ('you'), both of which devices help to directly involve the reader.

As well as this, however, the writer cleverly uses more generalised statements such as 'I doubt there are many parents who will not agree …' and 'there are not many jobs that require employees to take work home …' which give the argument a sense of authority. The overall balanced tone of the writing also serves to give greater force to the emotively-toned vocabulary ('they have already been forced to sit still …', 'some degree of mental trauma …') which occurs effectively throughout the piece.

The writer also skilfully controls her sentence structures using a mixture of complex and shorter sentences to great effect; this technique is used most effectively in the sentence which concludes the fifth paragraph and which emphatically sums up a key point in the argument.

Exercise 6

Now, using your summary of the main points made by the writer in 'Why Homework is a Bad Idea', write your own essay on the topic in which you present an opposing argument.

Exercise 7

Write an argumentative essay on the topic: 'Money Can't Buy Happiness'. How far do you agree with this statement?

Given below, in no particular order, are some comments which you may want to use as points in your argument.

Record amounts are being paid out by parents on birthday parties and celebrations to ensure that their child's big day is one to remember.

Ian Wright, one time professional footballer and now a TV presenter, spent three days in the wilderness with Kalahari Bushmen. 'I feel very humbled by the Bushmen,' he said. 'They don't know anything other than their life and they seem pretty happy.'

'Have you ever added up the cost of bringing up a child? Parents in the UK may spend up to £10,000 a year in bringing up their children.'

City traders can earn millions but their average retirement age has fallen to below 40; stress and sickness are the causes.

More and more people are finding that giving to those in need is more satisfying than buying luxuries for themselves.

Finally, here is a selection of argumentative essay titles similar to those that you might be given in an examination. Choose one and write between 350 and 500 words.

1 'The challenges of life bring out the best in young people.' What are your views?

2 'People are much too interested in their appearance nowadays.' Do you agree?

3 What aspects of your education do you think will be most useful to you in adult life?

4 'Animals and birds should never be kept in cages.' What is your opinion?

5 'Children do not spend enough time with their parents nowadays.' What is your opinion?

6 Discursive writing

Sometimes the requirements to recount personal experience, views and feelings, are tested individually through descriptive writing tasks (which allow you to recount your feelings) or argumentative tasks (in which you can express your views). Some essay topics, however, offer you a much wider scope as they allow you to refer to all three of these requirements; such essays are what are known as discursive writing tasks. You have a certain amount of freedom in the way you approach the tasks as you are able to make your own decision about the particular aspect of the task that you want to make the focus of your writing.

Exercise 1 : Music

Here is an example of a discursive topic and a sample essay. As you read it, make notes of what in your opinion make it an effective piece of writing. Are there any aspects of the essay which are less successful? In particular, you should consider the writer's use of language and the structure of the argument.

> William Shakespeare, one of the greatest writers who ever lived, said: 'If music be the food of love, play on.' Isn't that enough testimony to the power of music? Each one of us listens to music everyday, whether consciously or subconsciously. We hear it everywhere on the radio, on the television, on our compact disc player, and even perhaps, in the next door neighbour's whistling. Be it music from the 60s, pop music, grunge, rap, classical, baroque or Mozart symphonies, it is all from the same family — music.
>
> Music has evolved over the centuries. Two or three hundred years ago, everyone was listening to what we now call classical music. This was what made composers like Beethoven, Bach, Haydn and many others famous. Over the last one hundred or so years, a great range of popular music has developed including the music of the Beatles which

appealed to our parents in the 60s through to popular rock music of today from which bands such as My Chemical Romance and Nickelback are raking in millions of dollars.

Without a doubt, music has a positive effect on the psyche, as proven by studies around the world. Soothing music such as slow ballads or instrumental music calms the senses and helps us to relax. It helps us to unwind after a long day at work and therefore reduces stress levels.

Heavy metal and rock music, on the other hand, can also produce a beneficial effect, albeit in a different manner as some people prefer listening to loud music to release tension and stress as they feel that works for them. If it does them good, who are we to tell them to turn the volume down?

Studies have also shown that listening to classical music helps with brain development. This is why expectant mothers often put on music by Mozart in the hope that their child will grow up to be the next Einstein.

Music can break down barriers of distance, age, race and creed, as shown by the 'Live 8' concert which was held in 2005 at eight different locations around the world simultaneously. These concerts were held in the hope of raising enough funds to alleviate poverty in the continent of Africa. The project was a success and definitely proved that music can bring people together.

National anthems are also a form of music and, more importantly, they are national symbols for a country. Most champion athletes will say that the greatest moment in their lives is when their national anthem is played as they receive their Olympic or World Championship medals. Indeed, most organisations, including schools, have their own anthems with which their members can identify. These tunes symbolise oneness and unity and are sung by everyone who belongs to that organisation, regardless of their position within it.

However, too much of something is not a good thing. If we have our radio on at full volume throughout the day, seven days a week, sooner or later it could take a toll on our hearing as our hearing range will decrease and in some cases this may result in deafness. Therefore, we should always be sensible about what we do and listen to music in moderation.

Much has been said about music throughout history and, whether we like it or not, it is here to stay. Music allows songwriters to express their feelings through lyrics, pianists to express their emotions through their piano playing and it is a vast industry which provides many people with their daily living. So, why not look through that CD collection of yours, choose a song you like and spin it for, according to Auerbach, 'music washes away the dust of everyday life.'

The writer of this essay has sensibly decided to focus on only a limited range of ideas. (One of the potential problems with one-word titles is that without careful planning it is very easy for a student to try to include too many points and become confused.) This writer has deliberately chosen to write about the type of music which most appeals to him or her but has developed from writing about specific types of music to make some more general comments about the value of music to all people. The essay is well structured and the use of quotations at the beginning and end, to act as a kind of frame for the ideas included, is particularly effective.

Tools for discursive writing

Planning points

Discursive essay writing requires a different approach from writing an argumentative essay. A successful discursive essay covers a range of points which allows the writer to express his or her own experiences, views and feelings, although none of these points is necessarily any more important than another. This means that, very often, a discursive essay does not follow a single line of argument but instead contains a range of points linked by the common theme of the title. For this reason, when planning this type of essay, you may find that a spider diagram approach is the most effective way of doing so. For example, the essay on Music would have had a plan something like this:

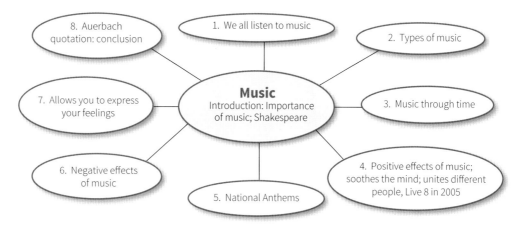

As you can see, there is no correct order in which these ideas can be expressed (apart from the introduction and conclusion); the skill of the writer lies in relating them together within the general framework.

Perhaps more than in other types of essay, the discursive essay is something in which the style of the writer is as important as the content of the essay. The real skill in producing this type of writing lies in the ability to take a single topic and then elaborate upon it, developing it in a variety of ways through making imaginative connections between different ideas.

Exercise 2

Here is an example of a professional writer dealing with the apparently uninteresting title 'Appetite'. Read through the essay carefully and when you have finished, write two or three paragraphs in which you comment on what makes it an effective piece of discursive writing. You should comment on the writer's use of language, his use of examples and the structure of his writing.

One of the major pleasures in life is appetite, and one of our major duties should be to preserve it. Appetite is the keenness of living; it is one of the senses that tells you that you are still curious to exist, that you still have an edge on your longings and want to bite into the world and taste its multitudinous flavours and juices.

By appetite, of course, I don't mean just the lust for food, but any condition of unsatisfied desire, any burning in the blood that proves you want more than you've got, and that you haven't used up your life. Wilde said he felt sorry for those who never got their heart's desire, but sorrier still for those who did. I got mine once only, and it nearly killed me, and I've always preferred wanting to having since.

For appetite, to me, is this state of wanting, which keeps one's expectations alive. I remember learning this lesson long ago as a child when treats … were few, and when I discovered that the greatest pitch of happiness was not in actually eating a toffee but in gazing at it beforehand. True, the first bite was delicious, but once the toffee was gone one was left with nothing, neither toffee nor lust. Besides, the whole toffeeness of toffees was imperceptibly diminished by the gross act of having eaten it. No, the best thing was in wanting it, in sitting and looking at it, when one tasted an inexhaustible treasure-house of flavours.

So, for me, one of the keenest pleasures of appetite remains in the wanting, not the satisfaction. In wanting a peach, … or a particular texture or sound, or to be with a particular friend. For in this condition, of course, I know that the object of desire is always at its most flawlessly perfect. Which is why I would carry the preservation of appetite to the extent of deliberate fasting, simply because I think that appetite is too good to lose, too precious to be bludgeoned into insensibility by satiation and over-doing it.

For that matter, I don't really want three square meals a day — I want one huge, delicious … table-groaning blow out, say every four days, and then not to be too sure where the next one is coming from. A day of fasting is not for me just a puritanical device for denying oneself a pleasure, but rather a way of anticipating a rarer moment of supreme indulgence.

Too much of anything — too much music, entertainment, happy snacks or time spent with friends, creates a kind of impotence of living which one can no longer hear, or taste, or see, or love, or remember. Life is short and precious, and appetite is one of its guardians, and loss of appetite is a sort of death. So if we are to enjoy this short life we should respect the divinity of appetite, and keep it eager and not too much blunted.

It is a long time now since I knew that acute moment of bliss that comes from putting parched lips to a cup of cold water. The springs are still there to be enjoyed — all one needs is the original thirst.

Source: from I Can't Stay Long by Laurie Lee

In this essay Laurie Lee has chosen to base his ideas on his own life experiences and his character and personality are clearly apparent, most noticeably in the third paragraph in which the example of the experience of eating a toffee as a child is developed into a detailed account which, despite its light-hearted tone, nevertheless contains a serious reflection on the nature of human experience.

Exercise 3

This is a sample essay written on the topic 'What lessons can we learn from the past?' As you will see, the writer has some quite good ideas but fails to make very much of them. Re-write the essay, developing fully the points originally made and adding ideas of your own. You may choose to conclude with a statement different from that of the original writer.

Lessons from the past don't always make our present life happier; sometimes those lessons make our life worse because we can never forget how we learnt those lessons. Parents always tell us that we can learn the hard way or the easy way; the easy way being we listen to them and do what they tell us to, and the hard way being to go out there, do something and actually realise that maybe we should not have done that but now we have learnt our lesson so we won't do it again. People say, 'Once bitten, twice shy'. I believe this is true and I've learnt a lot of my lessons this way such as now I know it's not a good idea to run into a wall because a broken arm and a sprained wrist have made me scared to go anywhere near a solid wall and I know I won't be running into one again soon.

But I don't think that lesson will make my present life happier because I am just left with memories and an arm I can't put any pressure on.

Some lessons I learnt make my present life happy. I'm glad I never walked off with a stranger as my parents told me not to do, but I don't think the lessons we learnt in the past have much influence on the way we live our present lives.

Exercise 4

Here are some discursive writing topics accompanied by some suggested opening paragraphs. Make your own spider diagram plans for each one of the topics and then write your own essay(s) on one or more of them, developing from the given paragraphs.

Weekends

Weekends never seem to arrive and when they do they are over too soon. They are times when the whole family can be together at home to do what they wish. For those of us who are at school they provide an opportunity to catch up with some much needed sleep, to complete those pieces of homework we've been intending to do every night of the week yet somehow never got round to and also, weekends are times for us to relax and spend time with our friends. Weekends provide opportunities for everyone no matter what their age or circumstances.

The Joys of Travel

What is meant by the word 'travel'? To some people it means spending a lot of money and flying to far-away places for a family holiday; to others it could simply involve leaving home in the morning and making the same journey to their place of work or study as they did the day before and the day before that. It depends on your outlook as to whether you see travel as being a functional or romantic activity.

Those who think in the latter way are likely to see their main means of travel as being either on foot or by using public transport such as buses and trains. On the other hand, those who seek the romance of travel may want to make long sea voyages or dream of riding round the world on a powerful motorcycle and camping under the stars at night. The joys of travel are many and varied.

Food

Food means different things to different people. Basically, it can be defined as substances which we ingest every day to keep us alive. To some people it is no more than this; to others it is a source of pleasure and excitement and to these people discovering and sampling different kinds of food and recipes from all parts of the world is one of the great motivations of their lives. In contrast to this, however, far too many people in some parts of the world suffer from shortage of food and are unsure as to where their next meal will come from. We need to keep all of these ideas in mind when writing about this topic.

Living in a City

'It's too noisy; I can't hear myself think. Everybody is rushing about with no care for anyone else. All I want to do is to leave this town and retire to the countryside where I can be at peace among the pleasures of nature.'

'There's nothing more exciting than living in the middle of a great city. You have all the entertainment you want—cinemas, theatres, concert halls, sports arenas. Everywhere you look, people are moving around purposefully; it's said that the city never sleeps—I wish that I could be awake 24 hours a day to make the most of what it has to offer.'

These are just two opinions about living in a city; where do your own views fit in?

Finally, here is a selection of discursive essay titles similar to those that you might come across in an examination. Choose one and write between 350 and 500 words.

Write about some of the things that make you happy and relaxed at the end of a school day.

- Cats

- Being Young

- Mistakes

- The Future is a Serious Matter

7 Personal writing

Sometimes the requirement to recount personal experiences is tested directly by essay titles which require you to write about an experience or occasion that has occurred in your own life. If you decide to tackle such a task, it is worth keeping some guidelines in mind.

- It is better to base what you write on something which actually happened rather than trying to invent a situation and claiming it to be true.

- The reader, however, will not know what really happened. So you can elaborate a little on the details or even combine two actual separate experiences into one.

- The reader will not know anything about your personal circumstances. Remember that you need to provide a context to your account and give some brief information about other people who were involved.

- Remember you are at the centre of the piece of writing — it is important that you make yourself interesting and communicate the key elements of your personality.

Exercise 1: Crab Racing

Here is an example of a piece of personal writing; the author is writing about an unusual sporting contest which she witnessed while visiting an island in the Caribbean.

Read it carefully and then make a list of the features which make it an effective piece of personal writing. In particular comment on how well it fulfils the rules printed above.

Crab racing turned out to be an inspiration. I don't know how long it had been since the creatures left their natural habitat but they looked as if they had resigned themselves to their fate. Even if the barrel they had just been taken from contained sea water or, alternatively, mud from their very own swamp, all memory of home had now gone.

They languished in the afternoon sun as if they hadn't a care in the world. Since ropes would be ridiculous on creatures that size, a sturdy piece of string was attached to the anatomy of each crustacean. The minders spent much time in examining claws and paying attention to details. In addition to the string, there was a second prop. It was one which could be described as the urging and steering mechanism—a stick. When the race began I tried not to rationalize or demand too much logic from what was taking place. But it was madness to the utmost degree. A number of male adults were holding a piece of string. At the other end of the string was a crab. The men were endeavouring to urge the creatures forward at a satisfactory pace with the aid of the stick. One crab was going backwards and continued to do so regardless of any attempts to the contrary. Three of them appeared to be moving diagonally. Two others seemed to be dancing a quadrille.

As always, there was a maverick. Slowly but surely he was inching forward. The crab was moving slowly but surely towards the finishing line. It was not so much a race as an exercise in patience. Not far removed from taking your pet snail for a walk. There was no longer any reason to scuttle. When you scuttle, you move with some intent to escape. If you are tethered by a string and the radius of your movement is governed by its length, then

what's the point? These crustaceans, in any case, looked as if they no longer knew the meaning of the word scuttle. Even worse, some seemed to be experiencing difficulty in moving a claw forward. I didn't know the rules of the race. Were there any? Was it my imagination or did I notice some tugging on the string? It would obviously serve to pull the crab forward at a speed not of its own volition. My eyes were riveted on the maverick some short distance from the finishing line.

The spectators were better behaved than the ones in Trinidad. However, one or two began voicing their doubts about the precise physical condition of the winner.

'You dirty cheat!'

'The crab dead! All you can't see the crab dead?!!'

I felt the protestors had a point. The only movement from the crab was the involuntary one made by any motion of the string.

'How all you people so stupid? All you can't see the crab already dead when he haul it across the line?!'

This was very interesting. The crab went into a series of jerks as the minder worked the string to demonstrate it was still in the land of the living. Alternatively, it could indeed have been involuntary. Death throes.

'How man in he right mind go want pin medal on dead crab?!'

Howls of laughter from the spectators. The winner sat unconcerned. Surely rigor mortis had now set in. At any rate, no attempt was being made to lift a claw in triumphant acclamation of victory.

'And I say it dead before it cross the line!'

A number of people formed a circle around the winner. There was much close inspection going on.

'He move! I see he move!' It was confirmed by another person in the circle. There was much jubilation. Everyone seemed happy. Everyone, that is, except the crab. And while we settled down to enjoy the rest of the afternoon, I was left with my doubts. Was there life in that body when the first claw slithered across the line?

Source: from *Sequins for a Ragged Hem* by Amryl Johnson

Here, the writer has chosen to describe her experience of an unusual event — crab racing. She skilfully captures the atmosphere of the occasion, in particular through her reproduction of the speech of the other spectators. However, what makes this a particularly effective account is the personality of the writer: she comes across as being fascinated, amused and a little bewildered and the informal tone she uses, reinforced by some direct questions, successfully engages the reader.

Exercise 2

The following example of a piece of personal writing was produced under time constraints. Teachers might consider it to be a good piece of work overall.

But, as you will notice when you read it, its structure, expression and the writer's focus on the topic could still be improved. The title is: Write about two occasions when you had great fun as a child.

Everybody has a <u>lot of memories to remember</u>, especially those during childhood. Whether they are sweet or bad memories they remain fresh in our minds. People always say that sweet memories are hard to forget. I really agree with this statement because we cannot deny it. Memories will always remain. I want to share with you two occasions when I had great fun as a young child.

The first is of when I entered primary school and the second is when my family celebrated my birthday without my knowing.

1994 was when I entered primary school. When my father drove me to Sunnyside Primary School I felt very scared because I did not know my new situation and environment. When we arrived at that school, my feelings changed from scared to excited because the environment of the school was very beautiful. It was surrounded by many plants and a few metres away from the school could be seen a beach. The beach is known as Golden Sands Beach.

When I entered the class, I saw many children with their own parents. Some of them were happy because they were going to meet new friends but others were crying. My mother always gave me support and encouraged me not to be scared but to be happy at all times. Moreover, my cousins were in the same class as me. I would soon be making new friends.

As the time passed by, we all got to know each other well and played together. It was a good time when I made new friends. Although I am seventeen now, it is hard to forget them because they were all kind and always helpful to me especially if I had any difficulties in a particular subject.

My second occasion when I had great fun as a young child was during the celebrations for my seventh birthday. One day before my birthday came, that is on the 4th April 1996, it seemed strange that my parents did not bring me and my brothers and sisters to go shopping because usually before a birthday they would bring us to buy stationery and new clothes.

My parents went shopping by themselves and when they got home, as usual, they had bought household goods and new stationery for my brothers and sisters. However, I felt very sad because they said that they had forgotten to buy new clothes and stationery for me. Because of my parents' lack of concern, I cried alone in my room.

Later, on the morning of April 5th 1996 as usual my brothers and sisters and I went to school and when we came back home, I was surprised because my parents celebrated my birthday party and had bought me a chocolate cake. I felt very happy when my parents gave me a big present that was a bicycle and then held me tightly.

Those are two occasions that were very exciting and fun. I will never forget either of them. They will always be in my mind.

The writer of this essay adopts a logical narrative approach to the topic. The content is relevant and gives a clear account of two separate occasions (although the description of the birthday celebrations tends to concentrate more on feelings of sadness than fun).

However, the account is a little lacking in excitement and interest; the character of the writer is not clearly apparent as although he makes an attempt to state his feelings he does not explore them in any great detail. Similarly, although the written expression is largely accurate, the vocabulary and sentence structures are a little repetitive and lacking in originality: these are further reasons why the writer's personality is not communicated strongly.

Some words and phrases in the essay have been underlined as more suitable expressions could be put in their place. Rewrite these passages, using words of your own, in order to make the account more interesting or to correct an error of expression.

Exercise 3

Write about your own first day at school (either at primary or secondary school). In particular, concentrate on describing particular details of the day which remain in your memory and try to bring out the feelings you had about the experience — be honest in your description; the feelings can be happy or sad.

Tools for personal writing

The key to effective personal writing lies in:

i   the selection and treatment of a suitable episode (or episodes) to describe

ii the way you present yourself as narrator.

Questions that ask for a piece of personal writing will usually suggest that you write about a specific occasion in your life, for example: Describe an occasion when you tried to be helpful but things went wrong. It is important that you focus what you write closely on what the question requires and avoid producing a mini- autobiography. You should not attempt to describe too complicated an event when writing under time constraints.

However, when thinking about approaching a personal writing task such as the one above, once you have decided on the episode about which you plan to write, you will need to make certain decisions.

• What shall I write about?

• How do I describe the event? Will I describe it exactly in the order it happened, or should I start from the disastrous conclusion and work back to the beginning?

• How much information do I need to give to provide the context for the episode?

• How will I conclude the account? Should I stop at the point when things went wrong or should I finish with saying what I learned from the experience?

• How much space should I give to describing what other people said and did?

• Should I treat the episode as comic or serious?

• If I decide to be humorous, how can I make it funny for the reader?

All of these are the sort of questions any thoughtful writer is likely to ask before beginning to write. There are, of course, no right or wrong answers. What is important is that you, as a writer, should have thought of these (or similar points) and used them to ensure that whatever approach you take will provide an account which is consistent and convincing.

Humour

Personal essay topics frequently allow the opportunity for writers to approach the account of their chosen episode in a humorous way. It is perfectly acceptable to take such an approach, but try to avoid being too heavy-handed in trying to communicate what you think might be funny.

It is likely that the events described are amusing in themselves — the most effective comic writing comes from the style of the writer and the language in which they are described: very often an understated approach is the most effective. The humour achieved by writers is very much dependent on the way they present their personalities as part of their narrative.

Exercise 4

Here are some possible answers to the questions posed above; write your own essay based on them.

- I'll describe the time I tried to cook the dinner and nearly set the house on fire.

- Perhaps I could start at the end with an opening sentence such as: 'Never again,' I thought as I gazed at the smoke-filled chaos which had once been mother's beloved kitchen.

- I'd better give a bit of background: how old I was; why I thought it would be a good idea to help out with the cooking. I did it as a surprise for Mum and Dad who were out at work. My elder sister was looking after me but she was on the phone with her friends.

- I think the approach I'm taking will allow me to make a reflective conclusion—things wouldn't have gone wrong if I hadn't left everything cooking in the kitchen to watch my favourite TV programme. Perhaps I could finish with my sister being blamed for the whole episode as she wasn't keeping her eye on me!

- I think I'll keep what other people said and did to the minimum—that will give greater emphasis to what Mum and Dad said when they saw what had happened.

- I think humour will provide the best approach. I need to concentrate on describing the things that went wrong in preparing the meal (upsetting bowls of flour etc.) as well as the final disaster. The most effective approach will be to present myself as well meaning and naïve and not really understanding how I finished up producing so much chaos.

Reading for enjoyment

Here is an example of a piece of humorous personal writing. It is taken from Gerald Durrell's autobiography '*My Family and Other Animals*'. Durrell became a famous naturalist and in this book he describes how his interest in living creatures was formed in his childhood on the Greek island of Corfu. In this episode, he describes how he unwittingly caused chaos at lunchtime by leaving a matchbox containing a mother scorpion and her babies on the mantelpiece. The other characters in this account are his mother; his brothers Larry and Leslie; his sister Margo; the family maid Lugaretzia and Gerald's dog, Roger. Much of the humour derives from the way in which the author builds disaster on top of disaster and describes it using an understated narrative voice. This is a very effective piece of humorous, personal writing; as you read it, consider closely how the different aspects of the passage combine to produce an overall description of chaos and confusion.

Lunch-time with scorpions

Then one day I found a fat female scorpion in the wall, wearing what at first glance appeared to be a pale fawn fur coat. Closer inspection proved that this strange garment was made up of a mass of tiny babies clinging to the mother's back. I was enraptured by this family, and I made up my mind to smuggle them into the house and up to my bedroom so that I might keep them and watch them grow up. With infinite care I manoeuvred the mother and family into a matchbox, and then hurried to the villa. It was rather unfortunate that just as I entered the door lunch should be served; however, I placed the matchbox carefully on the mantelpiece in the drawing-room, so that the scorpions should get plenty of air, and made my way to the dining-room and joined the family for the meal. Dawdling over my food, feeding Roger surreptitiously under the table and listening to the family arguing, I completely forgot about my exciting new captures.

At last Larry, having finished, fetched the cigarettes from the drawing-room, and lying back in his chair he put one in his mouth and picked up the matchbox he had brought. Oblivious of my impending doom I watched him interestedly as, still talking glibly, he opened the matchbox.

Now I maintain to this day that the female scorpion meant no harm. She was agitated and a trifle annoyed at being shut up in a matchbox for so long, and so she seized the first opportunity to escape. She hoisted herself out of the box with great rapidity, her babies clinging on desperately, and scuttled on to the back of Larry's hand. There, not quite certain what to do next, she paused, her sting curved up at the ready. Larry, feeling the movement of her claws, glanced down to see what it was, and from that moment things got increasingly confused.

He uttered a roar of fright that made Lugaretzia drop a plate and brought Roger out from beneath the table, barking wildly. With a flick of his hand Larry sent the unfortunate scorpion flying down the table, and she landed midway between Margo and Leslie, scattering babies like confetti as she thumped on the cloth. Thoroughly enraged at this treatment, the creature sped towards Leslie, her sting quivering with emotion. Leslie leapt to his feet, overturning his chair, and flicked out desperately with his napkin, sending the scorpion rolling across the cloth towards Margo, who promptly let out a scream that any railway engine would have been proud to produce. Mother, completely bewildered by this sudden and rapid change from peace to chaos, put on her glasses and peered down the table to see what was causing the pandemonium, and at that moment Margo, in a vain attempt to stop the scorpion's advance, hurled a glass of water at it. The shower missed the animal completely, but successfully drenched Mother, who, not being able to stand cold water, promptly lost her breath and sat gasping at the end of the table, unable even to protest. The scorpion had now gone to ground under Leslie's plate, while her babies swarmed wildly all over the table. Roger, mystified by the panic, but determined to do his share, ran round and round the room, barking hysterically.

'It's that boy again . . .' bellowed Larry.

'Look out! Look out! They're coming!' screamed Margo.

'All we need is a book,' roared Leslie; 'don't panic, hit 'em with a book.'

'What on earth's the matter with you all?' Mother kept imploring, mopping her glasses. 'It's that boy … he'll kill the lot of us …Look at the table … knee-deep in scorpions …"

'Quick … quick … do something … Look out, look out I'

'Stop screeching and get a book, for God's sake … You're worse than the dog … 'Shut up, Roger.'

'By the Grace of God I wasn't bitten … '

'Look out … there's another one … Quick … quick.'

'Oh, shut up and get me a book or something.'

'But how did the scorpions get on the table, dear?'

'That boy … Every matchbox in the house is a deathtrap … '

'Look out, it's coming towards me … Quick, quick, do something …'

'Hit it with your knife … your knife …Go on, hit it …'

Since no one had bothered to explain things to him, Roger was under the mistaken impression that the family were being attacked, and that it was his duty to defend them. As Lugaretzia was the only stranger in the room, he came to the logical conclusion that she must be the responsible party, so he bit her in the ankle. This did not help matters very much.

By the time a certain amount of order had been restored, all the baby scorpions had hidden themselves under various plates and bits of cutlery. Eventually, after impassioned pleas on my part, backed up by Mother, Leslie's suggestion that the whole lot be slaughtered was quashed. While the family, still simmering with rage and fright, retired to the drawing-room, I spent half an hour rounding up the babies, picking them up in a teaspoon, and returning them to their mother's back. Then I carried them outside on a saucer and, with the utmost reluctance, released them on the garden wall. Roger and I went and spent the afternoon on the hillside, for I felt it would be prudent to allow the family to have a siesta before seeing them again.

Source: from *My Family and Other Animals* by Gerald Durrel

Finally, here is a selection of personal essay titles similar to those that you might be given in an examination. Choose one and write between 350 and 500 words.

1 Write about some of the things that make you happy and relaxed at the end of a school day.

2 What changes have you seen in your school since you joined it?

3 Describe the biggest challenge in your life.

4 Describe a day when you were very unhappy.

5 Describe a special family celebration when things went unexpectedly wrong.

8 Narrative writing

Some essay topics require you to write a short story. Choosing one of these topics allows you to use your imagination and show how creative you can be. However, a narrative essay is not an easy option to do well. Before starting on it, you need to bear the following in mind.

- **Do not make the story too complicated**; you have only a limited period of time and it is important that you plan your answer carefully to keep it tightly focused.

- **Keep closely to the given title or topic**; many short stories written under time constraints fail to make a good impression because they wander away from the topic and lose credibility.

- **Try to write a story which contains events which could be within your own experience**; teachers do not find unsophisticated secret agent stories particularly enjoyable or convincing.

- **Try to break up long sections of narrative with passages of direct speech.** Remember, however, that making direct speech sound authentic and punctuating it correctly are difficult skills. If you don't get it right, your story will not be successful.

- **Do not repeat a story you have read or written elsewhere;** memorised stories seldom fit the given topic and teachers will always spot the joins.

Exercise 1

Here are two examples of narrative writing. The topic is to continue the story using the following opening sentences: *Having reluctantly agreed to meet them at 11 pm precisely in this deserted part of town, I anxiously scanned every moving shadow. I was afraid I would miss them, afraid also that they would not turn up.*

Both the examples deal with the same topic. Read through the two stories carefully and make notes of the good and less good qualities contained in each one. Discuss with a partner how they could be improved and which one you think is better and why.

Copying out and using the following grid will help you in making this comparison.

(The features listed in the grid should also provide a good checklist of points to cover when you are writing your own essays of all types.)

	Essay 1	Essay 2
Treatment of task		
Presentation of situation		
Narrative standpoint		
Tone/register		
Vocabulary/expression		
Structure		
Development of ideas		
Conclusion		
Structure of paragraphs		
Paragraph linking		
Technical accuracy		
Sentence structures: range/variety		
Punctuation		
Grammatical accuracy		
Use of idiom		
Spelling		

Essay 1

Having reluctantly agreed to meet them at 11 pm precisely in this deserted part of town, I anxiously scanned every moving shadow. I was afraid I would miss them, afraid also that they would not turn up.

I hadn't spent this much time alone in so long, it felt wrong. It felt like somehow I wasn't meant to be here. 'Shut up!' I said to myself. 'Don't be stupid.'

As my eyes eventually adjusted to the darkness, objects around me became clearer, much easier to distinguish. I was standing under a huge oak tree, where we had agreed to meet. I knew this must be the right one: there wasn't another tree for miles.

Eventually after what seemed like an age, I heard voices and they seemed to be getting closer. Not yet being able to make out what the voices belonged to, I strained my ears to hear what they were saying.

'No, I'll grab him and you can knock him out.' A cold fear rushed through my veins, I knew for sure that voice belonged to Rajeev.

I felt sick to my stomach when I realised that this had all been a plan, Rajeev had it in for me— big time.

I knew in that moment that I had to get away. I had to run. I ran until my heart was pounding my ears and my breath ached in my chest. I ran through fields, over fences and stone walls. I ran through gardens and dark alleyways. I ran along roads and streets that I had never seen before.

When I finally came to a stop, my legs didn't feel like they belonged to me anymore. I looked around and then it hit me. I didn't have a clue where I was. All I had thought about was running and getting as far away from Rajeev as was possible.

I tried to think back to when I was running. I could remember running but my surroundings were hazy. I wasn't even sure if I was in the same town anymore. I sat down on the cold, muddy floor, rested my back against a low wall and closed my eyes.

And then I felt it, a strangled sob, fighting to escape from the pit of my stomach. I had to hold it in, I couldn't cry now. What if someone walks past? I reopened my eyes and blinked to settle the tears. I knew that I wasn't upset about being lost. Well not upset enough to cry anyway. It was Rajeev that bothered me. Now that he had his own little gang, he had become worse than ever. It wasn't just name calling and joking anymore.

Tomorrow was Monday; there was no way I could go back to school. I had to stay away for as long as possible. Wait for things to calm down a bit. I couldn't go back home, I'd be made to go to school. I could sleep here. It was cold and it was muddy but if it meant that I didn't have to go to school tomorrow I was willing to. I curled up in a ball, pulling my knees up to my chest and closed my eyes. I promised myself that by the end of tomorrow I would have everything sorted out. There was just one question left—How?

Essay 2

Having reluctantly agreed to meet them at 11 pm precisely in this deserted part of town, I anxiously scanned every moving shadow. I was afraid I would miss them, afraid also that they would not turn up.

I then hear a crowd of voices, I look around but see nothing, the suspence is killing me.

After 5 months of being bullied, threatened, intimidated, it all comes down to today, this is my chance to show them that they can't do this to me anymore, I've had enough.

I then hear my name being called. 'Where are you?' They shouted.

Next thing there I am standing on my own, with a crowd of 7 boys walking towards me.

I told him to come on his own, but he was obviously too much of a coward, he had to bring his friends.

As they walk towards me, I hear loud footsteps, my heart begins to beat faster and faster.

I have to stay cool and calm. I'm not going to continue to be picked on all the time, I have to be strong.

As the boys are getting closer and closer to me, I'm very scared but I'm not going to show it, otherwise he'll see, and think his won and he can carry on bullying me, and other people, well, he cant, not anymore. It was 11:15 pm, pitch black, with only the streetlights on, I can honestly say this is the scaryist time in my life.

I then feel a hand over my mouth, then tape goes over it and a bag is placed over my head …

You will almost certainly have come to the conclusion that Essay 1 is the better of the two and your notes in the grid should provide a clear indication as to why. However, both essays share some positive qualities. Both deal with events which are convincingly within the experience of the narrator; neither of them is over-ambitious as each concentrates on one particular episode and develops it effectively without introducing too many complicated twists and turns. Also, each of the two writers appears to have planned for the essay to conclude at a particular point in order to leave the reader in some suspense.

Now we will look at the points in the grid in more detail to see how they can be used to help you in planning your own narrative writing.

Treatment of task

Presentation of situation and setting

The essential point about producing an effective short narrative is to be economical in the telling of the story. Lengthy scene-setting and description is better suited to a long novel. Your concern is to engage your reader as quickly as you can but also to ensure that the situation you are presenting can be understood straightaway. Before starting to write your story, you should try to put yourself in the position of your readers. Ask yourself a couple of straightforward questions such as, "What do my readers need to know?" "What important details about the setting of the story do I need to give them so that they can quickly understand the background of where the events happen?"

Remember, you may have a clear idea of the scene in your mind, but a reader will not have it unless you give a clear, but not over-detailed, description of it.

Narrative standpoint

The first decision you have to make is whether you intend to present your story through a first or third person narrative. A first person narrative is possibly more effective in allowing a reader to identify with the narrator (which is particularly important for a short narrative) and it also means that the events described can only be those within the narrator's experience — again, an effective way to limit the focus and range of your narrative.

On the other hand, using a third person narrative allows for a more omniscient approach. If you intend your story to conclude with, for example, the death of the central character, then a first person narrative standpoint may present problems!

Characters

When you are writing a short story (especially under time constraints), you should try to be as economical as you can in your description of characters and not to include too many of them in your story. It is important that you give some brief and pertinent details about your characters so that your readers can form an idea of them in their minds and can, therefore, build up an understanding of how those characters are likely to act and behave in the course of the story.

However, these introductory details need be little more than one sentence character summaries such as, "Rita, who was always on time for everything and never looked untidy or tired" or "David was the sort of person who never panicked and was always a reliable friend." Once you have established your characters, it is important that they then behave consistently with the character you have created for them. (The extract from *My Family and Other Animals* in the chapter on Personal Writing and the short story 'Coconuts' which concludes this chapter are both very good examples of economical presentation of characters and setting.)

Tone/register

The tone and register you use will, to some extent, depend upon the narrative standpoint you have chosen. A first person narrative allows for a more informal, colloquial approach which is suited particularly to the type of story told in the two examples above.

The narrator's tone of voice is an effective way of communicating his or her personality and character.

A short narrative can be made much more effective if a person's character is communicated through their language register rather than by a lengthy description of that character.

Vocabulary/expression

The vocabulary used by the narrator of the story and his or her sentence patterns are also an effective way of establishing character. An awareness of the associations and connotations of the vocabulary you use will also help to establish a suitable atmosphere for the story you are telling.

Structure

Development of ideas

Your narrative should quickly establish the direction it is going to take and the sequence of events should be planned to develop coherently. Keep your readers in mind at all times; if they find it difficult to follow what is happening, they will quickly lose interest. Remember that you have only limited time in which to write, so try not to produce too complicated a narrative. When making your plan, make sure that you decide on how to finish your story and keep the end point clearly in mind as you are writing.

Conclusion

When you plan your narrative be sure that you have a clear understanding of how it is going to conclude. You may decide that your final paragraph will wrap up all the loose ends of your story or you may want to leave your readers in mid-air.

What is important, however, is that, whichever the ending you choose, it should be the one you have planned for. The best narratives arrive at a logical conclusion, rather than just stopping because the author can think of no more to write. (The logically planned conclusion can, of course, be unexpected by the reader.)

Structure of paragraphs

You should use paragraphs to structure your story and their topic sentences are likely to provide the key stages of your narrative. Remember, each paragraph should be a unity within itself, but should also contribute to the overall unity of the story you are writing.

Although short, one or two-sentence paragraphs can be very effective for emphasising details, they should be used sparingly; too many short paragraphs result in a fragmented narrative.

Paragraph linking

Although it is important to link your paragraphs to form a coherent narrative it is equally important that you vary the ways in which you link them to ensure that you retain the interest of your readers. Try to vary the position of the topic sentences as well, to add variety to your style.

Technical accuracy

Sentence structures: range/variety

Just as you are concerned about varying your paragraph links and lengths, so you should also think about varying the length and structure of the sentences in your narrative. Repetitive sentence types (for example, having all sentences follow the same subject–verb opening pattern: 'It was…', 'He did…', 'She said…') very soon become monotonous.

Think about varying the word order and mixing simple and complex sentences and use each type as appropriate. For example, simple sentences can effectively create pace in your narrative while complex sentences are more suitable for reflective or descriptive sections.

Use of idiom

In an examination, you should be able to write accurately using Standard English. Although narrative writing sometimes requires a less formal tone than some other types of essay, it is important that you still use Standard English — although, if some of the characters in your story speak using a local dialect, it is perfectly acceptable to reproduce that at times to add authenticity to your narrative as long as this is not overdone.

However, if you are writing in an informal register, inappropriate or outdated colloquialisms will not convince your readers of the credibility of the character using them.

Punctuation, grammatical accuracy, spelling

As in all examination essays, it is important that you observe the conventions of correct spelling, grammar and punctuation. You may, of course, make one of the characters in your story speak ungrammatically for effect. But it is important to show that you can write accurately in the rest of the narrative so that the reader is aware of your including the ungrammatical sections deliberately to create an intended effect.

Exercise 2

Choose three of the following topics. (a) Produce a skeleton plan (using paragraph topic sentences) for each of them. (b) Write opening and concluding paragraphs for each one you have chosen using a first person narrator. (c) Write opening and concluding paragraphs for each one you have chosen using a third person narrator.

1   The Closed Door

2   Write a story beginning: 'It was just an ordinary weekday morning …'

3   Breaking the Rules

4   The Woman with the Bicycle

5   Write a story containing the words, 'I knew that it would never work.'

Exercise 3: Coconuts

Here is a short story by the writer, David Iglehart. Read it for pleasure in your groups. But while doing so, discuss with each other and make notes about how the author has presented his characters and their surroundings and circumstances, and how he has structured the story to develop to its conclusion. You should also consider the tone of the narrator and what message the story contains, if any.

When you have collated your comments, independently write your own analysis of the story, explaining what makes this an effective short story.

Coconuts

In the suburb of Adyar, just west of Chennai, a religious society dedicated to brotherhood, the study of comparative religion, and the unexplained laws of nature and man has built its international headquarters. With its large following and financial resources, it has filled its park-like estate, bordered by the blue Bay of Bengal and the ornate palace of a former maharaja, with churches and temples from every major creed in history. The temple is well attended by worshippers from the surrounding area. Germans, Lithuanians, and Argentineans in ochre robes meditate at graceful Buddhist stupas or wander contemplatively among the

flowering plants and trees brought in by members from around the world, and Hindu pilgrims by the thousands come to see an enormous banyan. With religious attractions like these, not to mention its famous library of rare books and ancient palm-leaf manuscripts, the society has a constant stream of visitors. And for years all of them had to pass before one small mystery that hardly anyone noticed – the life-and-death struggle between two women who sold coconuts, just outside the iron front gate.

To say that Chennai is hot is a ridiculous understatement. Anyone who walks outside in the fiery depth of summer and wants to stay sane, not to mention survive, has to have something to drink. Those visitors to the society who had the money and didn't mind walking several blocks out of their way could buy an iced, sugared milk at the stand of the Tamil Nadu Milk Cooperative. Those who had smaller budgets and had walked too much already, could buy an inexpensive coconut right at the gate and drink the milk. Business was steady, if not lucrative, and, miraculously, ninety-five percent of it always went to the woman who stood on the left of the gate. Naturally this drove the other woman crazy.

It takes a certain amount of capital to go into the coconut business, enough to buy a hefty knife to slice off the tops, a box of straws, and a pile of coconuts, not the small black kind found in American supermarkets but the big, oblong green ones full of clear, tangy milk. That may not sound like a lot of money, but for someone who lives on a couple of hundred rupees a month in a thatched hut that gets flooded out twice a year by the monsoon rains it's hard to save up. Otherwise ten or twenty women might have been selling by the gate. Still, the two women were equally well equipped.

Vijaya, on the left, was rounded, in her early sixties, and had long gray hair. She wore a threadbare sari but looked healthier and more prosperous than, say, the gangly bicycle repairman who had to live and work among the branches of the small banyan across from the milk stand or the wizened old bullock shoe-er who waited motionless by the main road with his tiny hammer, tiny anvil, strip of rope, and handful of tiny nails.

Sharada was also in her sixties, but she was thin and in bad tone and wore her hair short. Her sari was torn in many places, and she was obviously not doing well. Most of the day she stood alone, glowering before her unsold pile of coconuts.

When a festive crowd of pilgrims got off the city bus in front of the society, those who wanted coconuts were drawn magnetically to Vijaya. Only when Vijaya's line was long enough to make them completely impatient would one or two pilgrims drift over to Sharada, just enough to keep her hanging on, perpetually mystified.

A grey-haired man from the neighbourhood might walk up on his way to a lecture on devotion to Krishna, slender and dignified in his white shirt and linen dhoti. A beautiful young woman in a lavender and gold silk sari, with jasmine flowers in her thigh-length black hair, might arrive with her small children to see the holy sites. And although both women at the towering gate would hold up identical coconuts and quote identical prices, although Sharada even called out louder, each customer would go to Vijaya, leaving Sharada sputtering in rejection.

To Sharada, this was a terrible injustice. Years before, she had been the first of them to set up business there. A widow with grown children and a living to earn, she had searched through the area for a suitable spot for months, selling one coconut here, another there, wherever she wasn't driven away by other vendors. One day she passed before the society and noticed with surprise that the former coconut seller was gone. When she asked around and learned that the other woman had died, she seized the place as her own at once, intuitively selecting the more auspicious corner on the right. And at first she made decent money there for her trade, and thanked the gods for the good fortune that had come her way. Finally she had the chance to get out of the financial difficulties that had plagued her all her life and the near destitution she had been thrust into after her husband's death.

But after only a few months of success, she arrived one morning to find Vijaya setting up her own pile of coconuts on the left of the gate, which meant she'd been observing Sharada and should have known better. The perpetually bored, khaki-clad guard at the gate smiled at the implications, but Sharada was greatly offended. The previous seller had always worked alone, and there really wasn't enough business to be shared. Sharada glared at Vijaya and told her in loud, abusive terms that she'd better go away. But Vijaya merely nodded with a reserved politeness, pointed out that there was plenty of room, and then ignored Sharada and went about her work. After that, the two competitors didn't speak for more than a year. Their competition, however, began in earnest.

Sharada knew her business was bound to decline, but she believed she could hold on to most of it. For some weeks she watched with satisfaction as Vijaya hardly made a sale. She hoped the woman would admit defeat quickly and find some other place, but day after day Vijaya stood patiently and very still before her pile, holding up a green coconut for all to see, like a living effigy. And when someone finally bought one, her face would light up momentarily and she would hand over the coconut graciously, as if it were a blessing. Gradually more and more passers-by began to buy from her, especially repeat customers, and Sharada counted up a smaller profit each evening.

Appalled, Sharada did everything she could to stem her losses. She made it a point to arrive there first every morning. She arranged to have a larger pile of coconuts than Vijaya's, and even wiped them all down with a rag so that they looked clean and fresh. The straws in her box were pristine. She sharpened and re-sharpened her knife, and wielded it with a flourish when she sliced off the tops. But over the period of a year her sales plummeted for reasons she simply couldn't comprehend, while Vijaya's rose.

It would have been better for her to pick up her coconuts right then and move somewhere else, where her prospects might have improved. But the society had been the best location she'd ever found, and if she left she would not only face the search for a new one, but more quarrels with still more vendors, who covered literally every corner in the city. On top of that, it just didn't make sense to her that she couldn't compete. She had been there first! She had established customers! And she not only had the very same supplies, but more of them! Why should she be the one who was dislodged?

She began to observe Vijaya carefully to learn her secrets. Because Vijaya stood still with a raised coconut like a goddess, she did too. She also tried to imitate Vijaya's gratitude and graceful gestures, all to no effect. Besides, they made her feel self-conscious and ridiculous. What was it then, Vijaya's weight? Sharada ate rice ravenously for a while, but no matter how hard she tried she couldn't take on Vijaya's rounded shape. It was too expensive to eat like that anyway.

Then she tried a bold stroke. Early one morning she occupied Vijaya's corner. It was just possible that Indian pedestrians, who usually keep to the left, the way drivers there stay on the left side of the street, would also buy coconuts on the left, although everyone knew that everything on the right was always more auspicious. And her coup had immediate effects. When Vijaya arrived that day, she was plainly taken aback. Sharada watched with unconcealed amusement while the poor woman hesitated a good five minutes, but then Vijaya simply set up shop on the right.

For a few days Sharada's income increased, but then the balance of sales began to tip in Vijaya's favor again, as if on the great scale of life she had the heavier coconut. Sharada was incensed! It was like a slap in her poor face, when she had suffered so much already. Shortly afterwards she began to doubt herself, and she went that night to a temple of Lakshmi, goddess of good fortune, and prayed long and hard.

The following morning, filled with a new determination, she moved back to her old spot on the right. Vijaya let her. This time the relocation had no noticeable effect, and Sharada's downward spiral resumed as if her most earnest prayers had been ignored or rejected.

A note of hopelessness crept into Sharada's voice as she tried to hawk her wares, and she fumed and sulked bitterly when she failed, which did her business still more harm. It simply made no sense to her to lower her prices, since they were standard for the market and set at a pathetic minimum anyway. Instead, she began insulting Vijaya when no one else was there, to the guard's vast amusement. And in moments of frustration, watching her rival tuck away rupee notes in the folds of her sari, she began to mutter to herself venomously and swing her knife around, which scared many customers half out of their wits.

Finally the cauldron of hot emotions within her boiled over. One day when twenty pilgrims clustered about Vijaya for her sacred coconuts made of gold, while none at all went to Sharada, she dropped her coconut to the ground with an ominous thud. Shouting incoherently, she rushed at Vijaya with her knife still in her hand. The crowd around Vijaya parted. The khaki-clad guard at the society's gate shouted something and ran out. A tall man in the crowd grabbed at her, but she darted to the side and he missed. When she was in range, she insulted Vijaya brutally and raised her knife. Vijaya turned toward her with her damned coconut and her own knife, unraised, and looked at Sharada wide eyed but hardly moving, and took a deep breath. A sad sympathy filled her eyes, as if she understood Sharada's plight only too well. Sharada hadn't expected this. Dismayed, she felt frail and weak before her. In her confused state, she remembered the graceful image of Lakshmi from the temple the night before, which in its splendor seemed to merge somehow with Vijaya's rags. Trembling with a Hindu dread of what would happen to her if she went on, through the laws of karma in this life or the next, stronger by far than her fear of prison, Sharada lowered her knife.

The tall man grabbed her, and then the guard did too. But by then her fire had gone out. She realised she was muttering something even she couldn't understand. The two men sat her down by the gate, and the guard wet his handkerchief with cool water and washed her face with obvious annoyance and distaste. No one called the police because no crime had really taken place, just a moment of anger. Eventually Sharada wandered home without her pile of coconuts, went to bed without eating, and fell into an exhausted sleep. When she returned the next morning, dreading her losses because her coconuts sure to have been stolen, she found them all still there. Actually, they were back again, because Vijaya had paid a boy two of her own coconuts to take Sharada's home the night before and then return them to their place. It was an act of kindness for which Sharada never forgave her. Grimly Sharada took up her old position on the right, and her life resumed its apparently natural, downward course.

For her part Vijaya stood calmly on the left, doing a good trade, barely making money because that was the nature of the business, but surviving, even saving a little. A sweet-natured woman who was also widow and lived on the verge of destitution, she kept close watch of Sharada through the corner of her eye. But though she felt a sense of accomplishment and triumph that sometimes made her smile and glow when the customers crowded around her, she bore Sharada no ill will. By and large she ignored her. Instead, day in and day out for more than twenty years, she stood with perfect confidence at her post before the religious society and focused on her way in life, which was to provide refreshing coconuts as pleasantly as possible to whatever thirsty travelers might come to her, to pilgrims on their way to a banyan tree and holy places, until she came to seem serene and selfless and pilgrims were drawn to her naturally, as if she were herself a holy shrine.

Source: 'Coconuts' by David Iglehart (www.eastoftheweb.com)

Finally, here is a selection of narrative essay titles similar to what you might come across in an examination. Choose one and write between 350 and 500 words.

Write a story based on one of the following.

1 A person who was injured but kept it a secret and caused her friends great trouble.

2 The new bus driver.

3 Write a story with the title: An Unexpected Visitor.

4 Write a story beginning: 'I could tell by his face that he was angry'.

5 Write a story about the rivalry between two elderly people.

Directed writing

The Directed Writing task (sometimes referred to as Transactional Writing) differs from the Composition tasks as teachers look for evidence that you have read the information given in the question carefully besides assessing you for your writing skills. As with all writing tasks, it deals with those Assessment Objectives concerned with organisation of paragraphs, correct use of vocabulary, grammar, punctuation, spelling and the use of Standard English. In particular, however, it focuses on all of the following Assessment Objectives.

1   Articulate experience and express what is thought, felt and imagined.

2   Sequence facts, ideas and opinions.

3   Use a range of appropriate vocabulary.

4   Use register appropriate to audience and context.

5   Make accurate use of spelling, punctuation and grammar.

Task Fulfilment is an important consideration for assessing your work in Directed Writing. This means that you will be assessed on how well you:

* show an understanding of the purpose of the task

* show how clearly you are aware of the situation that you have to describe and the audience for whom you are writing

* show an appropriate use of the format in which you have been instructed to write

* develop and organise all three points that you are required to include in your answer

* can give your opinion and justify it

* adopt a tone and register entirely appropriate to the task.

As mentioned here, all Directed Writing tasks will contain three content points that you must include in your answer; at least one of these will require you to justify your personal opinion about the topic concerned or to make an interpretation of the information given in the task. It is important that you elaborate appropriately on the content points in your answer — it is not enough simply to mention them in passing.

Here is an example of a typical Directed Writing task.

> Your local youth group has arranged a camping trip for its members.
>
> As Secretary of the group, you have to write a letter to the parents of all those wishing to go on the trip informing them of the arrangements involved.
>
> As some parents may be concerned about the safety of their sons/daughters, you should, in your letter, attempt to reassure them of the precautions which are in place.
>
> Include in your letter the following information:
>
> • when and where the trip will take place
>
> • cost of the trip/travel arrangements
>
> • the activities involved and the measures taken to ensure the safety of those participating in the trip. Begin your letter, 'Dear Parent ...'

Now let us consider more closely what this task involves.

• You have been given a situation (the camping trip), a character or persona in which to write (secretary of a youth group), an audience to address (parents) and a genre (a letter).

• You have been given three specific points of detail to include in your letter.

• It is important that the letter you write is fit for purpose.

• The tone and register you use are, therefore, particularly important.

• Your approach should be friendly but not too informal. You should try both to encourage parents to let their children take part in the trip and to reassure them of the safety aspects involved.

• The information concerning details of the trip should be given clearly and unambiguously.

• You have been told how to begin the letter; there is no need to put your address at the top although you may want to make up a contact telephone number to include in the letter at an appropriate point.

• You should plan the order of your paragraphs carefully to ensure that all points are clearly communicated in a logical and reader-friendly way.

• Of the three points which must be included some, such as the cost and dates of the trip, must be stated clearly and comprehensively; information about the activities involved and the safety precautions will need some suitable elaboration in order to convince parents that their children will be safe.

• The opening and concluding paragraphs are particularly important in establishing an appropriate tone for your letter.

• Remember that your letter requires a suitable valediction (Yours sincerely) and you should include your position (Secretary) after your signature.

Exercise 1

Now, plan and write your letter, using the notes above.

Forms and purposes

Although only one Directed Writing task might be set each year in examinations, over a period of years, different forms of writing and different purposes for writing might be tested. It is important that you become familiar with the requirements needed for each of the main forms of writing that may occur. These are: letters, speeches/talks, reports, accounts and newspaper/magazine articles.

Letters

Letters may be either formal or informal. For example, you may be required to write a letter to a magazine or a newspaper; to a company or organisation asking for information or complaining about something; to a friend or acquaintance asking for their support in a venture you are undertaking or apologising for something which happened.

Of the above examples, the letters to a newspaper or an organisation are likely to be formal and the letter to a relative or acquaintance will be informal.

As a general rule, if you begin your letter by addressing the person to whom you are writing by his or her position or title (for example, Dear Editor, Dear Sir/Madam) then you are using a formal register.

However, if you are addressing the person by name (for example 'Dear Mr. Miah or Dear Rafiq' or 'Dear Aunt Urmi'), then you are writing informally. Different letter conventions apply, depending upon which sort of letter you are writing.

Formal letters should begin with your address and the date in the top right-hand corner of the page and with the title and address of the person to whom you are writing on the left-hand side of the page, starting below the last line of your address. The salutation (Dear Mr ...) should be written directly under the last line of the recipient's address and, if you have been asked to quote a reference, this should be placed on the middle of the following line. Your letter should conclude with either 'Yours faithfully' or 'Yours truly' and you should sign both your first name and surname or family name.

A formal letter will, therefore, look something like the one given below.

```
                                                    Your address

                                                    Date:

Recipient's name and title

Recipient's address


Dear Mr
                              Ref: AXGTY/2007
_____
_____
_____
_____
_____
_____
_____
_____
_____
_____
_____


Yours faithfully


```

Informal or personal letters are, by their very nature, less detailed in their layout. Again, your address and the date should be written in the top right hand corner of the page but it is not necessary to include the recipient's address.

You should place the salutation (Dear Urmi) at the left of the page on the line immediately below the date. If you address the person by their title and name (Dear Mrs. Patel) then you should conclude the letter with the standard valediction for a personal letter which is 'Yours sincerely'.

However, if you are writing to a close friend or relative, 'Yours sincerely' usually sounds too stilted so you need to decide on a valediction which reflects the closeness of your relationship to the recipient such as 'With love' or 'Yours affectionately'.

A personal letter will, therefore, look something like the one given below.

```
                                              Your address

                                              Date:

Dear Urm

_____

_____

_____

_____

_____

_____

_____

_____

_____


Yours affectionately

Soraya
```

The main difference between a formal and a personal letter will be found in the tone of what you write. Formal letters will be more objective in tone and written in formal Standard English; personal letters will be more colloquial with a greater use of abbreviations.

Similarly, formal letters will focus almost exclusively on the issue with which they are concerned, whereas personal letters are likely to ask questions about the recipient's health and that of his or her family besides dealing with the main topic of the letter. However, you should be careful not to make a personal letter so colloquial that your teacher reading it cannot understand what is being said.

The advice above is concerned with the format to be used when writing letters in everyday situations; as already stated, letters set as part of Directed Writing tasks will not require you to give details of the sender's or recipient's addresses unless such details are provided for you in the instructions to the question. You should, however, always include an appropriate date.

Exercise 2

Choose one of the topics below and write an appropriate letter.

1   You have recently bought an expensive piece of electronic equipment which has developed a fault. Write a letter to the retailer explaining when you bought the item, what the fault is, and asking for either a full refund or a brand new replacement for the item.

2   Write a letter to your aunt who lives in another town. You are visiting that town for the purpose of attending an interview and you wish to ask your aunt if she could provide you with overnight accommodation for two nights.

3   Write a letter to the Editor of a local newspaper, in which you explain why there should be more leisure facilities provided for young people of your age group in your local area, and asking for support from other people in your campaign for suitable facilities.

Speeches and talks

If you are asked to write the words of either a speech or a talk, it is important that you show some awareness of an oral register in your writing. A speech is generally a more formal form of spoken address than a talk and is likely to be aimed at a larger audience. For example, a talk may be addressed to members of your own class at school, whereas a speech could be delivered as part of a public speaking competition to an audience with whom you are unfamiliar. In the latter case, it would be sensible to begin your response by introducing yourself ('Good evening, my name is ... and I am going to speak about ...'), whereas with the former such an introduction would be unnecessary as your listeners would already know who you are; in this case, your introduction could be much more low-key ('Hello, everyone, you all know me and you won't be surprised that I am going to talk to you about ...').

Remember, also, that both speeches and talks may require you to be persuasive or informative, and you should ensure that the register you use is appropriate to the task.

The instructions to the task will indicate who your audience is. It is important that you keep this audience clearly in mind while you are writing your response as teachers are likely to be appreciative of the use of a tone which is appropriate to the audience.

For example, if you are addressing an audience of 16-year-old students within a school classroom, your language is likely to be more colloquial than if you are addressing an audience of local dignitaries, teachers and parents at a school speech day.

One of the main difficulties when writing the words of a speech or a talk is to ensure that what you write sounds like something which is spoken but avoids being so informal in its structure and vocabulary that it is difficult to assess as an example of Standard English.

The best approach is to ensure that you place your words clearly within an oral framework by starting with a direct address to your audience and concluding in a similar way ('Thank you for listening to what I have had to say.').

Once you have given yourself this type of structure, try to ensure that, at regular points throughout your speech, you address your audience directly (through the use of either the second person pronoun 'you' or the inclusive first person plural 'we') and that you include your audience in what you are saying by directing rhetorical questions towards them.

Much as the speech genre is a central element of the question, you should not concentrate on this at the expense of the structure of your argument and the need to include the points stated in the question.

Finally, it is not necessary to embellish what you write with stage directions such as 'Spoken passionately, while raising both arms in the air'; as a successful writer, you will convey emotions and so on through well-chosen vocabulary and a suitable variety of sentence structures.

Exercise 3

You have been asked to talk to a small group of students in your year group at school about a local tradition or ceremony which you consider to be important. In your talk you should:

- Say what the tradition or ceremony is and when and where it takes place
- Give details of what the ceremony or tradition involves and why it is important to you and your family and friends
- Say what it reveals about the life and culture of your area and why it should be preserved.

Reports

There are two possible types of report that you may be required to write as a Directed Writing exercise. One is a report for a newspaper or magazine giving an account of an event or an episode; the other is a formal report written to be read by someone in authority (the Principal of a school or the police) in which you provide information about something which you have witnessed or in which you have assembled facts and details to support a particular proposition (such as suggestions for redesigning a student common room).

Whichever type of report you write, it is important that you organise your response carefully. You must ensure that the facts you are communicating are followed easily by the reader. You should keep the audience for your report in mind at all times and write using a register appropriate to that person's position.

Remember that, with a formal report, the person for whom you are writing is likely to be busy and will not, therefore, appreciate something that is too full of digressions and unnecessary description and does not convey the facts directly.

As a general rule, you should include a main heading at the start of your report ('Proposals for Redesigning the Students' Common Room'). Each paragraph should contain one key point, and the topic sentence should clearly state what this is and point the way forward.

At the end of the report there should be a business-like summing up of the main points with a suggestion as to the next stages to be considered if the task requires this.

If you are asked to write a report for a newspaper or magazine, then certain specific features need to be considered. One of these is that it may be necessary to make the report more immediate or dramatic than would be the case with a formal report. It is important to keep the purpose of your report clearly in your mind and make sure that you avoid the temptation to drift into a narrative style. For example, if you are required to write a report for the police, giving details of a robbery at your house, then make sure that you focus clearly on the facts — for example, the time when you discovered that it had occurred; how long you had been away from home, etc. There is no need, however, to go into details of what you did while you were away because, however interesting it might be to you, it is unlikely to help the police solve the crime!

Newspaper reports, in particular, should start with a headline which will prepare the reader for both the facts and the tone of what follows. They may also contain statements given by other people who were present at the incident being reported. These statements can be written either as reported speech or included in your report as direct quotations (in which case it is, of course, important that you punctuate them correctly as direct speech).

Exercise 4

An incident occurred in your English lesson the other day. Your teacher had had to leave the room on urgent business and while she was gone, a window was accidentally broken. As the class representative, you have been asked by the Principal to submit a formal written report explaining what happened. Your report should include the following details:

- why the teacher had to leave the room and who had been left in charge
- what happened/who was involved
- whether anyone was at fault.

Examples of Directed Writing responses

Here are two sample responses to the same task. Read through each carefully and discuss its strengths and weaknesses with a partner. In particular, make notes on how well the writers have dealt with the following features:

- layout

- tone

- treatment of required details.

- arrangement of ideas

- suitability of salutation and valediction

Exercise 5

You have been chosen to represent your school in a general knowledge competition. You must choose one friend to be in your team. Write a letter to your friend inviting him or her to be in your team. You must include the following points.

- when and where the competition will take place and prizes involved

- a request to your friend to join you in the team and why you think your friend is the best choice for your team

- what preparation you should both do.

Adapted from *Cambridge O Level English Language 1120 Paper 1 Part Two, November 2005*

You must cover all three points in detail. You may also add further details if you wish. Make your letter friendly and enthusiastic. Start with 'Dear ...'.

Letter 1

Dear Sanjeev

It has been a very long time since I ever spent with you or even seen you. This is why I am writing to you, to inform you that there is a general knowledge competition that I believe that you and I could win together. I am writing you to become part of our team and take yet another title.

The competition will be held in my school hall, where you and I captured our first ever public speaking tittle. The competition will be held on 16th November 2007 which gives us a month to prepare for the competition.

In general preparation, our General Studies teacher, Mrs. Charles, has prepared some notes to further our general knowledge. This will help us tremendously and reduce the time taken to research information. I think that this information will be retained in your mind easily for you understand work easily.

I advise that you enter the competition for the prizes is worth the work and time. The third prize is fifty thousand rupees to be shared amongst the team. The second is sixty thousand rupees and three computer towards our school. The first prize is seventy-five thousand rupees also to be shared and five computers towards the school.

I strongly believe that you are the best person to join our team and fill the vacant space. Your mental capacity and quick understanding can help our team to be victorious. Please reply as soon as possible to inform me of your choice.

Yours truly

Sunil

Letter 2

> *Dear Yash*
>
> *How's life with you? I hope everything is fine. Please give my regards to the rest of your family. As I have already told you, I have been named captain of the team which will represent our school in the forthcoming general knowledge competition organised by the Rotary Club. The competition will take place on the 25 November during the summer holidays so it does not clash with our end-of-year examinations. The Rotary Club has already reserved the Town Hall for the occasion.*
>
> *The team consists of three members and I would be glad if you would be one of them. I have already asked Leena and she agrees with me that I should invite you to join us. I sincerely hope that you will as I'm looking forward to working with you.*
>
> *I believe you are the best choice for our team because I know you travel abroad quite frequently. I'm sure your vast experience of foreign countries will be an important catalyst in our success. I also chose you as you have been learning Biology, a subject which neither Leena nor I has studied.*
>
> *If you agree to form part of our team, please make a list and learn everything you can about important towns and cities abroad like London, Paris, New York etc. Leena is studying as much history as she can of all the places she can think of. I have taken up researching details of celebrities and major sporting achievements. I know our teamwork will be central to our success.*
>
> *The winners of the competition will each receive a cheque for 5000 rupees and a week long holiday to a top hotel in Mauritius with all expenses paid. I will be thrilled if you accept this request. Please reply as soon as possible; I must stop now or I'll miss the post.*
>
> *Best regards Sarwan*

Both of these responses cover all the required points for inclusion but the second is a more successful response for various reasons. It is better organised; it has a more consistently persuasive tone and it develops details relating, in particular, to the preparation for the task in a more convincing manner. Whereas, the first answer contains an inappropriate valediction ('Yours truly'), the second uses a more suitable formula for a letter to a friend ('Best regards'). It should also be noted that the written expression of Letter 1 is less accurate than that of Letter 2.

Finally, here is a selection of Directed Writing tasks similar to those that you might come across in examinations. Choose one and write between 200 and 300 words.

Exercise 6

Your school/college has been left a significant sum of money in the will of a former pupil. It is stipulated that this money should be used to provide a facility which the school does not at present possess.

Your Head Teacher/Principal has asked students for written suggestions as to how this money can be best used.

Write a letter to the Head Teacher/Principal. You must include the following information:

- the amount of money involved and what it should be spent on
- a description of the new facility and what it should involve
- the ways in which the whole school will benefit from the new facility.

You must cover all three points in detail. You could also add further details if you wish and make your report clear and helpful.

Exercise 7

You have recently represented your school in a nation-wide, inter-school competition. Although you and your team did not win the competition, you reached the final rounds and found the whole experience to be very rewarding.

Write a letter to your Uncle who lives in another country telling him about your experience in the competition.

In your letter you should include:

- what the competition involved and where it was held
- how your team prepared for the competition and what happened in the competition itself
- what you and your team found rewarding about the whole experience.

Cover all three points in detail. Your letter should be friendly and informative. you should begin your letter 'Dear Uncle...'.

Exercise 8

Your school is holding a writing competition. You are asked to write an article about a person with whom you would like to change places for a day. It could be a famous person or someone you know. Write your article which will appear in your school magazine.

You must include the following:

- which person you would like to change places with and what you admire about that person
- what you would do on that day
- what you think you would learn from changing places with that person.

You must cover all three points in detail. You should add further details if you wish and make your article lively and interesting for your fellow students.

Adapted from *Cambridge 1115 P1 Part 2 A, Oct/Nov 2004*

Exercise 9

While shopping in your local market you witnessed a theft taking place. Although many stallholders and customers chased, the thief was not caught. The police were called and they asked all witnesses to write a report of what they saw.

Write your report; you must include the following details:

- when and where the theft took place
- how the theft was carried out and a description of the thief
- why the thief escaped capture.

You must cover all three points in detail. You may add other details if you wish but make sure that your report is focused on the episode.

Exercise 10

You have just returned from a three-day outdoor activity camp. You have decided to write a letter to a friend about your experiences at the camp.

Write your letter including the details below:

- who organised the camp and where and when it took place
- the activities in which you took part
- the benefits you gained from the experience.

You must cover all three points in detail. You may add further relevant details if you wish.

Writing: Frequently asked questions

Question
How will it affect my performance if I write less than the recommended word limits?

Answer
Answers which are slightly less than the recommended number of words might be acceptable overall but such answers are likely to be self-penalising as ideas may not be developed fully. This could result in your work being considered less successful than if it had been of the required length.

This principle applies to both Directed Writing and Composition.

Question
How will it affect my performance if my answers are longer than the recommended word limits?

Answer
It is likely that by writing too much, especially for Composition, you will penalise yourself. When you are writing under time constraints, the more you write, the less time you will have for planning and checking your work. This means that there is a greater chance of making careless mistakes of written expression which the teacher will not accept or excuse. Remember, also, that if you write too much for the Directed Writing task, you will leave yourself insufficient time to produce an adequate response for the task in Composition.

Question
Will every spelling and punctuation mistake I make affect my performance?

Answer
No. Your writing is likely to be assessed by the overall impression in which the teacher takes into account the linguistic competence you display as well as the relevance and interest of what you write.

The more easily you communicate your meaning to the teacher, the better impression it will make on him/her. However, if your answer contains so many errors of expression, punctuation and spelling that the teacher's understanding of what you want to say is impeded and she or he has to re-read what you have written to make sense out of it, then it will affect your performance negatively.

Question
If I write a really interesting and exciting story, will this compensate for making spelling and grammatical mistakes?

Answer
Only to some extent. The main purpose of the writing task is to assess your linguistic competence; if your expression is not secure, then you will not be fully successful in conveying an exciting piece of work.

Remember that you can make what you write interesting by successful vocabulary choices and controlled, positive punctuation. Do not try to write something which is too ambitious; you will run into difficulties with time.

Question
If I'm not sure how to spell a word, but think it is the best one to use, should I use it anyway?

Answer
The spelling errors which are most serious are those where you misspell simple vocabulary (e.g. freind, dinning room) or when you misspell the same word in different ways in different parts of your essay. An occasional error in spelling, where otherwise your use of a word is correct and appropriate, might be excused by teachers.

Question
How are the Directed Writing tasks assessed by teachers?

Answer
Overall, the linguistic qualities teachers usually look for are very similar to those required for the essay in Composition.

However, for Task Fulfilment there will be a particular emphasis on how well your answer suits the purpose of the task, for example, if you are required to write a friendly letter, it is important that you write in an appropriate tone and are not overly formal; if you are asked to write a newspaper report, then you should show an awareness of the common features of journalistic style, etc. How effectively you incorporate and develop the three content points in your answer is also a very important consideration in this.

Question
How much detail should I give to making the content points?

Answer
It is not enough to just mention the points. Your work must show that you have fully understood the points. This means that you should develop each point sufficiently to show that it has been made clearly. When you are planning your answer for Directed Writing, it is a good idea to use the content points as the basis of your plan so that you can give a clear focus to each point and make it an essential part of your answer. Remember to be precise; if you are asked to give the date when an event occurred, do not just write something general like 'last week' as this is unlikely to provide sufficiently detailed information; the actual day and date would be much more useful.

Writing: Practice in writing

Finally, here is a complete exam-style paper on Writing for you to answer. Try to complete it in the time allowed and make sure that you put into practice all the advice you have picked up from previous chapters.

Directed Writing

Begin your answer on a fresh page. You are advised to write between 200 and 300 words. Total marks for this part: 30

*You have recently been the victim of a minor crime in a public place. When you read the account of the incident in the local newspaper you are angry to discover that the reporter thinks you are the guilty person. You decide to write a letter to the Editor to convince him of the truth. Write your letter to the Editor. You must include the following:

1 when and where the incident took place

2 what the report said had happened and what really happened

3 a request for an apology to be published in the newspaper.

You must cover all three points above in detail. You should make your letter convincing and persuasive to the Editor. Start your letter with 'Dear Editor,' and remember to provide a suitable ending.

Composition

Write on one of the following topics. At the head of your composition put the number of the topic you have chosen. You are advised to write between 350 and 500 words. Total marks for this part: 30

1 Describe someone you know personally who is a mixture of attractive qualities and odd behaviour.

2 If you could live for a month in any other country, which would it be and why?

3 Write about an occasion when someone reacted too quickly and spoilt a perfectly sensible scheme.

4 Imagine you have started a job. Write about a perfect day or a disastrous one.

5 Write a story based on the sentence 'Only when we rushed into the library did we understand why he had shouted out.'

Reading skills

Reading skills are very valuable as they underpin many aspects of our lives, and not just within school. Because of that, it is important to develop strong reading skills outside the context of any examination for which you are preparing.

If you take a few moments to think of the importance of reading, you will realise just how much reading you do in your everyday lives, for example navigating your way round the signposts of town, information on the school noticeboards, the instructions for your homework, etc. At home you may have to read manuals for electronic gadgets, use cookery books – or watch your parents do this –, check times in newspapers of local events or television programmes, etc. Letters arrive at your home from banks, from charities looking for donations, or from businesses trying to sell some goods or services. Newspapers may be bought or delivered to your home, enabling family members to keep up with current affairs and world events.

Reading all of these types of materials – and this is not a comprehensive list – requires many skills, including the ability to scan for information, to follow the line of an argument, to make judgements and to understand vocabulary. Reading for pleasure is a pastime many people find delightful: to lose yourself in the gripping plot of a novel, to be transported in your imagination to an interesting setting or to identify with the fictitious lives of others, all enhance reading skills. The advantages of developing reading skills is something of which you should be aware; these skills have a much wider context than their assessment in an examination. It is also valuable to understand how these skills will be assessed under examination conditions and to practise and develop your reading skills throughout your course.

The key reading skills which you will be developing throughout the course are given in the assessment objectives as follows:

R1: Demonstrate understanding of explicit meanings.

R2: Demonstrate understanding of implicit meanings and attitudes.

R3: Analyse, evaluate and develop facts, ideas and opinions.

R4: Demonstrate understanding of how writers achieve effects.

R5: Select for specific purposes.

The Cambridge O Level English Language Syllabus will develop your skills in reading and answering questions within time limits and therefore you will need to learn to manage your time and to practise questions against the clock. It is important to strike a balance between time spent on reading and writing your answers, and the best way to arrive at this balance is to practise. The aim of this section of the book is to give you that necessary practice in manageable and progressive sections.

In order to build your reading skills, you should try day by day to increase your ability to read a variety of texts accurately and with confidence. Almost certainly you are already doing that, even if you have never stopped to think about it.

Exercise 1

Working with a partner, make a list of the different types of written English to be found in your own homes.

The most obvious types will be books, and the most obvious division of books is into non-fiction and fiction.

Exercise 2

Working with a partner, divide your list of types of written English into non-fiction and fiction.

For non-fiction, you might have something like this: biography, autobiography, travel, information books on, for example, sport or entertainment. But other non-fiction material in your home might also include recipe books, a telephone directory, magazines and manuals on, for example, a computer or a washing machine.

For fiction texts, you might have something like this: science fiction, war, historical, crime, romance, human interest, thriller, adventure, school, childhood. These broad headings for fiction texts are called genres.

Having strong skills in reading English means that you will be able to read a *wide* variety of texts. The more experience you have of reading written English on your own, the better you will develop these skills – and your chances of succeeding in examinations.

The passages you are asked to read in an examination will be either non-fiction or fiction, one of each. Non-fiction passages may be from any one of a variety of topics, whether about modern issues or of a more historical nature; fiction passages may be from any genre.

It is therefore extremely important to familiarise yourself with different types of written English and be able to recognise the characteristics of different types of written English.

Exercise 3

Working with a partner, read the following very short texts of written English. Write each one down and beside each write whether it is non-fiction or fiction.

1   The damage being done to coral reefs in the twenty-first century is a cause of great concern to governments and environmentalists alike.   _____

2   Standing in the shadows of the huge house's garden, he watched and waited. His opportunity would arise soon, he was sure of that.   _____

3   There can be no doubt that computers have brought about a revolution in the way schools are run.   _____

4   'What do you want?' came the robotic voice from the other space ship. Ajay stepped forward, terrified.   _____

5   It was a terrifying sight all right. But at least, thought Sachin, they would soon know the truth. It had been a long, hard battle.   _____

6   It was good that the two families were pleased at the match. Already preparations were under way for the big day.   _____

7   The girls crowded into the assembly hall, where the results would be announced.

    It was hard not to be anxious, although some girls disguised it well by giggling nervously.   _____

8   Television is undoubtedly a useful and pleasant means of relaxation. It can also be educational.   _____

9   The men marched on, their eyes dimmed with fatigue, their feet blistered in their ill-fitting boots, the scream of dropping shells behind them.   _____

10 Many foods contain high amounts of unsaturated fat, which is unfortunately contributing to increased levels of obesity in some parts of **the world**.   _____

Exercise 4

Working with a partner, look back at the texts in the previous exercise which you have judged to be fiction. Against each, write down what genre of fiction you consider it to be. At the end of your list of texts from the previous exercise, write a sentence of your own in which, by referring closely to the language of the text, you justify your choice of genre.

Exercise 5

Write ten short texts of your own, each one not more than thirty words. Write five fiction and five non-fiction texts. It should be clear from the language of each text whether it is fiction or non-fiction, and what genre each of the five fiction texts is.

Exercise 6

Swap your ten texts with a partner. Copy each of your partner's ten texts. Beside each one write whether it is fiction or non-fiction and, in addition, write beside each fiction text what genre it is. When both you and your partner have finished this exercise, swap your work back and correct it for each other. Take time out to explain errors which have occurred in identifying the texts.

Exercise 7

This is an exercise which must be started at home. Bring in to class six types of writing from your own home. These should be a mixture of fiction and non-fiction, and different fiction genres.

Prepare a short talk to the class in which you identify your texts as fiction or non-fiction, identify fiction genres, and single out features of language, giving examples of particular words and phrases which back up your identification.

The purposes of the exercises covered so far in this chapter are to highlight the different types of written English which you already know and to help you to focus on the means of identifying these different types of written English. This in turn will help you to cope with whatever type of comprehension text you are asked to deal with in examinations and to sharpen your focus and hence your ability to perform well.

The most basic task for you in any reading situation is to glean information, which might be no more than simple facts.

Exercise 8 : A Visit to My Grandparents

Read the following short passage, which is fiction, childhood genre, and write down three pieces of information which are contained in it.

I was finding it hard going, pushing on the pedals. The tyres slipped on the stones and the clods of dry earth. The closer I got to the house, the bigger the yellow house grew in front of me, and the heavier the weight that crushed my chest, taking my breath away.

My grandparents lived there, but what if they thought I shouldn't be out on my bike on my own? What if they phoned my mother and asked her to come right over to collect me, bike and all? How grown up would I feel then?

Exercise 9: Computers in Education

Read the following short passage, which is non-fiction, discursive genre, and write down three pieces of information which are contained in it.

Computers in the classroom have brought about a revolution in education. No longer are all lessons taught by the teacher using the board and a piece of chalk, or by children reading books. These methods of learning have their place of course, and an invaluable one at that, but computers allow individual learning—children can also work at their own pace, which increases their motivation.

Exercise 10: Another Working Day

Read the following short passage, which is fiction crime genre, and write down three pieces of information which are contained in it.

> Sergeant Smith was not very fond of his boss, the Chief Superintendent. But they had a reasonable working relationship, which was just as well, thought Sergeant Smith, as the two of them drove to their latest crime scene—a house where the owner had been attacked by two young men who had broken in to steal anything of value they could find, especially jewellery.

Exercise 11: The Retreat

Read the following short passage, which is fiction war genre, and write down three pieces of information which are contained in it.

> The air was grey with diesel fumes, and straggling wearily through the stench, and for the moment moving faster than the traffic, were hundreds of soldiers, most of them carrying their rifles and their awkward greatcoats—a burden in the morning's growing warmth. Walking with the soldiers were families hauling suitcases, bundles, babies, or holding the hands of children. The only human sound Turner heard, piercing the din of engines, was the crying of babies.
>
> Source: from *Atonement* by Ian McEwan

Exercise 12: Space Travel

Read the following short passage, which is non-fiction, discursive genre, and write down three pieces of information which are contained in it.

Perhaps the strongest proof of the ingenuity of mankind is the fact that human beings have begun the exploration of space. People in the second half of the twentieth century saw men walking on the surface of the moon, which a short time before must have seemed more like science fiction than reality. Spacecraft in orbit has become a familiar, if not a commonplace, phenomenon, and we are no longer surprised to hear about the exploration of space in newspapers or television.

Exercise 13: Nelson Mandela

Read the following short passage, which is non-fiction, autobiography genre, and write down three pieces of information which are contained in it.

When I was not much more than a newborn child, my father was involved in a dispute that deprived him of his chieftainship at Mvezo and revealed a strain in his character I believe he passed on to his son. I maintain that nurture, rather than nature, is the primary moulder of personality, but my father possessed a proud sense of rebelliousness, a stubborn sense of fairness, that I recognise in myself.

Source: from *Long Walk to Freedom* by Nelson Mandela

Exercise 14: Examinations

Read the following short passage, which is non-fiction, discursive genre, and write down three pieces of information which are contained in it.

There can be no doubt that the examination season is a tense time for students. Months, and sometimes years, of preparation have gone into each examination, and students feel under great pressure to perform to the best of their ability and achieve their potential. Sometimes their parents, however unwittingly, add to their pressure by talking about the examination results of other members of the family, stressing how important it is to succeed at school if one is to succeed in life. Teachers, too, in their desire to prepare their classes well for the impending examinations, put an additional burden on to the poor students, who sometimes dread the possibility of letting down their hard-working teachers who have done so much for them.

12 Selecting content points in summary questions

A key reading skill, and one that you will be assessed on, is to scan and analyse a text, by identifying and summarising required information, such as similarities and differences, or advantages and disadvantages, or problems and solutions, or causes and effects, or actions and consequences. A question which deals with your ability to demonstrate these skills is a summary question. In any summary question, you are asked to read a passage and show that you have understood it by writing a short text of your own based on the original. The subject matter of your short text, or summary, will depend on what you have been asked to do.

What follows is a list of typical summary tasks. What you are asked to do here is called the **rubric**.

1   Write a summary of the problems encountered on the journey.

2   Summarise the skills the writer thinks are necessary to become a good swimmer.

3   Summarise the advantages and disadvantages of recorded music.

4   Write a summary of the ways in which advertisers use celebrities to sell products, and the disadvantages of this strategy.

5   Summarise the ways in which coral reefs are under threat.

The first stage is to read the rubric properly and be quite clear in your mind what you are being asked to do.

The second stage is to read the passage carefully, or the area of the passage which you are being asked to summarise, at least twice. Read it the second time with the summary rubric in mind.

The third stage is to select the content points. These are the pieces of information which you need to follow the rubric. So, in the first example listed earlier, the content points will be problems encountered, in the second example the content points will be skills necessary to become a good swimmer, and so on. At this stage, you are free to use note form or to write in sentences; you are can use words from the passage or your own words. We will say more about this at a later stage; at this point, we are thinking only of content points and how to select them.

At first, silk was the monopoly of the Chinese Imperial family, who used it for sunshades and banners. As it became more plentiful, it was utilised for clothing, but exclusively for members of the court. Only the Emperor and his first wife wore yellow silk—the colour of the sun. His other wives wore violet, as did high-ranking officers. Those of the second rank wore red and the rest had black. Later, the favour of being able to wear silk was extended to landowners and merchants who sought to out-dazzle each other in a riot of colour. Eventually, ordinary people could wear silk clothes, although they were not so elaborately embroidered, nor did they have the tea-cups of lacquered silk, customary with the wealthy. Silk achieved importance in other ways. Until the invention of paper, people wrote on it. It became a popular currency, with even taxes paid in it.

Working with a partner, make a list of the six things people used silk for.

The first stage is to read the rubric carefully and be quite clear in your mind what you are being asked to do. In this case, the task is to list the uses of silk. These words — 'used' and 'silk' — should be at the front of your mind as you approach stage two.

The second stage is to read the passage carefully at least twice. Remember to keep the key words — 'used' and 'silk' — at the front of your mind as you read.

The third stage is to select the content points. These are the pieces of information which you need to follow the rubric.

The word 'used' appears in the first sentence and it is easy to link it to 'sunshades' and 'banners', which follow closely after the word 'used'. The word 'utilised' appears in the second sentence, and 'utilised' is a synonym for 'used'. Good writers avoid repeating words and so this writer has used a synonym, but because we have the rubric key words — 'used' and 'silk' — at the front of our minds, we do not miss the signpost. So it is clear that silk was utilised, or used, for clothing.

The third, fourth, fifth and sixth sentences, and the first part of the seventh, give details of the groups of people who were entitled to wear silk and the colours each group wore. These groups are the Emperor, his wives, high-ranking officers, landowners, merchants and ordinary people. However, because we have the key words at the front of our minds — 'silk' and 'use' — we are not tempted to use any of this material in our list of uses of silk, because this material gives extra information about the use of silk which we have already found, namely that it was used for clothing.

But when we read on into the seventh sentence, with the key words — 'used' and 'silk' — at the front of our minds, we see that silk was used by wealthy people to make tea-cups. The eighth sentence repeats the idea that silk was used and so, although no particular use is specified in the sentence, it is a further signpost and alerts us to the possibility that by reading on we will find other uses for silk.

And so, in the ninth sentence, we see that silk was used as writing material, and finally in the tenth sentence we see that it was also used as money. The extra information about taxes is not a separate point, any more than the information given about the groups of people who wore silk and the colours that they wore. The information about taxes is linked to the idea of money, which we have already found as a point.

People used silk for:

1 sunshades	2 banners	3 clothes
4 tea-cups	5 paper	6 money

These six points are called the content points.

We saw that there are two sections of extra information in the passage. The first section is the detail about the people who were entitled to wear silk and the colours they wore. The second section of extra information is the reference to taxes. These sections of information are not content points because they do not refer to particular uses of silk, which was the rubric.

The purpose of these sections is to give additional information and colour to the passage, to elaborate on the basic information given about the uses people found for silk. They are called elaboration points.

Exercise 2: The Wearers of Silk

Working with a partner, make a list of seven people or groups of people who wore silk, and write beside each group what colour of silk they wore. Do not include ordinary people in your list.

You should have something like this:

1 emperor – yellow

2 emperor's first wife – yellow

3 emperor's other wives – violet

4 high-ranking officers – violet

5 second-ranking officers – red

6 other officers – black

7 landowners and merchants – many colours.

In the exercise we have just done, we see that the section of the passage about people who wore silk and the colours they wore is not a section of elaboration. It is a section of content points because the rubric has changed.

> ### Remember
> Before looking for content points, it is important to be sure of the rubric and to isolate the key words and keep them at the front of your mind as you read the passage.

Exercise 3: A Bad Start

Read the passage and answer the question which follows it.

The day started off badly and got steadily worse and worse. My sister spent ages in the bathroom, even longer than usual, and so I was late with my shower. When I was halfway to the bus stop, I realised I had left my bus pass on the kitchen table and had to go back for it, after which I raced back to the bus stop, sweating, dishevelled and breathless. My sister, of course, was already there, looking relaxed, demure and very well-showered.

She smiled a knowing smile at me as if to say: 'Aren't brothers awful?' to her equally well groomed friends. To make matters worse, one of my sister's friends, Padma, was standing there with her; because I found Padma fascinating and pretty, and had been trying to pluck up the courage to speak to her for months, I felt awkward and embarrassed. Clearly, this was not the day for doing it; I quietly cursed myself for appearing so silly before her.

I dashed off the bus, glad to get away from my sister and Padma. As soon as I reached the class—it was science first period that day—I remembered that we had been given homework the last day. How could I have forgotten to do it? Groaning inwardly, I waited for the teacher to ask for the homework notebooks. I took a deep breath and put up my hand to confess.

'What do you mean, no homework?' hissed the teacher. 'It's lunchtime detention for you, and a letter home to your parents. I'm surprised at a boy like you forgetting your homework.'

My heart sank. My father would be furious with me.

Working with a partner, make a list of the seven problems which the writer experienced that day. Use the three steps already outlined to complete this task.

You should have something like this:

1 He was late having his shower.
2 He left his bus pass on the table.
3 He was embarrassed to see Padma/behaved awkwardly with Padma.
4 He had forgotten his science homework.
5 The teacher gave him lunchtime detention.
6 The teacher was to going to send a letter to his parents.
7 His father would be angry with him.

Exercise 4: Cafe India

Read the passage and answer the question which follows it.

Aruradhu loved Cafe India and went there whenever she had a free afternoon. The coffee which was served there was perfect, the right blend of beans, not too strong but with a full flavour. The service was excellent and she had come to know the waiters well, particularly the charming young man called Sajjad, a university student who worked part-time in Cafe India to pay for his studies.

Sitting there today, Aruradhu looked around the familiar space — with its checked table covers, cream walls, slightly fraying carpet — and thought that its familiarity was comforting. Sometimes, when it wasn't too hot, she liked to sit on the balcony, which gave a bird's eye view of the street below. She watched people chatting, young men watching girls passing by, and once she had witnessed a pickpocket in action, unaware that he was being watched from above. On other days, she met up with her friends, former teachers like herself, and they passed a happy time reminiscing about the good old days in the classroom.

On other occasions, like today, she could read a book — crime novels were her favourites—and sip coffee contentedly as she pretended not to be listening in to other people's conversations, a secret delight.

Working with a partner, make a list of the seven things which Aruradhu likes to do in Cafe India. Use the three steps already outlined to complete this task.

Exercise 5: A Frightening Experience

Read the passage and answer the question which follows it.

Salman was terrified. He had been on his way back home from his friend's house when the street lights had gone out and he was walking in pitch darkness. The wind had started howling, which was always enough to make him frightened. Suddenly Salman was reminded of a newspaper article he had read in his local paper, describing a robbery that had taken place on a nearby street only the week before. The thief had come from nowhere, it seemed, and stolen a young man's wallet. Safe in the security of his warm home, Salman had barely thought the article important, and had forgotten it instantly, but now it came back to his mind vividly. He realised that there was no-one about on the street, despite the fact that it was early evening. What if his watch had stopped, and it was much later than he thought? He would certainly be in for a row when he reached home. That thought did nothing to make him feel better. Suddenly he heard footsteps behind him. What was that? They got louder and louder, and closer and closer. He was petrified, his heart racing, his tongue sticking to the roof of his mouth. Was it the thief he had read about? Instinctively he held on to the wallet in his pocket. Should he stand still or make a dash for his home, which was only a few yards away now? Almost crying with relief, Salman realised that the walker was none other than his elder brother, walking quickly to catch up with him. His imagination had been playing tricks on him.

Working with a partner, make a list of the seven things which happen to make Salman terrified. Use the three steps already outlined to complete this task.

Exercise 6: Anna

Read the passage and answer the question which follows it.

Malini drove along Ansari Road, concentrating on her driving, which was especially necessary at this time, the rush hour. However, she couldn't help thinking of her friend, Anna, and the news she had received that day that Anna's long–term relationship with her boyfriend, Chris, had come to an end. Anna had put a brave face on as she told Malini about the fact that Chris had decided to go to Australia to study and that she wouldn't see him for at least three years.

More than that, it seemed that his parents had never approved of Anna, something which clearly upset her and made her angry. Her own parents did little to make her feel better, she said, by complaining so much about Chris that she had started avoiding them, something she wasn't proud of, as they were getting older and needed her support more than she needed theirs. Her father was to go into hospital soon for an operation, which was very much in her thoughts. As Malini climbed into her car to drive home, Anna smiled ruefully. 'And I failed my driving test last week,' she said.

Working with a partner, make a list of the seven things which are troubling Anna. Use the three steps already outlined to complete this task.

A word about note form

The rubric describes the selection of content point as 'notes'. This means that (a) you are free to write in sentences or notes and (b) you are free to use the words of the passage or your own words. If the point is sufficiently made, teachers are likely to give you credit. However, 'notes' does not mean something like lecture notes, which have to be intelligible only to the writer; the point has to be intelligible to the teachers reading your work too! For example, if the rubric asks for the advantages of television, and the passage states that television is entertaining, then it is possible to write 'entertaining' as the answer, as long as you put the word 'entertaining' under the category called 'advantages'. However, if another content point according to the passage is that television enables us to see world events as soon as they happen, it will not be sufficient to write 'events' or 'as soon as they happen'; such a note may be meaningful to you, but does not make sense on its own. The invitation to write in note-form is not an invitation to be imprecise: as always, the question must be answered.

A word about using your own words

As far as the first part of a summary question is concerned, you are free to make the content points either by lifting words from the passage or by using your own words. However, you must bear in mind that in the second part of a summary question, you will be rewarded for the extent to which you produce a piece of writing which is relevant to the task, as well as being a piece of coherent formal continuous prose which is easy to follow. You will also be asked to use your own words as far as possible, as using your own words is the best way to ensure relevance and coherence. So you may wish to deal with the re-casting into your own words when you get to the stage of writing in relevant and coherent formal continuous prose, or you may wish to deal with it at the note-writing stage of content points. It's up to you, under the direction of your teacher of course.

A word about fiction and non-fiction summary tasks

In examinations, you might be required to write a summary of a non-fiction text. In this book, you will be dealing with summaries of both fiction and non-fiction. This does not matter; the basic skills in summary writing are the same, whether you are dealing with fiction or non-fiction.

Exercise 1: Queen

The passage which follows describes a journey the writer made with his elephant, Queen. With a partner, make a list of the problems the writer encountered with Queen during the journey. There is no need at this stage to write in paragraphs or to try to write coherent formal continuous prose in your own words. We will deal with that later. Concentrate in this exercise on content points.

As we were reaching the outskirts of the village, I saw a bus approaching us.

Queen swerved abruptly, causing the collapse of a tea-stall. We came to a halt amongst a cascading river of cups and teapots. Glaring at us, his face a mottled purple, was the enraged owner.

'Er … I'm frightfully sorry, sir,' I gasped. 'You see my …'

'You! you!' the man shouted furiously. 'Everything gone, I'm ruined, I'll take you to court.'

'Now, sir,' Aditya said. 'There's no need for that. I am sure we can come to some financial agreement.' After the man had cooled down, we assessed the damage and compensation was paid. We couldn't get out of that village quickly enough; the drain on my nerves and on my pocket had been considerable. Besides, Queen unashamedly kept on helping herself to the cakes which were laid out on some market stalls. Understandably her greed annoyed the owners and Salim would smack her trunk, whereupon she would squeeze her small brown eyes shut like a naughty little girl.

Eventually, we emerged into open countryside, and to our relief followed a track free of the din of traffic and the possibility of Queen's thieving. After a while we noticed that Queen was limping, a bad sign for our future progress, let alone Queen's comfort. Salim discovered the cause — a metal leg chain with small spikes had obviously been used on her by her previous owners. One of the spikes had caused an ulcer, but, Salim told me, hot-water and salt dressings applied nightly would cure it. Although his knowledge of elephant ailments reassured me, it took some time to make and apply these dressings.

Days passed and our journey continued. Queen plodded along, her trunk plucking at branches from overhead trees, munching with contentment. Nevertheless, it was evident that her leg was still troubling her. Soon we came to another little town. The animal doctor there explained that Queen had a serious infection, and that she would need injections of antibiotics. Moreover, this difficult task was to be mine — and I was distinctly uneasy about it.

After mentally marking a spot in Queen's enormous side, I shut my eyes and nervously plunged in the needle. I realised my attempt had failed when, with a squeal of rage, Queen trundled away with a broken needle wobbling precariously out of her side.

'That was incorrect,' the vet remarked needlessly. 'Place the needle in straight. Now, we will try again.'

You should have something like this:

1   Queen swerved to avoid a bus
2   and knocked over a tea-stall
3   the owner was angry
4   and shouted at them
5   the writer had to pay compensation to the owner
6   Queen helped herself to cakes from market stalls
7   which annoyed the stall owners
8   Queen was limping
9   because a metal chain with spikes had been used on her leg
10 it took time to make and apply the dressings to Queen's leg
11 we found out/the animal doctor told us that Queen had an infection
12 she would need antibiotics
13 which I would have to give her
14 I failed to give her the injection properly

Source: from *Travels on my Elephant* by Mark Shand

Exercise 2: The Lonely Lighthouse

In the passage which follows, the crew of a delivery ship are approaching a lighthouse to deliver supplies to the three lighthouse keepers who live there. It is clear that something is wrong. With a partner, make a list of the problems which alerted the crew to the fact that something is wrong. There is no need at this stage to write in paragraphs or to try to write coherent formal continuous prose. We will deal with that later. Concentrate in this exercise on content points.

The delivery ship drew near the island and the crew noticed immediately that something was wrong. There was no welcoming flag flying from the lighthouse pole, although the delivery ship would have been expected. However, it was possible that the keepers were busy working out of sight on the other side of the island and, therefore, had not noticed the ship approaching. The captain ordered the ship's whistle to be sounded, but the shrill blast brought only thousands of sea-birds, from the cliff face, noisy and angry at being disturbed. There was no movement in or around the lighthouse. With mounting astonishment, the captain ordered a rocket to be fired over the island and, although it burst its colourful contents with a loud explosion, still nothing was seen of the keepers.

A small group of sailors was instructed to go ashore and find out what was wrong. Perhaps, they thought, the keepers were ill and could not venture out of the lighthouse.

They climbed aboard a small boat and rowed ashore. The sailors' leader went to the top of the cliff on which the lighthouse perched, and began running along the pathway, calling out the names of the keepers. But the only answer that came was the howling of the gales.

The keepers normally opened the entrance gate of the yard when a delivery was expected, but on this particular day the gate was closed; it creaked open at his touch and he moved towards the lighthouse itself. He was surprised to find the front door was wide open and cautiously he entered. He continued to call out the names of the three men, but still no-one answered his shouts.

In the kitchen, two chairs stood next to the table, but the third chair had been knocked over and was lying on its side. Although it was freezing winter weather, the ashes in the fireplace were cold, showing that it was some time since a fire had been lit. All the pots and pans were clean and stacked neatly in their usual places. The clock on the shelf above the fireplace had stopped.

The leader then went into the bedrooms and found that the beds were unmade, just as they would be if their occupants had just risen from them and left hurriedly. By now, he was finding it difficult to control his feelings. The hairs were standing up on the back of his neck, and he ran all the way back to the landing point. He breathlessly explained to the rest of the crew what he had found, and two of the men volunteered to go back with him to the lighthouse.

This group of three combed the outbuildings and the lighthouse itself. On reaching the top of the tower, they found that the warning lamp of the lighthouse was in working order, but there was a thin film of dust over it, suggesting that it had not been lit for some time. In addition, the last entry in the lighthouse's record book was for ten days earlier, although the normal practice was to complete the record daily. There was still no trace of the three keepers. It was becoming increasingly clear after this second search that no-one was there.

Source: from *Scottish Mysteries* by Donald M. Fraser

Exercise 3: School Uniform

The passage which follows describes the advantages and disadvantages of school uniform. With a partner, make a list of these advantages and disadvantages. There is no need at this stage to write in paragraphs or to try to write coherent formal continuous prose. We will deal with that later. Concentrate in this exercise on content points.

Many schools insist that the students wear school uniform. Probably the most popular type of school uniform is a shirt for both girls and boys, with black trousers and black skirt for male and female students respectively. A tie might also be worn. The heads of schools tend to favour the wearing of uniform for their students because it encourages a sense of belonging to the same group, like being in one big family. Furthermore, school uniform puts an end to any possibility of some students being seen to be better off than others. If rich kids have more money to spend on designer clothes which are popular with the younger generation, the poorer kids know nothing about it. All students look the same, both rich and poor, and so school uniform is a great leveller of social groups. Children can concentrate on their studies without worrying whether or not they're dressed in the latest fashions. Fashion items can be kept in better condition because they are not being worn out in the rough and tumble of hectic school life. Students are able to concentrate on their studies better as there are no distractions of wondering who is the 'coolest' in the class and where everyone fits in the clothes competition.

Outside school, students are clearly identified. This is a good thing because they are ambassadors for their school and, if they misbehave outside school, the school is easily identified. A fear of bringing their school into disrepute, or a fear of being identified and their teachers or parents notified, might prevent some antisocial behaviour, especially in big cities. Conversely, good behaviour admired outside the school day could cause adults to see a particular school in a good light and want their children to attend it — well behaved students in uniform are an eloquent advertisement for their school. Very young children might aspire to be pupils at that school when they are older because the students inspire them by their exemplary behaviour.

On the other hand, some students are not so keen on wearing uniform, arguing that it suppresses their individuality and freedom to express themselves. What is the point, they say, in everyone being identically dressed? Doesn't that lead to robots rather than human beings, a bland group of people who are unable to think for themselves or to be creative? Others might say that parents have to buy yet more clothes for their children when they have to buy school shirts, trousers, ties, even special shoes, and so school uniform costs rather than saves money in the family, and puts an extra burden on the finances of a family. This is clearly more significant in a family with a limited income.

Exercise 4: Titanic

The passage which follows describes the events leading up to the sinking of the ship Titanic. Working with a partner, make a list of all the things that went wrong and eventually became contributing factors in the sinking of the ship.

Reports showed icebergs nearly in the path of the huge ship; unfortunately, not all these reports reached her control room. Nevertheless, the captain and his officers clearly knew there was a distinct possibility, even likelihood, of encountering an iceberg during the night. The captain must have known the risk he was taking in maintaining Titanic's speed, but decided to take it anyway; to have slowed his ship under the circumstances would have suggested a degree of timidity out of keeping with his character. Also his reputation was involved; he was understandably proud of it and did not want to damage it at this stage in his career. This marvellous vessel he commanded was on her first voyage while he, ironically, was on his last.

The lookouts were specifically warned to watch for icebergs, yet they did not seem particularly concerned about this possibility. Nor had any extra lookouts been posted. No special instructions were given to the ship's engineers to stand by for possible emergency manoeuvres. The advisability of slowing the vessel to allow more time to react should an iceberg be sighted ahead does not appear to have been considered by the captain. This is hardly surprising as it would have thwarted the hope for an even higher speed on the following day.

When further messages about icebergs came in from the ship Californian, the young radio operator on Titanic ignored them. Although he was dedicated to his profession, he did not have that degree of judgement which comes from years of experience. Besides, the glamour of his job had made him arrogant.

Meanwhile, as one of the lookouts neared the end of his watch, an ominous smudge about the size of his hand loomed on the horizon dead ahead. The object grew rapidly in size and distinctness. Convinced that one of the icebergs he had been warned about was directly in Titanic's path, the lookout raised the alert and watched helplessly as the ship hurtled towards the sheer grey wall of ice.

Source: from *Disasters at Sea* by Captain Richard A. Cahill

Exercise 5: Cycle Rickshaws in Dhaka

With a partner, make a list of the six ways in which rickshaw cyclists put themselves and other people in danger. There is no need at this stage to write in paragraphs or to try to write coherent formal continuous prose. We will deal with that later. Concentrate in this exercise on content points.

So crowded are the city centre streets of Dhaka that sometimes the cycle rickshaw is the fastest means of transport. But cycle rickshaws can also be dangerous. Weaving in and out of traffic may save time but it is not always safe. Rickshaw cyclists sometimes try to shorten their journey times by going against the line of oncoming cars, and run the risk of being knocked off their cycles and seriously injured.

Damage to cycle rickshaws has become quite commonplace too — it is easy to dent a tyre as you accidentally bump into the kerb in your attempt to dodge a wide vehicle like a bus or a car. Scraping the wheel of a cycle can also occur in this way, and it can be so expensive to have a cycle repaired that it causes financial hardship in many households. Cyclists would be safer if they wore helmets, but unfortunately they don't, as again this would put additional strain on the family budget. Passengers in cycle rickshaws would be safer if they were strapped in, but there are no safety belts installed in these colourful vehicles.

Exercise 6: Tourists in Sri Lanka

With a partner, make a list of the six reasons why tourists come to Sri Lanka. There is no need at this stage to write in paragraphs or to try to write coherent formal continuous prose. We will deal with that later. Concentrate in this exercise on content points.

Sri Lanka, which means 'Beautiful Lanka', is a favourite place for tourists. They enjoy its wonderful climate, its all-year-round heat, especially those from colder, Western countries. They are drawn to the beauty of the island — the coastal regions and the mountainous areas — and it is hardly surprising that millions of visitors arrive each year to enjoy the delights of

this country. Tourist hotels are of a high standard, which is yet another attraction. They are well designed and modern, with facilities appreciated by their residents. The capital, Colombo, ensures an abundance of stores and boutiques to suit every taste and wallet, whether in the latest fashions, more traditional clothing, jewellery, perfumes ... the list is endless.

Everyone can afford to shop in Colombo; there are many low budget shops and hawker stalls, as well as the glittering, glamorous stores. Tourists enjoy walking through neighbourhoods where Ceylonese food is on sale in a variety of welcoming restaurants, and where the very best and tastiest of food is sure to be served.

Writing summary content points: relevance and cohesion

Summary writing

As we have seen in the previous chapters, the first stage in summary writing is the selection of content points, in accordance with the question asked. You are free to write these content points in note form or in sentences; you can also write them in the words of the text or in your own words.

The next stage in summary writing is to write up these content points in relevant and coherent formal continuous prose. Continuous prose means that it must be written in sentences and at least one paragraph, clearly punctuated. You probably know what is meant by formal writing, but some guidance on this will be given later. When you write your content points in relevant and coherent formal continuous prose, you will be assessed for the extent to which your writing is relevant to the task and coherent, i.e. easy to follow. These are all skills which are required in good summary writing, and later we will look at ways in which these skills can be developed and improved.

Organising and writing your summary

You have been given advice on organising a piece of writing in the section of the book on Writing. Organising a summary is easier than organising a piece of Composition, where you have only a topic to work on, and little or no guidance. Organising a summary is more like organising a piece of Directed Writing, in which the task is detailed for you. So far, you have written down the content points in a list. Now is the time to think about how to write up these content points so that the best possible summary is produced with them.

If you have produced your content points in note form, you will have to flesh out the notes into relevant and coherent formal continuous prose. Of course, you may have decided to write the content points already as coherent sentences and not notes. There are several variables here. The important point is to know in advance of an examination your preferred strategy — notes or sentences — at the first point of the summary writing, namely the selection of content points. The day of any examination is too late to start experimenting. Your teacher may wish to offer you a variety of strategies over your years of study, to ascertain the method most appropriate to you.

Paragraphing your summary

Paragraphing your summary is easy. Because it is a short piece of writing, it may be written in a single paragraph. In cases where there is more than one section to the rubric you may find it more logical to use each section to write a separate paragraph. But there is no need to do so — it's up to you. You will be neither penalised nor rewarded in examinations for the number of paragraphs which you use to write your summary. The same is not the case, of course, in Composition and Directed Writing, with which the section on Writing in this book deals.

The length of your summary

The rubric usually indicates the recommended number of words you should use in your summary, and the range is quite wide, possibly between 150 and 180 words. You are not likely to be penalised for exceeding that limit. However, you will not have enough space to write much more than the recommended number of words in any case; furthermore, long summaries are self-penalising, as a long summary loses the focus of what a summary is intended to be and becomes verbose, thus lacking the coherence that would make it easy to follow. You may also be tempted to include details which are irrelevant to the task.

On the other hand, there is no benefit in writing much below the recommended number of words, because if you use considerably fewer words than the number prescribed in the rubric, you will probably penalise yourself by not writing enough content points.

Correct punctuation

If you are studying under an English curriculum, it is generally assumed that you are familiar with the basic rules of punctuation — in other words, that you can use full stops and capital letters accurately in order to produce correct sentences. You will already have done some work on sentence structure and punctuation in the section of this book on Writing.

Exercise 1: Punctuation

Check your basic punctuation skills by redrafting the following passage using correct punctuation.

the moment had arrived all those weeks of preparation had been moving them towards this day it was a difficult syllabus but the class had had a good teacher how happy they were about that all the students filed into the examination hall with butterflies in their stomachs was there anyone who was not really nervous what would the comprehension passage be about this year would it be narrative or discursive would it suit everyone everyone was silent the papers were give out they were thinking about what they had been taught about literal comprehension and inferential comprehension not to forget of course the summary question which carried half of the marks everyone started to read the passage but they could not believe their eyes it was impossible to understand there was no punctuation whatsoever.

Exercise 2

Go back to the lists of content points you made in Chapter 12 for each of the short passages in exercises 4, 5 and 6. For each of these, write the list of content points into a paragraph.

Your paragraphs should be headed as follows:

- Cafe India

- A frightening experience

- Anna.

Exercise 3

Go back to the lists of content points you made for each of the passages in exercises 1, 2, 3, 4, 5, and 6 in Chapter 13 . For each of these, write the list of content points into a paragraph.

Your paragraphs should be headed as follows:

- Queen

- The Lonely Lighthouse

- School Uniform

- Titanic

- Cycle Rickshaws in Dhaka

- Tourists in Sri Lanka.

Writing summaries which are relevant and coherent

Once you have made your list of content points, either in note form or sentences, (and we have discussed in Chapter 12 what is meant by 'notes' in this context) you will be asked to write these notes into a summary which is relevant and coherent formal continuous prose.

Relevance

Using material which is relevant means using only information which answers the question and avoiding:

- material which merely repeats a previously made point

- material which gives particular information merely illustrating a previously made point

- material which is a topic sentence, or introduction, to the subject being discussed or described.

> **For example**
> Look at the following passage, already used to find content points, to answer the question: *Why do tourists visit Sri Lanka?*

Sri Lanka, which means 'Beautiful Lanka', is a favourite place for tourists. They enjoy its wonderful climate, its all-year-round heat, especially those from colder, Western countries. They are drawn to the beauty of the island—the coastal regions and the mountainous areas—and it is hardly surprising that millions of visitors arrive each year to enjoy the delights of this country. Tourist hotels are of a high standard, which is yet another attraction. They are well designed and modern, with facilities appreciated by their residents. The capital, Colombo, ensures an abundance of stores and boutiques to suit every taste and wallet, whether in the latest fashions, more traditional clothing, jewellery, perfumes ... the list is endless. Everyone can afford to shop in Colombo; there are many low budget shops and hawker stalls, as well as the glittering, glamorous stores. Tourists enjoy walking through neighbourhoods where Ceylonese food is on sale in a variety of welcoming restaurants, and where the very best and tastiest of food is sure to be served.

- *'Sri Lanka is a favourite place for tourists'* is a topic sentence, i.e. it sets the scene by introducing the context for the question asked.

- *'which means 'Beautiful Lanka''* is a detail which illustrates the topic sentence

- *'the coastal regions and the mountainous areas'* illustrates or gives extra information about the beauty of the island

- *'it is hardly surprising'* is an opinion, and not a detail, which supports why people go to visit Sri Lanka

- *'which is yet another attraction'* underpins the content points, but need not be repeated in your answer

- *'whether in the latest fashions, more traditional clothing, jewellery, perfumes'* elaborates on why stores and boutiques suit every taste and wallet.

Exercise 1

Re-read the passages 'School Uniform' and 'Cycle Rickshaws in Dhaka' from Chapter 13 and answer the question that follows.

School Uniform

Many schools insist that the students wear school uniform. Probably the most popular type of school uniform is a shirt for both girls and boys, with black trousers and black skirt for male and female students respectively. A tie might also be worn. The heads of schools tend to favour the wearing of uniform for their students because it encourages a sense of belonging to the same group, like being in one big family. Furthermore, school uniform puts an end to any possibility of some students being seen to be better off than others. If rich kids have more money to spend on designer clothes which are popular with the younger generation, the poorer kids know nothing about it. All students look the same, both rich and poor, and so school uniform is a great leveller of social groups. Children can concentrate on their studies without worrying whether or not they're dressed in the latest fashions. Fashion items can be kept in better condition because they are not being worn out in the rough and tumble of hectic school life. Students are able to concentrate on their studies better as there are no distractions of wondering who is the 'coolest' in the class and where everyone fits in the clothes competition.

Outside school, students are clearly identified. This is a good thing because they are ambassadors for their school and, if they misbehave outside school, the school is easily identified. A fear of bringing their school into disrepute, or a fear of being identified and their teachers or parents notified, might prevent some antisocial behaviour, especially in big cities. Conversely, good behaviour admired outside the school day could cause adults to see a particular school in a good light and want their children to attend it — well behaved students in uniform are an eloquent advertisement for their school. Very young children might aspire to be pupils at that school when they are older because the students inspire them by their exemplary behaviour.

On the other hand, some students are not so keen on wearing uniform, arguing that it suppresses their individuality and freedom to express themselves. What is the point, they say, in everyone being identically dressed? Doesn't that lead to robots rather than human beings, a bland group of people who are unable to think for themselves or to be creative? Others might say that parents have to buy yet more clothes for their children when they have to buy school shirts, trousers, ties, even special shoes, and so school uniform costs rather than saves money in the family, and puts an extra burden on the finances of a family. This is clearly more significant in a family with a limited income.

Cycle Rickshaws in Dhaka

So crowded are the city centre streets of Dhaka that sometimes the cycle rickshaw is the fastest means of transport. But cycle rickshaws can also be dangerous. Weaving in and out of traffic may save time but it is not always safe. Rickshaw cyclists sometimes try to shorten their journey times by going against the line of oncoming cars, and run the risk of being knocked off their cycles and seriously injured.

Damage to cycle rickshaws has become quite commonplace too — it is easy to dent a tyre as you accidentally bump into the kerb in your attempt to dodge a wide vehicle like a bus or a car. Scraping the wheel of a cycle can also occur in this way, and it can be so expensive to have a cycle repaired that it causes financial hardship in many households. Cyclists would be safer if they wore helmets, but unfortunately they don't, as again this would put additional strain on the family budget. Passengers in cycle rickshaws would be safer if they were strapped in, but there are no safety belts installed in these colourful vehicles.

With a partner, pick out and write down clusters of words or even whole sentences which are either:

*   material which merely repeats a previously made point

*   material which gives particular information merely illustrating a previously made point

*   material which is a topic sentence, or introduction, to the question.

A word about the assessment of relevance

When you make a list of content points in the first part of a summary question, under 'Notes', you may come up with any number of points between none at all (and that is to be avoided!) or twelve, thirteen, fourteen, even fifteen or sixteen. When your teacher is assessing your work after you have written up your notes into a piece of relevant and coherent formal continuous prose, and even under examination conditions, this number will not be checked. In other words, if you made eleven content points under 'Notes', these eleven points remain, and would be given eleven marks if the exercise was done under examination conditions. When assessing the work you do, in writing up your notes into a piece of relevant and coherent formal continuous prose, no teacher or Examiner checks the number of content points you have made in that piece of writing.

However, as a general rule, the number of content points you have made in the piece of writing under relevant and coherent formal continuous prose will partly determine the credit you are given when it is assessed. If you have an excellent understanding of the task, this will be demonstrated in a large number of the passage's points, ideas or arguments. Conversely, if your understanding of the task is limited, this will be reflected in far fewer of the passage's points, ideas or arguments. In practice this means that you need not reproduce every single point you made under 'Notes', and this will not be checked when you write your summary as a piece of writing which is relevant and coherent. However, the greater number of content points you reproduce the better when it comes to assessment of relevance.

Coherence

Summaries which are coherent are easy to follow. One of the ways of making sure your summary is easy to follow is to write it in Standard English.

Standard English means vocabulary which would be understood by all speakers of English, in other words vocabulary which would be found in an English dictionary, free from slang or jargon. Standard English sentence structures would be understood by all speakers of English and would not infringe any of the rules of English grammar.

Another signpost of coherence, that is the extent to which your piece of writing is easy to follow, is the way in which it is written in a natural, unstilted style. One way of doing this is to combine information in compound or complex sentence structures. This is not obligatory, but often helps the flow of a piece of writing. If the sentence structures which you use are compound or complex, but copied from the text, you will not make as good an impression on teachers as you would if you wrote in original compound or complex sentence structures, i.e. sentence structures that have been created by you and not by the writer of the original passage.

Copying whole stretches of structures from a text means you run a greater risk of copying over material which is not relevant. Writing original compound or complex sentence structures, as well as writing original simple structures, means you are using your own words. This is not assessed separately, but will help with the general coherence of the piece of work which you produce.

Signposts of compound and complex sentences

- **More than one finite verb:** Sentences with only one finite verb are called simple sentences. An example of a simple sentence is: '*The boys played cricket*'.

- **The conjunctions '*and*' or '*but*':** What could have been written as two or more simple sentences have been combined to create a single **compound sentence**, i.e. a sentence where each part is of equal value and could stand on its own as a simple sentence. An example of a compound sentence is: '*The sun shone and the boys played cricket*'.

- **Conjunctions other than '*and*' and '*but*':** What could have been written as two or more simple sentences have been combined to create a single complex sentence, i.e. a sentence where only one part could stand on its own as a simple sentence.

  The other parts of the complex sentence are secondary to, or subordinate to, the main, independent part of the sentence. An example of a complex sentence which has been created using two conjunctions is: '*Before their mothers called them in for lunch, the boys played cricket because the sun was shining*'.

  Examples of conjunctions other than '*and*' and '*but*' include '*when*', '*while*', '*after*', '*before*', '*because*', '*until*'.

- A **relative pronoun**, i.e. 'who', 'whom', 'whose', 'which' and 'that': An example of a complex sentence which has been created using a relative pronoun is: '*The sun shone, which meant that the boys could play cricket*'.

- A **present participle**, i.e. the part of the verb which ends in '-*ing*': An example of a complex sentence which has been created using a present participle is: '*Playing cricket, the boys were very happy*'.

Exercise 2: Conjunction

Combine the following sentences by using conjunctions. An example has been done for you.

Lucky was excited going to school. She was going to be studying sentence structure in English that day.

Answer: *Lucky was excited going to school because she was going to be studying sentence structure in English that day.*

1   Lucky was very tired. She had been studying sentence structure all day.
2   Lucky got home. Her mother was there to greet her.
3   Lucky ate her lunch. She went straight to her room to study.
4   Lucky revised that day's lesson on sentence structure. She felt very cheerful. She felt she understood how to use conjunctions.

Exercise 3: Relative Pronouns

Combine the following sentences by using relative pronouns. An example has been done for you.

In Bangladesh there are many dedicated English teachers. All the teachers want all their students to succeed.

Answer: *In Bangladesh there are many dedicated English teachers who all want all their students to succeed.*

Notice that sometimes the word order has to be changed when combining sentences using relative pronouns.

1   Tulen was an English teacher. He worked in a high school in Bangladesh.
2   Tulen taught English in a high school. The school had almost five hundred students.
3   Tulen met one of his former students. He had taught this student for three years of high school.
4   Tulen lived next door to Nath. He had taught Nath's son for two years of high school.

Exercise 4: Present Participles

Combine the following sentences by using present participles. An example has been done for you.

Indrani woke up early. She jumped out of bed, eager to go to work.

Answer: *Waking up early, Indrani jumped out of bed, eager to go to work.*

Notice that sometimes the word order has to be changed when combining sentences using present participles.

1   Indrani walked to school. She met an old friend from high school.
2   They chatted together. They walked along the street.
3   Indrani heard that her friend was a teacher. She told her friend that she was a teacher too.
4   Her friend smiled. She told Indrani that she had heard from many colleagues that Indrani was a wonderful teacher.

Exercise 4A: Studying for an Examination

Combine the following list of summary content points to produce a paragraph of Standard English, with original complex sentence structures if possible. Write between 150 and 180 words, including the opening ten words given below.

Begin your answer like this:

Because Minhajul and Sajjad were students at the same school . . .

1   Minhajul invited Sajjad to his house
2   spent three hours there on Saturday
3   English examination coming up
4   worried about sentence structure
5   particularly worried about spelling
6   teacher had told them not to worry too much
7   teachers were kind about spelling
8   teachers did not deduct marks for every single error
9   Minhajul and Sajjad were hungry
10 they left their books on the table
11 they went to the kitchen
12 they drank some water
13 they ate some sandwiches
14 Minhajul's mother came in from the shops
15 she asked them how their studies were progressing

Exercise 4B

Swap your answer with a partner. For your partner's summary:

1   Count the number of sentences.
2   Check that they are all sentences. (Do they all have verbs? Do they all make sense on their own?)
3   Count the number of simple sentences, i.e. sentences with only one verb.
4   Check to see if there are any compound sentences, i.e. Sentences joined by 'and' or 'but'.
5   Check to see if there are any complex sentences, and whether or not these are original.
6   For each complex sentence used, check the way in which the structure has been created, i.e.
    •   has a conjunction been used? ('because', 'when', 'after', 'before', 'since', etc.)
    •   has a relative pronoun been used? ('who', 'whose', 'whom', 'which','that')
    •   has a present participle been used? (the part of the verb ending in '-ing' e.g. 'going', 'seeing')
    •   have linking words been used appropriately? ('however', 'moreover', 'nevertheless', 'furthermore' etc.).

Make a list of your findings for your partner. Your partner will be doing the same with your piece of work.

Exercise 4C

Take your own piece of work back from your partner. Study carefully what your partner has written.

Redraft your summary, trying to make the necessary corrections and/or improvements to it as suggested by your partner.

Exercise 5A: A New job in Male

Combine the following list of summary content points to produce a paragraph of Standard English, with original complex sentence structures if possible. Write between 150 and 180 words, including the opening ten words given below.

Begin your answer like this:

The flight from Pakistan was long and exhausting for Amrita . . .

1. Amrita was a mathematics teacher
2   she was pleased to have a job in Male

3   she arrived in Male by boat from the airport

4   she checked into her new lodgings

5   she went for a walk to see her new surroundings

6   she went to the fish market

7   tuna was the main fish caught and sold

8   they lay around on the floor of the market

9   there was a strong smell of fish

10 and a lot a noise

11 shoppers were mainly women

12 the women selected the tuna they wanted

13 and took it to the salesmen and it was weighed and paid for

14 Amrita bought a piece of tuna

15 she went back to her lodgings to have the tuna for supper

Exercise 5B

Swap your answer with a partner. For your partner's summary:

1   Count the number of sentences.

2   Check that they are all sentences. (Do they all have verbs? Do they all make sense on their own?)

3   Count the number of simple sentences, i.e. sentences with only one verb.

4   Check to see if there are any compound sentences, i.e. sentences joined by 'and' or 'but'.

5   Check to see if there are any complex sentences, and whether or not these are original.

6   For each complex sentence used, check the way in which the structure has been created, i.e.
    •   has a conjunction been used? ('because', 'when', 'after', 'before', 'since' etc.)
    •   has a relative pronoun been used? ('who', 'whose', 'whom', 'which' ,'that')
    •   has a present participle been used? (the part of the verb ending in 'ing' e.g. 'going', 'seeing')
    •   have linking words been used appropriately? ('however', 'moreover', 'nevertheless', 'furthermore' etc.).

Make a list of your findings for your partner. Your partner will be doing the same with your piece of work.

Exercise 5C

Take your own piece of work back from your partner. Study carefully what your partner has written. Redraft your summary, trying to make the necessary corrections and/or improvements to it as suggested by your partner.

Exercise 6A: Light Street and Heavy Street

Combine the following list of summary content points to produce a paragraph of Standard English, with original complex sentence structures if possible. Write between 150 and 180 words, including the opening ten words given below.

Begin your answer like this:

The volume of traffic in streets produces contrasts between them . . .

1   in Light Street (street with light traffic) people consider the street as home territory

2   in Heavy Street (street with heavy traffic) only the building they live in is considered as home

3   in Light Street people make use of the street

4   people sit on the front steps and chat in Light Street

5   children play on the pavements in Light Street

6   Heavy Street is seen as a corridor between the safety of individual homes and the outside world

7   there is no community feeling in Heavy Street

8   people keep to themselves in Heavy Street

9   in Heavy Street motorists view pedestrians, cyclists or children playing in the street as intruding into their space

10   as the speed of the traffic increases in Heavy Street the attitude of motorists to pedestrians becomes increasingly ruthless

11   in Heavy Street the pavement eventually disappears

12   there are no more pedestrians or children playing in the street

13   the pavement becomes a no-man's land and the street loses its main attraction

14   people on Heavy Street no longer use their front gardens

15   they cannot relax in their gardens because of the continual noise

Exercise 6B

Swap your answer with a partner. For your partner's summary:

1   Count the number of sentences.

2   Check that they are all sentences. (Do they all have verbs? Do they all make sense on their own?)

3   Count the number of simple sentences, (i.e. sentences with only one verb).

4   Check to see if there are any compound sentences, (i.e. sentences joined by 'and' or 'but').

5   Check to see if there are any complex sentences, and whether or not these are original.

6   For each complex sentence used, check the way in which the structure has been created, i.e.

   •   has a conjunction been used? ('because', 'when', 'after', 'before', 'since' etc.)

   •   has a relative pronoun been used? ('who', 'whose', 'whom', 'which', 'that')

   •   has a present participle been used? (the part of the verb ending in 'ing', e.g. 'going', 'seeing')

   •   have linking words been used appropriately? ('however', 'moreover', 'nevertheless', 'furthermore' etc.)

Make a list of your findings for your partner. Your partner will be doing the same with your piece of work.

Exercise 6C

Take your own piece of work back from your partner. Study carefully what your partner has written. Redraft your summary, trying to make the necessary corrections and/or improvements to it as suggested by your partner.

Exercise 7A: The Changing Relationship between Man and Animals

Combine the following list of summary content points to produce a paragraph of Standard English, with original complex sentence structures if possible. Write between 150 and 180 words, including the opening ten words given below.

Begin your answer like this:

The farming of wild animals produced various changes in their …

1   the physical appearance of farmed animals changed
2   most farmed animals became smaller
3   some farmed animals developed more distinctive markings and/or bright colours
4   the jaw muscles in grazing animals became smaller
5   the faces of grazing animals became shorter
6   the brains of farmed animals became smaller
7   the senses of farmed animals became less acute
8   before the farming of animals, man respected the animals he hunted
9   man depended on animals for his needs, like food and clothing
10   the bones of animals became the weapons of man
11   hunters feared and admired the animals they hunted
12   in some societies animals were idolised as gods
13   farming certain species of animals led to a bond of mutual affection between them and the farmers
14   shepherds often risked their lives to rescue their lambs
15   dogs and horses became inseparable companions of their masters.

Exercise 7B

Swap your answer with a partner. For your partner's summary:

1   Count the number of sentences.

2   Check that they are all sentences. (Do they all have verbs? Do they all make sense on their own?)

3   Count the number of simple sentences, i.e. sentences with only one verb.

4   Check to see if there are any compound sentences, i.e. sentences joined by 'and' or 'but'.

5   Check to see if there are any complex sentences, and whether or not these are original.

6   For each complex sentence used, check the way in which the structure has been created, i.e.

   *   has a conjunction been used? ('because', 'when', 'after', 'before', 'since', etc.)

   *   has a relative pronoun been used? ('who', 'whose', 'whom', 'which', 'that')

   *   has a present participle been used? (the part of the verb ending in '*ing*'e.g. 'going', 'seeing')

   *   have linking words been used appropriately? ('however', 'moreover', 'nevertheless', 'furthermore' etc.)

Make a list of your findings for your partner. Your partner will be doing the same with your piece of work.

Exercise 7C

Take your own piece of work back from your partner. Study carefully what your partner has written. Redraft your summary, trying to make the necessary corrections and/or improvements to it as suggested by your partner.

Exercise 8A

Make up your own list of summary points. These can be of a narrative nature or a discursive nature. There should be fifteen points and you should provide the ten opening words.

Exercise 8B

Swap your list of content points with your partner. Write a summary based on the content points your partner has given you. Use the opening ten words your partner has provided. Write between 150 and 180 words, including the ten opening words. Write in relevant and coherent formal continuous prose. Try to use a variety of sentence structures, some simple and some complex. Check your spelling and punctuation. Check that you have created complex sentences by the use of present participles or conjunctions or relative pronouns. Check that you have included no irrelevant information.

Exercise 8C

Swap your work again with your partner. Write a short paragraph about the summary your partner has produced with the content points you gave him/her. Assess the extent to which he/she has written relevant and coherent error-free prose and the extent to which he/she has used a variety of sentence structures.

Exercise 9

Look at what your partner has written about your summary: the good points and the points which might be improved. Decide how your work on summary writing in relevant and coherent formal continuous prose might be improved in the future.

A word about linking to produce coherent writing

Sometimes a good way to produce a piece of coherent writing is to use linking words. These may be adverbs or phrases, which show a continuation in the argument or points in the passage, or which show a change of direction in the argument or points in the passage.

Some adverbs or phrases which show continuation include, 'moreover', 'similarly', 'again', 'in the same way', 'likewise' and 'furthermore'.

Some adverbs or phrases which show a change of direction include, 'on the other hand', 'however', 'in contrast' and 'nevertheless'.

However, these words and phrases should not be used without clear understanding of their purpose and they should be used sparingly. A liberal sprinkling of such words, particularly if their appropriateness is unclear, will do little to enhance a piece of writing and indeed may spoil it.

Each exercise which follows gives you a sample first draft summary. For each one, produce a redrafted version. This means you will have to:

- correct any mistakes of grammar, punctuation, agreement, wrong preposition, spelling

- insert links, such as 'however' or 'furthermore', where appropriate

- combine groups of simple sentences into complex or compound sentences where appropriate

- redraft legibly and in your best handwriting.

Exercise 1: The Lighthouse 1

The ship's crew noticed immediately that something was wrong because there were no welcoming flag from lighthouse when the ship is near. Whistle and rocket are used, still there is no response from those lighthouse keepers. The gates that should be open was close, the door of the lighthouse was widely open.

The fire had not being lit for some time. The last entry of the lighthouse record book were the fifteenth of december, this puzzled the searchers. The lamp covering with dust showing that it also had not been lit for some time, the beds was unmade. Two of the three sets waterproof clothing was missing from cupboard. The grass along the edge of cliff was torn away when they investigate outside the lighthouse. The railings around the platform where the crane stood was broken. A huge boulder which was part of cliff had been move a great distance down the starecase and blocking it.

Exercise 2: The Lighthouse 2

The ship's crew noticed immediately that something was wrong because the welcoming flag should be wave for our welcome. They thought that the keepers may busy working out of sight. The wistle was blown to call the keeper but no responce. The ship's captain order his crew to fire a rocket but it didn't make the keepers noticed.

A small group of sailor was ordered to check the area. They found out that the warning lamp was working order and when they check the record book, it haven't been filled for 11 days. The sailor told their captain that they didn't found the keepers, the next day they search the lighthouse and found out that two of the three waterproof clothing was missing. The railing around the platform was broken and huge boulder was move down stairway. There were no trace of the three keepers later than. All the crew of the ships thinks there a mystery their.

Exercise 3: The Lighthouse 3

The ship's crew noticed immediately that something was wrong because there was no welcoming flag flew from the ashore. The captain asked to fly a rocket over the island but still nothing was seen of the keepers. Some sailors are order to find what happend inshore, they started calling the keepers names and there is no answers. The entrance gate were closed, it should be open by the keepers as they came there. The main door was open and again calling the name of the keeper. In the kitchen too chairs stood next to the table and one of it knocked over and lying on it's side. The bedroom were unmade seems that the occupants had just risen from them and left hurriedly. There is a this dirty dust over the warning lamp. They found two waterproof clothing were missing and one still hung there. They also found that the grass had been torn away along top edge of cliff.

Exercise 4: Threats to Coral Reefs 1

When hotel developers near coral reefs compete for land, thus raise it's price and as result forced local people to leave thier homes. Infact, in some places, hotels have been built on burial sites on the coast. Little by little the construction of golf courses for tourists have been proved fatal to the coral reefs as the golf courses are treated by fertilisers, pesticides and large amount of water when all of substences contains deadly loads of waste materials and chemical.

However, airport runways are built and thos its construction produces to much waste which are sufficient to kill coral. Local people lacking of food caused by the distruction of coral. Even, the increase of pollution, noice, raods and the destruction of natural habitats of animals from the arrival of tourists. Sailing ships create severe on coral reefs with their heavy anchor, coral continues to damage from the submarines power and diver also damage coral reefs consideribly.

Exercise 5: Threats to Coral Reefs 2

When hotel develops near coral reefs compete for land they force local people out of their homes, it is easy to understand the location of hotels in this magnificent areas but way of live of country is exploitd to great extent. Tourist attractions like golf courses deprives the local people for shorelines which is necesary for their way of life.

Pollution is important factor in the destruction of wonderful coastal areas. Pollutants is dumped into the coral reefs which destroy life in the reef, the rock from coral reef have been use on a small scale to build houses but the rocks are now been excavated in large quantities for hotel development and yet again depriving the local people from their own houses. Lagoons are being dig deeper affecting the area where fish breed and the prices of popular fish has been raised so high that the people cannot aford them, boats that carry people cases severe damage to reefs.

Exercise 6: Threats to Coral Reefs 3

When hotel develops compete for land they forced local people out of their homes, the country is frequently exploit for tourist entertainment. The construction of golf courses for tourists deprive local people of coastal area. The water used by golf courses drains out on the coral reefs carries deadly load and chemical, building of airport along the coast are built on coral reefs. Their construction produce large quantities of waste.

Rock from coral reef are taken in uncontroled quantities to built tourist hotel thus depriving local people of building material. Pleasure boat distroy the areas were fish breed, deprives local people's food. Some fish are too expensive because they can only afford by tourist. Villages are destroyed by pollution created by tourists. Huge jetties and docks is built over coral reefs, Hotel often lack of proper sewage facilities. Boats carrying people to dive. These boats increases the destruction of coral. Everyday boats send there anchors crashing down on reef.

17 Choosing vocabulary suited to its purpose

In summary writing, and indeed in all writing, you must choose a vocabulary which is suited to its purpose and audience. You had an opportunity to consider appropriate vocabulary, tone and register in earlier chapters in this book which dealt with Composition and Directed Writing. The matter of vocabulary, tone and register is more complex in Writing than it is in Reading. This is because you might be writing to amuse or entertain, or to persuade and argue, or to reflect on past events; you might be writing a letter, or a report, where the purpose and audience are given in the rubric of Directed Writing.

However, choosing vocabulary suited to its purpose is much simpler in Reading.

You might be relieved to know that in comprehension questions teachers focus on reading rather than writing, and so there are usually no penalties for the wrong type of vocabulary (provided, of course, that the sense is clear), tone or register. The part of Reading where vocabulary, tone and register become important is the summary question, and this is relatively straightforward because the golden rule is formality.

A definition of formal language is probably best given by a definition of what it is not. Signposts of informality are chatty or conversational language or tone, abbreviations or contractions, the active rather than the passive voice of the verb and the use of direct speech. So, signposts of formal language could be seen as being:

- no chatty or conversational language or tone, for example, 'It is clear to see that …' rather than 'Let's be clear about …'

- no abbreviations or contractions, for example, 'Coral reefs cannot be looked after if …' rather than 'Coral reefs can't be looked after if …'

- the passive rather than the active voice of the verb, for example, 'It can be seen that' rather than 'I can see that.'

- no direct speech, for example, 'The captain said that the crew should go to the lighthouse', rather than ' I am going to the lighthouse,' the captain said.

- no slang or colloquial expressions, for example, 'The children thought that their teacher was efficient and friendly', rather than 'The kids thought that their teacher was cool'.

Exercise 1

Working with a partner, look at:

1   a copy of a novel, either your own or from the class or school library, and

2   a more formal text of your own choice, which can be a non-fiction text such as an instruction manual, an autobiography or a book designed to give information on a particular topic.

From these texts, write down ten examples of informal language and ten examples of formal language. Beside each example, write a sentence or two to explain why your choices of examples are either formal or informal language.

Informal Language	Formal Language
1.	
2.	
3.	
4.	
5.	
6.	
7	
8.	
9.	
10.	

Analysing, evaluating and developing facts, ideas and opinions

To analyse, evaluate and develop facts, ideas and opinions means to follow a sequence or argument, to distinguish fact from opinion, or to identify conclusions, criticism, advice, warning or disagreement that the writer may have in connection with the ideas presented in the passage.

The idea of being tested on this in an examination may be relatively new to you, but in fact this skill is one which you have always been working on in your English class, perhaps without realising it. You are frequently evaluating, and forming judgement and responses to what you read and what you hear in the classroom and in the world around you.

In an examination, you will be required to analyse, evaluate or develop facts, ideas or opinions in a non-fiction passage. You will have already summarised the passage by selecting content points and writing them in relevant and coherent, formal continuous prose. Therefore, when you reach this stage, you will already be quite familiar with the passage and will have begun to formulate ideas and opinions about it.

Distinguishing fact from opinion

A fact is something which is demonstrably, or objectively, true. An opinion is based on subjective judgement, in other words, not everyone would agree that it is true.

Signposts in opinions are emotive words, for example, '*like*' or '*love*' or '*hate*', or words in which judgement is implied, for example, '*beautiful*' or '*wonderful*' or '*favourite*', or words which are comparatives or superlatives, for example, '*better*' or '*best*' or '*perfect*'.

Exercise 1: Distinguishing Facts and Opinions

With a partner, look at the following statements and decide whether each is a fact or an opinion.

1   Some people think that pandas are cute.

2   All people think that pandas are cute.

3   Pandas are undeniably cute.

4   My brother thinks that pandas are cute.

Statement 1 is a fact, or at least probably a fact. There is enough use of the panda in, for example, picture books or films, to suggest that they appeal to people; the panda was chosen as the logo of the World Worldlife Fund for a purpose, probably because many people find it an attractive creature.

Statement 2 is an opinion. There can have been no research of everyone in the world on their feelings about pandas. Such statements are often used to arouse interest in particular topics, but can be seen only as a type of exaggeration which needs to be classified as an opinion.

Statement 3 is also an opinion. As long as only one person does not find pandas cute, then the assertion is not 'undeniable'.

Statement 4 is a statement. The brother has an opinion, namely that panda are cute, but the writer is merely telling us what the brother's opinion is, and so the entire statement is a factual one – the fact is that the brother has an opinion that pandas are cute.

Exercise 2: Facts and Opinions

Write down each of the following sentences and beside each one write whether it is a fact or an opinion.

1   Rice is eaten in many parts of the world.   _____

2   Kandy is a city in Sri Lanka.   _____

3   Everyone likes rice.   _____

4   My cousin thinks he is very handsome.   _____

5   The countryside in the hills above Islamabad is beautiful. _____

6   Television is the most important invention of the twentieth century. _____

7   Television was invented in the twentieth century.   _____

8   Islamabad is the capital of Pakistan.   _____

9   There is nobody who wouldn't want to visit Kandy. _____

10 My cousin is very handsome.   _____

Exercise 3: More Facts and Opinions

Read the short passage below and write down two facts and two opinions from it. You may need to alter the wording of the passage to do this.

> Everybody likes travelling by train, and it is easy to see why. For a start, there are no security checks, as there are on planes, and security checks are very upsetting. There is nothing nicer that zipping through the countryside on a train, watching rural scenes: villagers gathering crops or tending animals.
>
> Most trains nowadays have air conditioning, which makes travel even more comfortable than it used to be.

Exercise 4: More Facts and Opinions

Read the short passage below and write down two facts and two opinions from it. You may need to alter the wording of the passage to do this.

Some people think that television was the best invention of the twentieth century. It cannot be denied that watching television is a great way to relax, but at what cost? Too much lounging in front of 'the box' as it is called, takes people away from other pursuits, such as reading or playing sport. People who watch too much television are boring individuals who eventually are unable to distinguish the real world from the fantasy world of soap operas.

Exercise 5: More Facts and Opinions

Find a short non-fiction passage in a book or newspaper. Make sure it has a mixture of fact and opinion. If it has not, rewrite it and edit it to make it does have such a mixture.

Write down a list of five statements from your chosen passage. Swap with a partner and ask him/her to write beside each statement whether it is a fact or an opinion.

Identifying conclusion

Sometimes a passage invites you not only to work out your own ideas or opinions, but to work out the conclusion to which the writer has come.

Exercise 6: Sport and Study

Read the following short passage. After the passage there are three statements. Write down which of the statements is the writer's conclusion.

It is important for all people, including young people, to keep fit. One way to do this might be to play cricket or rugby, or to attend classes in aerobics or dancing. Young people also have to set aside enough time to complete homework assignments and to work on areas of particular concern in their studies, whether it is quadratic equations in Maths or metaphors in English. Achieving the balance between physical and mental achievement is not easy.

Possible conclusions:

1   The writer thinks that sport is more important than studying.

2   The writer thinks that sport is just as important as studying.

3   The writer thinks that studying is more important than sport.

Exercise 7: Pakistan

Read the following short passage. After the passage there are three statements. Write down which of the statements is the writer's conclusion.

> Pakistan is a fascinating country. The mountains of the north offer some of the most spectacular scenery in the world, and attract walkers and climbers who are stunned at the spectacular views. The snow-capped mountains look like pictures from fairytales. In the south, at the coast, it is still possible to charter a sailing boat for a couple of hours of fishing. Even better is the opportunity to shop in the country's many bazaars, with their busy tea-stalls and roadside barbeques, with the pungent aroma of delicious food.

Possible conclusions:

1   The writer prefers the coastal area of Pakistan.

2   The writer prefers the mountains of Pakistan.

3   The writer prefers the bazaars of Pakistan.

Identifying criticism, advice, warning or disagreement

Exercise 8: Mobile phones

Read the following short passage. Working with a partner, identify the criticism the writer is making. You may need to alter the words of the text to do so.

> Mobile phones sit well with the fast pace of life in the twenty-first century. Gone are the days of wondering if one's children are late coming home from school because the bus has broken down or they are stuck in a traffic jam. Lunch with a friend can be arranged via text from the train and dental appointments can be arranged while waiting in a supermarket queue. It is rather pathetic to see a parent phoning home to find what the kids want for dinner, instead of making that choice for them, but it is a small price to pay for convenience.

Exercise 9: Mobile phones

Read the following short passage. Working with a partner, identify the advice the writer is giving. You may need to alter the words of the text to do so.

> Mobile phones sit well with the fast pace of life in the twenty-first century, even if sometimes we are out for dinner with friends and can become more caught up with the people we're not with than the people we are actually with! Gone are the days of wondering if one's children are late coming home from school because the bus has broken down or they are stuck in a traffic jam. Lunch with a friend can be arranged via text from the train and dental appointments arranged while waiting in a supermarket queue.

Exercise 10: Criticism, advice, warning and disagreement

Write a short non-fiction passage of your own which has either a criticism, a piece of advice or a warning in it, or which contains conflicting information which might be construed as a disagreement. Swap your piece of writing with a partner and ask him or her to identify the criticism, advice, warning or disagreement in it, and do the same with your partner's piece of writing.

19 Exercises in fact gathering from short texts

We have already seen that, in an examination, you might be given a non-fiction text and asked:

1 to identify content points,

2 reproduce these content points in a piece of formal continuous prose and

3 answer some questions which test your ability to respond to the main ideas of the passage.

You will thereafter be given a fiction passage and asked to answer a variety of questions, which will include literal comprehension, inferential comprehension, own words questions, quotation questions, vocabulary questions and questions on writer's craft. Do not worry if you find all of this daunting at the moment; this book will break down the types of questions and show you how to identify them and also how to answer them.

A word about fiction and non-fiction

Fiction is the name we give to any writing which is narrative, i.e. a story. Fiction is not based on fact, but rather on the results of the imagination of the writer. You probably know various types, or genres, of fiction already, starting with the fairy stories which were read to you when you were very young. There are many other genres of fiction, such as science fiction, crime, adventure. On the other hand, non- fiction is factual, i.e. based on facts which are true. Some of the non-fiction texts you have probably seen are biography, autobiography, travel writing, books on sport, etc.

In this book you will be given a mixture of fiction and non-fiction passages. The techniques for answering each type of question remain the same, whether fiction or non-fiction.

Exercise 1: Joseph and Rohit

Read the following short passage, which is fiction, school genre, and answer the fact gathering questions which follow.

Rohit always dreaded going into the chemistry class because Joseph intimdated him. No matter how hard Rohit tried, his marks for class tests just never matched up to Joseph's. Only last week, Rohit had spent hours on a detailed assignment given to the class by their teacher. At home, Rohit's finished assignment had looked splendid, but when Joseph took his own assignment out of his bag and handed it to the teacher, Rohit was dazzled by the brightness of its colourful front cover and depressed by its obvious length. The trouble was, it was difficult not to like Joseph. It would have been much simpler to dismiss him as the class swot, or some strange workaholic, but, no, Joseph was great company, with a quirky sense of humour, who looked out for everyone and was very thoughtful and kind-hearted. It wasn't his fault he was so clever.

1 Why did Rohit dread going into the chemistry class?   [1]
2 Was Rohit pleased or disappointed with his assignment as soon as he had finished it
   at home?   [1]
3 Did Rohit like or dislike Joseph?   [1]
4 Write down one thing about Joseph which made him a popular pupil.   [1]
5 Write down the one thing about Joseph which made people wary of Joseph.   [1]

[5 marks]

Exercise 2: Anna

Read the following short passage, which is fiction, childhood genre, and answer the fact gathering questions which follow.

The bus was already crowded when it arrived, and Anna and her mother barely managed to find room to sit. Off it went, rattling along over the dirt road, until it eventually trundled to a stop outside the market area. Anna's mother bundled her off, eager to join the jostling crowds thronging the narrow streets. They hurried by the displays of flashy jewellery spread out on the walk-ways, with their coloured bangles, crudely fashioned rings, and roughly polished stones, making for the stall selling clothing material. Anna's mother quickly began sifting through their repetitive patterns of colour, fashioning in her mind's eye some new dress for herself, no doubt, or a best shirt for father.

Anna, however had her mind set on the caves near the market. She had heard of the attractions there; the tempting iced drinks, street musicians performing, and the fascinating puppet shows. Up till now she had not been allowed to go on her own. For the moment, though, the displays of luscious fruit across the road were temptation enough. She counted the coins in her purse, and treated herself to a small bag of juicy plums.

1 Why did Anna and her mother find it difficult to find a seat on the bus?   [1]
2 Where were Anna and her mother going?   [1]
3 Which stall were they heading for?   [1]
4 What was Anna's mother thinking of making?   [1]
5 Where did Anna really want to go?   [1]
6 Was Anna allowed to leave her mother at the market?   [1]

[6 marks]

Exercise 3: Modern Travel

Read the following short passage, which is non-fiction, and answer the fact gathering questions which follow.

In the twenty-first century, ordinary people can travel more than they were ever able to do before. One reason for this is the vast improvement in transport and communications. Jet planes can travel from one end of the world to the other in a matter of hours.

People work shorter working weeks than in the past and therefore have more leisure time, which they often spend taking holidays to far-flung destinations. Places they would only ever have dreamed of, or have seen in magazines or read about in books, have become accessible to the ordinary traveller.

Low price airlines are a modern phenomenon; sometimes called 'no frills' airlines, they keep prices down by cutting back on many of the extra services of their more expensive counterparts — for example, a seating plan on the plane, or elaborate meals and drinks. Affluence and higher incomes also mean that ordinary people are able to do more than feed, house, clothe and educate their families—they are able to indulge themselves in luxuries which in the past were reserved for the rich. One of the most appreciated of these luxuries is travel.

1   In what one way, according to the writer, is the twenty-first century different from those which went before?   [1]

2   Why do people nowadays have more leisure time than in the past?   [1]

3   What is different about the destinations of the modern traveller compared to the destinations of travellers in the past?   [1]

4   How do 'no frills' airlines keep their prices down?   [1]

5   Why are ordinary people nowadays able to have luxuries which were not available to ordinary people in the past?   [1]

6   What, according to the writer, is one of the most appreciated luxuries available to ordinary people nowadays?   [1]

[6 marks]

Exercise 4: A Bad Day

Read the following short passage, which is fiction, school genre, and answer the questions which follow.

The day had started off badly for Rahman. Firstly, his alarm clock had not rung because, he realised later, the battery needed to be replaced. When he got up, late of course, he remembered that he had forgotten to pack his schoolbag the night before. How often his mother had told him to be well prepared for school by having an organised bag sitting at the front door. He scrambled around frantically, picking up notebooks, textbook and pencils and dashed out for the school bus. As he reached the bus stop, he was just in time to see the school bus drive off in a cloud of exhaust fumes. Feeling very sorry for himself, and feeling hunger pangs because he had not had time for breakfast, he felt like crying, although tears were, he thought, hardly appropriate for a boy of his age.

1   Why did Rahman not wake in time for school?   [1]

2   What advice had Rahman's mother often given him?   [1]

3   How did Rahman normally get to school?   [1]

4   What went wrong with his travel arrangements on this particular day?   [1]

5   Apart from feeling sorry for himself, why does Rahman feel like crying?   [1]

6   Why does he think he should stop himself from crying?   [1]

[6 marks]

Exercise 5: The Intruder

Read the following short passage, which is fiction, crime genre, and answer the fact gathering questions which follow.

He stood in the dark, at the edge of the quiet street, ready to walk quickly away if anyone passed by who might later be able to identify him. He was dressed in a nondescript way — black jogging trousers, baggy black sweater — and he had been careful to shield his eyes with a baseball cap. He would be difficult to identify, all right, although the chances of that ever becoming an issue were slim in this deserted part of town. He pulled himself back further into the shadows as the front door of the house, the house he had been watching for weeks, opened and the owner, a dark haired, rather burly man of about forty, he'd reckoned, came out and got into his parked car. As the car drove away, he smiled to himself.

This was his moment. The rest of the inhabitants of the house — the mother and the two children whom she took out every Tuesday — had already left. That meant that the house was empty. It was up to him now to avail himself of this opportunity, and make his move. Having checked that no-one was around, he walked briskly in the front gate and round to the back garden, where his bag of tools, including a crowbar, had already been hidden. He grinned to himself, pleased that his weeks of planning and surveillance were about to be rewarded. 'How smart I am!' he smiled to himself, as he removed the crowbar from the bag.

1   What is the character in the story planning to do?   [1]

2   Why would he walk quickly away if anyone passed by?   [1]

3   Write down one of the things he did to make sure he would be difficult to identify.   [1]

4   Why was the matter of identification not likely to become an issue?   [1]

5   How many people lived in the house?   [1]

6   Who left the house first?   [1]

7   On what day of the week does the story take place?   [1]

8   What had he already hidden in the garden?   [1]

[8 marks]

20 More about fact gathering questions

Now that you have examined a variety of written texts and completed some exercises on them, it is time to think about the skills that you need to develop in Reading for Meaning.

Reading for Meaning is different from Reading for Ideas. Reading for Meaning deals with your ability to demonstrate skills in Assessment Objective R1 and Assessment Objective R2, which are to show understanding of explicit meaning and to show understanding of implicit meaning. As you may realise from these objectives, there are a range of skills within Reading for Meaning and therefore there are several types of questions which test them. You will be working through the different types of questions in the chapters which follow.

There are techniques which you can learn to make the process of answering questions easier, so that you are more likely to be successful. For example, you need to ask yourself the following.

- Is the answer lying on the surface of the text or is there something I need to work out?

- How long need my answer be?

- How short is my answer allowed to be?

- Am I allowed to use the words of the original text?

- Do I need to use my own words?

- Is the question asking only about the story or argument of the text?

- Is the question asking about particular features of language, for example figures of speech, or the way language is used to invite evaluation of character or plot?

Literal and inferential comprehension

The key to distinguishing between literal and inferential questions lies in the difference between Assessment Objectives R1 and R2.

Assessment Objective R1 requires you to '*demonstrate understanding of explicit meanings*' and Assessment Objective R2 requires you to '*demonstrate understanding of implicit meanings and attitudes*'.

We will start with answers to the first question above.

- Is the answer lying on the surface of the text or is there something I need to work out?

In literal comprehension questions, the answer lies on the surface of the text; in other words, the answer is explicit. In inferential comprehension questions, you are required to work something out, to make a deduction, based on the information in the text; in other words, the answer is implicit.

> **For example**
> The sky was grey and full of heavy clouds. Rain ran in little rivers down the roads and traffic was travelling much more slowly than usual.

Question 1: What was the weather like that day?

Answer: It was raining.

The answer to this question lies on the surface of the text. The word 'rain' occurs in the text and is reinforced by the reference to the cloudy sky. This is a literal comprehension question.

Question 2: From the evidence given in the text, why do you think the traffic was travelling more slowly than usual?

Answer 1: The traffic was travelling more slowly than usual because it was raining and there might have been an accident if they had travelled at a normal speed.

Answer 2: The traffic was travelling more slowly than usual because the drivers were worried that they might skid on the wet road.

Answer 3: The traffic was travelling more slowly than usual because there was a traffic jam.

Both answers 1 and 2 are correct. Each answer makes a deduction, or inference, about the text, namely that if the rain was running in little rivers down the road, it might be dangerous for drivers to proceed at their normal pace. Answer 3 is incorrect because although it makes a deduction, that deduction is not based on the information given in the text. Answer 3 comes from the student's imagination, not the text. There is no evidence whatsoever in the text of a traffic jam.

> ### Remember
> The answers to literal comprehension questions lie on the surface of the text. The answers to inferential questions do not lie on the surface of the text, but can be worked out or deduced by looking at the context of the question, i.e. the area of text on which the question is based. The first step in selecting the correct answer to a comprehension question is to identify whether it is literal or inferential comprehension.

Signposts towards inferential comprehension questions include the following.

* Why do you think …
* Suggest a reason …
* Why might …
* What possible explanation is there for …
* In what way could it be thought that …
* How can you tell that …

Exercise 1: Literal and Inferential Questions

Write down each of the following questions. Although they are not attached to any text, it should be possible for you to tell which can be answered by literal comprehension and which require an inference to be made. Beside each one write down whether it is signposted as a literal or as an inferential question.

1 How many people were in the restaurant?
2 What was the name of Anna's brother?
3 Suggest a reason why the shop was empty.
4 At what time of day is the story set?
5 What possible explanation is there for Michael's absence on that day?
6 Why might you be surprised to find that the trip was well organised?
7 Why did he not know where the sound was coming from?
8 Why do you think the writer tells us that the countryside was beautiful?
9 What colour was the girl's dress?
10 How might you be able to tell that the journey was made during the night?

Exercise 2: City Life

What follows is a short passage with questions which can be answered by literal comprehension. Read the passage carefully and then answer the questions which follow.

Many of today's major social problems have arisen because the population has been crowded into urban areas. The drawbacks of city life are obvious: traffic, cost of living and increased crime.

The advantages of city life include access to work, services, education, entertainment and friends. If the population of a city were reduced by even ten per cent, the result would be a major difference in property values and a deterioration in services paid for by public money, like transport.

1   Give one advantage and one disadvantage of city life.   [2]

2   Give one result of reducing the population of a city by ten per cent.   [1]

[3 marks]

Exercise 3: Classroom Computers

What follows is a short passage with questions which can be answered by literal comprehension. Read the passage carefully and then answer the questions which follow.

Some people are afraid that computers used in education will lead to a deterioration in educational standards. However, anyone who has ever watched kids round a classroom computer, or witnessed computer exchanges between students in classrooms separated by oceans, knows that technology can actually improve the learning experience by making it more enjoyable.

Despite a common view to the contrary, computers will not become a substitute for teachers. Indeed, computers will bring together the best work of countless teachers and students.

1   According to 'some people', what will be the result of using computers in the classroom?   [1]

2   According to the writer, what aspect of technology leads to an improvement in education?   [1]

3   What is the 'common view' about computers?   [1]

4   According to the writer, what is the advantage of using computers in the classroom?   [1]

[4 marks]

Exercise 4: Inferential Questions

Now answer these inferential questions on both 'City Life' and 'Classroom Computers'.

1   If the population of a city were reduced, why do you think there would be 'deterioration in services'?   [1]

2   Suggest a reason why the writer refers to 'kids' in the second line of the passage and to 'students' in the third line of the passage.   [2]

[3 marks]

Now go back to some of the other questions posed at the start of this chapter.

•   How long need my answer be?

•   How short is my answer allowed to be?

The answer to these questions is simple. As long as you answer the question, the length of your answer doesn't matter. You will not impress teachers with elaborate sentences. In fact, as you will almost certainly be working against the clock, it is a good idea to keep your answer to the shortest form possible, as long as you answer the question, of course.

Look back at the answers to the inferential question on page 125: From the evidence given in the text, why do you think the traffic was travelling more slowly than usual?

There were three answers for consideration, two of which were acceptable and one of which was not. Each of the answers started:

•   The traffic was travelling more slowly than usual because . . .

However, it would not have affected the correctness or otherwise of the answers if they had simply been written as:

•   It was raining and there might have been an accident if they had travelled at a normal speed.

•   The drivers were worried that they might skid on the wet road.

•   There was a traffic jam.

All of these sentences answer the question (although the third is wrong) in a way which does not repeat the stem of the question.

What these answers do is more than selection of information. They also retrieve the information necessary to answer the question, without wasting time in words which do not contribute to a correct answer but merely pad out a correct answer. To retrieve information is to do more than select it. It is to home in on as small an area of the text as is sufficient to answer the given question. Retrieval of information imposes a kind of economy on your answers to questions.

Remember
There is no need to copy out the stem of the question when you write an answer to it.

Exercise 5: Writing Shorter Answers

What follows are some questions and answers. Even though you have not been given the original texts, write answers shorter than those given below to show that your answer has been both selected and retrieved.

Question 1: How can you tell that the girl is upset?

Answer: It is obvious that the girl is upset because she is crying.

Question 2: If the people had realised that the storm was coming, what precaution might they have taken?

Answer: If the people had realised that the storm was coming they would have taken the precaution of tying up all the boats in the harbour.

Question 3: From your reading of the passage, how many days was the journey likely to last?

Answer: From my reading of the passage it seems likely that the journey would last six days.

Question 4: Suggest a reason why, in spite of the rising cost of materials, the factory continued to manufacture furniture.

Answer: In spite of the rising cost of materials, the factory continued to manufacture furniture because it had been given a subsidy by the government.

Question 5: The writer refers to 'an often expressed' fear. What is this fear?

Answer: The 'often expressed fear' to which the writer refers is the fear that soon there will be a shortage of teachers.

Question 6: The writer states that 'technology should be at the service of everyone'. Which group of citizens does he fear will be the only ones to benefit?

Answer: He fears that, although technology should be at the service of everyone, the only group to benefit will be the rich.

Question 7: Feelings between the two men became strained. From the evidence of the paragraph, what is the first example of this tension?

Answer: The first example of feelings between the two men becoming strained was when they stopped talking on the journey.

Question 8: 'Each man looked after himself'. What is surprising about this in view of the journey they were undertaking?

Answer: It was surprising that each man looked after himself in view of the journey they were taking because it was a dangerous journey and it would have been safer if they had worked together.

Question 9: Apart from feelings of wild excitement, how was Emma feeling at the end of the marathon?

Answer: Apart from feelings of wild excitement, Emma was feeling exhausted at the end of the marathon.

In the following exercises, you will find passages with questions for you to answer. Use the signposts you have learned to decide which questions are literal and which are inferential. It is best to answer in sentences, but remember not to waste time in repeating the stems of the questions in your answers.

Exercise 6: Exploring a Cave

Read the passage and then answer the questions which follow below.

Exploring a cave can be an unpleasant experience: there is a damp, sometimes dusty smell which seems to be the same in all caves. You can see nothing at first but, when your eyes adjust to your unfamiliar surroundings, the strange light casts eerie shadows on the walls. Sometimes you are aware of creatures like mice scurrying across your path.

If you are exploring a low cave, at the start of the walk stooping is rather a joke, but it is a joke that wears off as soon as you have travelled a short distance. You not only have to bend; you have also got to keep your head up so that you can see the roof of the cave. You have, therefore, a constant pain in the neck and aching thighs, but this is nothing compared to the pain in your knees.

After about a kilometre it becomes an unbearable agony. You begin to worry whether you will ever get to the end — still more, how on earth you are going to get back. Your pace grows slower and slower in response to the difficulties.

Sometime it is hard going underneath your feet, with jagged pieces of rock littering the ground and frequent pools of stagnant water. You certainly need to tread very slowly.

1 Why does the writer describe exploring a cave as 'unpleasant'?   [1]
2 What does the writer suggest is frightening about exploring a cave?   [1]
3 What would happen to someone walking in a cave who didn't keep his head up?   [2]
4 What is the worst pain experienced by someone walking in a low cave?   [1]
5 What are the two main worries of a person walking in a low cave?   [2]
6 Why do you think a walker's pace 'grows slower and slower'?   [1]
7 What two aspects of the cave mean that the walker 'needs to tread very slowly'?   [2]

[10 marks]

More exercises in literal and inferential comprehension

Each of the exercises which follow gives you a passage to read, and for each passage there are some literal and inferential questions for you to answer. You are free to lift the answers from the passage.

Exercise 1: Julia

She had lived most of her life alone. Her mother had borne her late in life and Julia believed that, and the strain of trying to please her tyrannical father, had probably contributed to her mother's early death. When her mother died, a few weeks after her sixtieth birthday, Julia was not quite fifteen.

She had escaped from her father as soon as she could, going to Girton College, Cambridge on a scholarship, which paid her way. Although he had tried to make her departure from the family home as unpleasant as possible, there was not much he could do to prevent it and once away from him a part of her had felt she could never again face living with another man.

There had been female friends, such as Vera, and there had been Harriet whom, she now concluded, pounding the streets, she had not treated as well as she could have done. Harriet had been more than a friend; but, blindly, she had taken Harriet for granted. Yet she had loved Harriet, she now knew, and she knew it because she had learned to love someone else.

If you spend most of your life alone often you do not know that you are lonely. It was not until the 'discovery' that Julia Garnet knew that she was lonely and that she had been so for most of her life.

Source: from *Miss Garnet's Angel* by Salley Vickers

1   Give two reasons given by the writer to explain why Julia's mother died relatively young.
    Number your answer (i) and (ii).   [2]

2   How old was Julia when her mother died?   [1]

3   What one piece of information are we given about the behaviour of Julia's father which
    suggests that Julia did not have a good relationship with him?   [1]

4   Why was Julia's father unable to prevent her taking up her university place?   [1]

5   Once she left home, what effect did Julia's relationship with her father have on her?   [1]

6   What two aspects of her relationship with Harriet does Julia now regret? Number your
    answers (i) and (ii).   [2]

7   What does the word 'blindly' suggest about Julia's behaviour towards Harriet?   [1]

8   How does Julia now know that she loved Harriet?   [1]

9   According to the writer, what often happens to people who live most of their lives alone? [1]

10 Why do you think the writer begins and ends the extract with a reference to the fact
    that Julia has lived most of her life alone?   [1]

[12 marks]

Exercise 2: Selling the Flat

There were matters to attend to: the solicitors, Mr Akbar. And it's right too, she thought, as the plane taxied out and up and over the sea. There is a life to close down.

London was dirty and hot after a cold July, and Ealing particularly stuffy. Mr Akbar, however, was overjoyed to see her.

'Madam, come in, come in,' he gestured hospitably down her own hall. 'It is wonderful that you have come.'

He made her sweet mint tea and they sat on the balcony overlooking the gardens. The gardens, which had been a source of joy to Julia during her years at Cedar Court, looked seedy: the turf parched and the flowerbeds municipal.

'These I love,' said Mr Akbar, pointing at a pair of bedraggled mallard ducks which had wandered onto the lawns.

'Do you, Mr Akbar? Then I am happy you are going to buy my flat.'

'You accept my price?'

Julia had taken the precaution of visiting a local estate agency before their meeting and had gleaned that the sum he was offering was rather below the market value. She had come intending to be firm on this point.

But the eyes of Mr Akbar, looking pleadingly at her, made her waver.

She had bought the flat for a good price after the original landlord died, leaving her as the sitting tenant. It seemed greedy to take advantage now of her own good fortune and besides, had Mr Akbar not made overtures to her she might never have had the idea to sell up. He did not have the appearance of wealth.

And the hassle of selling the place elsewhere would delay her. Anyway, she owed him something for putting the idea of her permanent remove to Venice into her head.

Source: from *Miss Garnet's Angel* by Salley Vickers

1. Julia plans to 'close down' her life in London. What is the first thing she has to do? [1]
2. Give three pieces of evidence to suggest that Mr Akbar 'was overjoyed to see' Julia. Number your answers (i), (ii) and (iii). [3]
3. Mr Akbar and Julia 'sat on the balcony'. How can you tell that Julia's feelings about her former home have changed? [1]
4. How does the writer make it clear from his description of the gardens that the weather was hot? [1]
5. Why might it be surprising that Mr Akbar loves the ducks? [1]
6. What had Julia discovered when she visited the local estate agent? [1]
7. Before she came to visit Mr Akbar, what had Julia planned to do when it came to selling the house to him? [1]
8. What made Julia change her mind about her earlier decision? [1]
9. (i) What had been Julia's 'good fortune'? (ii) Whose idea has it been to sell the flat in the first place? [2]
10. Apart from the difficulty involved in selling her flat to someone else, give two reasons why Julia decides to accept Mr Akbar's offer. Number your answers (i) and (ii). [2]

[14 marks]

Exercise 3: Anna's Journey

'Just remember, Anna, your father and I are very proud of you.' Her mother's words to her before she left rang in Anna's ears and she felt tears prick her eyes. She forced herself to stop thinking about her mother, afraid of making a spectacle of herself in such a public place as an airport.

Her heart sank when she realised that there were crowds of people waiting to have their passports checked. In a state of great anxiety, she chose what seemed to be the shortest queue, and fished in her overloaded handbag for her passport. Panicking, she was convinced she had lost it, only seconds later to find it. All around her were people of different nationalities, united in their common purpose – to have their passports checked as soon as possible, leave the bustle of the airport and enter the country.

'Now for my baggage,' thought Anna, following the appropriate airport signs. Her mother had told her that all the suitcases from her aircraft would be placed on a moving conveyor belt, and that she would have to identify and retrieve her own suitcase from among all the others. Anna searched for her own suitcase, but with no success. Bags were collected, people came and went, until Anna was left standing tearfully in an empty hall.

By now she had been spotted by a uniformed official. 'Please come with me,' he said to Anna, not unkindly, leading her to a little office, where he picked up a pen and printed form. Clearly this was mere routine for him. 'Now, please give me details about your missing bag – make, colour, size.' Because she was by now wildly agitated, Anna's mind had gone blank and she was unable to answer any of these questions. With a disdainful sigh, the official informed her that when her baggage was traced it would be delivered to the city address which Anna was able – miraculously, his look suggested – to give him. He glanced at his watch and sighed again.

When she reached the student accommodation, she was disappointed that no suitcase awaited her in her room, although she consoled herself with the thought that, given the time-scale, this was hardly surprising. She surveyed the tiny room which was to be her home for at least the next year. It seemed so empty and unfriendly after the warmth of home. 'Perhaps I shall feel better about it in the morning,' thought Anna, as she climbed into bed. The last thing she remembered before sleep overtook her was an ache of homesickness in the pit of her stomach.

In the morning, she felt considerably brighter and searched in her handbag for clean clothes and toiletries, determined to make the most of her free day by investigating her new environment. The coolness inside provided a refreshing change to the heat outside. Dizzily scanning the buildings, Anna could appreciate why they were called skyscrapers. People surged past, their faces set impassively, as they hurried towards their destinations. Cars gave off clouds of exhaust fumes as they inched along the road, their drivers tapping their fingers in impatience on the steering wheels. The traffic lights changed; Anna was propelled across the road by the crowd standing on the pavement, and found herself outside a huge covered market.

There was an aroma of spices and fruit, and the sound of voices echoed around the high space. Fearfully, Anna took the precaution of clutching her bag tightly as she walked around, nevertheless relishing the vastness of the market and the variety of goods on display. By now, it was raining outside. People pushed into the market, many with newspapers over their heads, rain running in little rivers from their chins, their hair, their sandals. A queue for taxis had formed and people edged to the front of it, watching intently every vehicle that screeched round the corner. The sun blazed down again and steam hissed up from the pavement. It was time for Anna to go back to her little room. 'Back home?' she wondered, amazed at the difference a day could make. As she opened the door of her room, she found that she was not entirely alone. Standing in the middle of her floor, with make, colour and size clear to see, was the suitcase she had lost the previous day. Happily, Anna went downstairs to phone her mother.

1   What did Anna fear she might do to draw attention to herself? [1]

2   Give **two** reasons which might explain why Anna was unable to find her passport immediately. [2]

3   When dealing with her missing baggage, the uniformed official showed **two** separate attitudes to Anna. What were these two attitudes? Number your answers (i) and (ii). [2]

4   Anna was 'disappointed that no suitcase awaited her in her room'. Why do you think this was an unreasonable reaction? [1]

5   'People surged past, their faces set impassively'. What **two** impressions of city people do you think this suggests? In your answer, do not copy from the passage. [2]

6   Why were the car drivers impatient? [1]

7   Anna was fearful as she walked around the market. What was she afraid of? [1]

8   Suggest **two** reasons why Anna went 'happily' to phone her mother. [2]

[12 marks]

Adapted from Cambridge O Level English Language 1120 Paper 2 Q1, Q2a, Q3b, Q5b, Q6a, Q7, November 2006

22 Selecting and retrieving information by lifting

Now we will look at some of the other questions asked at the start of Chapter 20.

- Do I need to use my own words?

- Am I allowed to use words of the original text?

The answer to these questions is that you may use the words of the original text unless you are told otherwise. In questions where you are required to use your own words, the wording of the question will make that clear. You will look at such questions later. Right now you will deal only with questions where you are allowed to use the words of the text. This is called lifting from the text.

> **Remember**
> Unless the question specifies use of own words, it is acceptable to lift from the text.

However, when you lift from the text to answer a question, you must make sure that you do not include material from the text which is not necessary in your answer.

If you do include extra, unnecessary information, your answer might not be considered acceptable by teachers. Look at the short passage below.

> The appearance of land at the end of a long sea voyage must be a welcome sight for any ship's captain. Yet he has to be particularly alert at this stage of the voyage, for in many parts of the world there are often rocky islands close to the shore he is approaching.
> Source: from *Scottish Mysteries* by Donald M. Fraser
> *Cambridge O Level English Language 1120 Paper 2 Q1a, June 2005*

Question: At what stage of a sea journey must a captain be 'particularly alert'?

Answer 1:   He must be alert at the end of the voyage.

Answer 2:   He must be alert when land appears.

Answer 3:   The appearance of land at the end of a long sea voyage.

Answer 4:   The appearance of land at the end of a long sea voyage must be a welcome sight for any ship's captain.

Answers 1 and 2 are correct. Each of them has selected and retrieved key words from the passage which answer the question and recast them in a sentence.

Answer 3 is also correct. It is a direct lift from the passage but this is acceptable because, unless otherwise stated, this is not an own words question. This is a literal comprehension question and the answer lies on the surface of the text.

It would have been better if the answer had been given in a short sentence but that does not prevent the answer from being considered acceptable.

However, Answer 4 is incorrect because, although it lifts the correct answer, it goes on to lift so much of the text that the question is not in fact answered. This answer does not give 'a stage of a journey' but a lifted sentence which ultimately does not answer the question.

> **Remember**
> Although it is acceptable to lift from the text in answering a question, you must be careful that what you lift does not include extra information which might distort your answer or prevent the question from being answered.

Exercise 1: Coral Reefs

From the passage which follows answer the questions by lifting.

> A thriving coral reef is one of the most glorious sights on our planet. Anyone swimming underwater near a coral reef for the first time is likely to find it a beautiful place teeming with life of every description set among a rich and random pattern of colours.
>
> Coral reefs are second only to rain forests in the huge number of plants and animals they support. Just as forest plants have been used for hundreds of years for medicinal purposes by people living in the rain forests, so some reef plants and animals have been used by people in coastal communities to help cure diseases like malaria.
> Source: Adapted from *The Greenpeace Book of Coral Reefs*

1   Why does the writer describe coral reefs as 'one of the most glorious sights on our planet'?   [1]

2   In what ways are coral reefs almost as important as rain forests?   [1]

3   What common benefit do people living in rain forests and people living near coral reefs get from local plants?   [1]

[3 marks]

Text adapted from *Cambridge O Level English Language 1120 Paper 2 Q1 a & b, Q3 a, November 2004*

Exercise 2: Grandfather

From the passage which follows answer the questions by lifting.

> She loved to sit on her grandfather's knee while he read her stories for what seemed like hours. He never tired of reading to her and it would never have occurred to her that he would refuse to do so. His voice was gruff but comforting; it was his reading voice just for her.
>
> Sometimes she took a peek at his face; his skin was wrinkly and she liked to trace with her eye particular lines as they meandered from one side of his face to the other. He had a white, bushy moustache which curled up at the edges and twitched as his lips moved over the mysterious symbols on the page which she did not understand but loved to listen to. She had to sit very still as his clothes were scratchy and made her legs red if she moved too much.

1   Why did the little girl like to sit on her grandfather's knee?   [1]

2   What one feature of her grandfather's voice might have been frightening to the little girl?   [1]

3   Apart from the moustache, what was it about her grandfather's face which interested the little girl?   [1]

4   Why did the little girl have to sit very still on her grandfather's knee?   [1]

[4 marks]

Exercise 3: Friendship with Jennifer

From the passage which follows answer the questions by lifting.

> She spent a day with an old friend and felt really refreshed. She and Jennifer as a team had a long history. They made their shy introductions on their first day at primary school and since then have shared many high — and low — points in their respective lives. They joined the local youth club together, and walked and talked and went shopping together. They discussed each other's boyfriends.
>
> In a nutshell they grew up together. Her day with Jennifer restored her well-being, her happiness, her sanity. But more than that, it made her reflect on the nature of real friendship —having someone value you for what you are.

1   What had made the woman feel 'really refreshed'?   [1]
2   When did the woman and her friend meet each other for the first time?   [1]
3   Give an example of one activity that the two friends did together.   [1]
4   What was the main advantage gained by the woman from her day spent with her old friend?   [1]

[4 marks]

Exercise 4: The London Marathon

From the passage which follows answer the questions by lifting.

> Chris's best friend had told him he was mad even to consider running the London marathon, and, as his friend was a doctor, Chris took his comment seriously. However, for months he was out running on the pavements around his home trying to forget that his build was neither slim nor athletic. Not for him the lure of fame or fortune; he had committed himself to raise money for charity. More than twenty six miles — he told himself not to think about it as he sweated on the treadmill in his local gym. He tried, unsuccessfully, to think of it as fun, but that was stretching his imagination too far. But when it was over Chris did feel just that little superior — and he had had a great tour of London!

1   Why did Chris take his friend's comments seriously?   [1]
2   What two reasons does the writer give to suggest that Chris was not suited to running a marathon?   [1]
3   Why was Chris determined to run the marathon?   [1]
4   In what two ways did Chris train for the marathon?   [2]
5   Apart from making Chris feel superior, what was the other advantage to him of running the marathon?   [1]

[6 marks]

> **Remember**
> Although all of these questions can be answered by lifting, they could be answered in other ways. But the important point here is that, although some questions can be answered by lifting, you must not copy over sections of the text which do not in fact answer the questions. In such cases, the excess in your answer makes it unacceptable. It tends to be easier, literal comprehension questions which can be answered by lifting.

> **Remember**
> When you answer a question by lifting, make sure that you do not stray into areas of the text that are irrelevant to the correct answer.

For each of the exercises which follow:

- read the passage carefully twice

- answer the questions by lifting (do not try to use own words at this stage)

- answer the questions in sentences, but do not waste time copying out question stems

- be careful that what you lift does not include extra information which might distort your answer or prevent the question from being answered.

Exercise 1: Grandfather's Study

In Pappachi's study, mounted butterflies and moths had disintegrated into small heaps of iridescent dust that powdered the bottom of their glass display cases, leaving the pins that had impaled them. Cruel. The room was rank with fungus and disease.

Rahel (on a stool, on top of a table) rummaged in a book cupboard with dull, dirty glass panes. Her bare footprints were clear in the dust on the floor. They led from the door to the table (dragged to the bookshelf) to the stool (dragged to the table and lifted onto it). She was looking for something.

On the top shelf, the leather binding of grandfather's set of 'The Insect Wealth of India' had lifted off each book and buckled like corrugated asbestos. Silverfish tunnelled through the pages, burrowing arbitrarily from species to species, turning organised information into yellow lace. Rahel groped behind the row of books and brought out hidden things. A smooth seashell and a spiky one. A plastic case for contact lenses. An orange pipette.

Behind the books, Rahel's puzzled fingers encountered something else. Another magpie had the same idea. She brought it out and wiped the dust off with the sleeve of her shirt. It was a flat packet wrapped in clear plastic and stuck with Sellotape. A scrap of white paper inside is said 'Esthappen and Rahel'. In Ammu's writing. There were four tattered notebooks in it.

Source: from *The God of Small Things* by Arundhati Roy

1   What had happened to Grandfather's collection of moths?   [1]
2   Where in the study had Grandfather kept his collection of moths?   [1]
3   Apart from the dead moths, what else about the study might have made Rahel dislike it?   [1]
4   The cupboard had 'dirty glass panes'. What else was dirty?   [1]
5   How had Rahel got the table to the bookshelf?   [1]
6   How had Rahel got the stool on to the table?   [1]
7   Explain fully what had happened to Grandfather's set of books entitled 'The Insect
    Wealth of India'.   [2]
8   What did Rahel have to do to retrieve the 'hidden things'?   [1]
9   Explain fully how you can tell that the notebooks had been hidden by Ammu.   [2]
10 Explain fully how you can tell that the notebooks were important to Ammu.   [2]

[13 marks]

Exercise 2: The Brazilian Rain Forest

Once a year the skies of western Brazil grow dark by day as well as by night. Farmers and cattle owners burn down vast areas of the great rain forests around the river Amazon to clear land for crop-growing and cattle rearing. Smoke from the fires blots out the sun. Scientists, now keenly aware of the dangers to the earth's environment, see this great annual destruction as a major peril for Brazil, and also for the rest of the world. Politicians have joined scientists to try to stop the foolish waste of the precious resources of the planet.

For more than four hundred years settlers and farmers have been attacking Brazil's forests in one way or another. They tried to snatch land for themselves from the seemingly indestructible jungles, but their power of recovery defeated their efforts. New trees continually filled in the small patches of land that they cleared. Nowadays, modern machinery can cut down trees at an alarming speed, and the controlled burning down of the forests has meant that areas larger than some whole countries have been permanently stripped bare.

One result of this destruction is becoming alarmingly obvious. The forests contain an astonishing variety of animal and plant life which is slowly but surely disappearing. One type of tree may maintain more than four hundred insect species, each square kilometre of forest its own assortment of birds and mammals.

Source: from *World's Apart: An Explorer's Life*, by A. R. Hanbury-Tenison

1   Once a year, what is unusual about the skies of western Brazil?   [1]

2   Why do farmers and cattle-owners burn down the forests?   [1]

3   In the first paragraph, what evidence does the writer give to suggest that vast areas are
    burned?   [1]

4   Explain fully why scientists are worried about the burning of the forests.   [2]

5   How can you tell that politicians agree with scientists?   [1]

6   Is the destruction of the forests a new phenomenon? Give a reason for your answer.   [1]

7   What feature of the jungles meant that settlers were unable 'to snatch land for themselves',
    and what evidence of this feature does the writer give to support his claim?   [2]

8   In the second paragraph, what evidence does the writer give to suggest that vast areas
    are burned?   [1]

9   Apart from burning down forests, how else is land obtained for farmers and cattle owners?   [1]

10 What is 'one result' of the destruction of the forests?   [1]

[12 marks]

Exercise 3: Estha and Rahel

They were nearly born on a bus, Estha and Rahel. The car in which Baba, their father, was taking Ammu, their mother, to hospital in Shillong to have them broke down on the winding tea estate road in Assam. They abandoned the car and flagged down a crowded State Transport bus. With the queer compassion of the very poor for the comparatively well off, or perhaps only because they saw how hugely pregnant Ammu was, seated passengers made room for the couple and for the rest of the journey Estha and Rahel's father had to hold their mother's wobbling stomach (with them in it) to prevent it from wobbling.

According to Estha, if they'd been born on the bus, they'd have got free bus rides for the rest of their lives. It wasn't clear where he's got this information from, or how he knew these things, but for years the twins harboured a faint resentment against their parents for having diddled them out of a lifetime of free bus rides.

They also believed that if they were killed on a zebra crossing, they'd have got free bus rides for the rest of their lives. They had the definite impression that that was what zebra crossings were meant for. Free funerals. Of course there were no zebra crossings to get killed on in Ayamenem, or, for that matter, even in Kottayam, which was the nearest town, but they'd seen some from the car window when they went to Cochin, which was a two hour drive away.

Source: from *The God of Small Things* by Arundhati Roy

1   Where were Estha and Rahel's parents going when their car broke down?   [1]

2   How did they complete their journey after the car broke down?   [1]

3   Why might we be surprised that the passengers on the bus felt sorry for Baba and Ammu?   [1]

4   Why might we expect the passengers on the bus to feel sorry for Baba and Ammu?   [1]

5   Why did Baba have to hold Ammu's stomach on the bus journey?   [1]

6   What did Estha think would have happened if he and his sister had been born on the bus?   [1]

7   How did Estha know what would have happened if he and his sister had been born on
    the bus?   [1]

8   Why did the twins feel resentful towards their parents?   [1]

9   According to the twins, what was the advantage of being killed on a zebra crossing?   [1]

10 Why were the twins unlikely to be killed on a zebra crossing?   [1]

[10 marks]

Exercise 4: The Domestication of Animals

There are thousands of species of wild animals, and yet surprisingly few, for example the goat and the cow, have been domesticated. The reason is that it takes special qualities to make animals suitable for domestication. They must be strong enough to withstand removal from their mother at an early age and find food for themselves so that her milk can be used for human consumption. They must breed freely in captivity — a guarantee that the farmer has a living — and be easy to look after. Domestic or farm animals must be able to develop a

liking for man, enjoy comfort, and accept confinement and control. And, of course, they must be useful: primarily as a source of food, but also in the provision of wool or hide for clothing and sometimes as a means of transport or pulling power.

Animals suitable for domestication only emerged with the spread of grass. Millions of years ago, the world's rainfall decreased, forests diminished, low-growing plants appeared, then grass, and, with them, grazing animals developed. Thus sheep and antelope appeared on the scene, followed by cows, goats and horses. Not until about 10,000 years ago did man develop the idea of taking animals into captivity. There was wild game in abundance, so what prompted the idea?

It could have come naturally from his experience as a nomadic hunter. As he followed his prey on their yearly migrations he gradually began to influence their movements and behaviour in certain situations. For example, some animals would be driven into a narrow, steep-sided valley where they could more easily be rounded up and some of them slaughtered. Or perhaps the idea arose out of keeping young animals as pets. Predators trying to steal food from the hunters' camp were fed by the men and encouraged to become part of the community: the predator changed into the pet.

Source: Adapted from *Animal on the Farm* by Judy Urquhart

1 According to the passage, what do the goat and the cow have in common?   [1]

2 Why are domestic animals taken from their mothers at an early age?   [1]

3 Why do animals removed from their mothers at an early age have to be strong?   [1]

4 What must happen to ensure that the farmer makes a living?   [1]

5 What are the three uses to which domestic animals can be put? Number your answers (i),
   (ii) and (iii).   [3]

6 What is the main reason for the development of domestic animals?   [1]

7 What two things happened after the forests diminished which led to grazing animals?
   Number your answers (i) and (ii).   [2]

8 According to the writer, why might we be surprised that man started to take animals into
   captivity?   [1]

9 What did early man do which shows he was a 'nomadic hunter'?   [1]

10 What was the advantage of driving animals into a 'narrow, steep-sided valley'?   [1]

11 Why did men feed predators which were trying to steal their food?   [1]

[14 marks]

24 Answering in your own words

We will now move on to techniques for dealing with questions which require you to answer in your own words. In an own words question, you go beyond merely selecting and retrieving the information required to answer the question.

Go back to a question asked at the start of Chapter 22.

• Do I need to use my own words?

We have already established that the answer to this question is that you may use the words of the text unless the question tells you specifically not to. In cases where you are required to answer in your own words, the question wording will make that clear.

Answering an own words question means that you will have to render key words from the text into words which do not come from the text. Usually, in an examination, you will not be required to select and retrieve these words from the text yourself, as they will be incorporated into the question you are asked, although this chapter includes some questions where you are required to select and retrieve the key words yourself before re-casting them into your own words.

Example 1

In time, our early ancestors learned to communicate knowledge to one another. This enabled them to find more food.

Question: Using your own words, say what our ancestors learned which enabled them find food.

Step 1
In answering this question the first step is to identify it as an own words question. This is not difficult as the question wording makes it quite clear that you are required to answer in your own words. Such questions are usually clearly signposted in an examination — there are no tricks there! Similarly, you must realise that, if you do not use your own words, you are wasting your time. Lifting is pointless in an own words question.

Step 2

The next step in answering this question is to be sure of the key words you are being asked to re-cast into words or expressions of your own. Careful reading of the question and the text should lead you to see that 'communicate' and 'knowledge' are the key words.

Step 3

The final step in answering this question is to evaluate the key words you are being asked to re-cast into words or expressions of your own. This means that you must weigh up their meaning in the text and come up with synonyms or other equivalents.

So your synonyms for '*communicate*' might be '*pass on*', '*tell*', '*share*' or '*inform*', while your synonyms for '*knowledge*' might be '*information*', '*what they had learned*' or '*what they had found out*'.

Your answer might be: They passed on to one another what they had found out.

Notice that we established that own words questions ask for synonyms or other equivalents. You do not need to give a single word to re-cast a single word. Nor do you need to give the same part of speech, i.e. a noun for a noun or a verb for a verb. So 'what they had learned' is a perfect answer to re-cast 'knowledge' although it is not a single word answer. However, 'what they know' would not be an acceptable answer because 'know' is a derivative of 'knowledge' which means that it comes from the same family.

> ## Remember
> In an own words question, a single word synonym is not necessary for a correct answer. However, answering in a derivative of the key word will not be acceptable to teachers.

> ### *Example 2*
> The island's isolated location and hostile weather meant that the lighthouse took four years to complete.

Question: What features of the island meant that it took four years to build the lighthouse? Answer in your own words.

Step 1

This is an own words question.

Step 2

Key words are '*isolated*' and '*hostile*'.

Step 3

Possible synonyms for '*isolated*' are '*far away*', '*lonely*', '*separated*', and '*cut off*'. Possible synonyms for '*hostile*' are '*unkind*', '*inclement*', '*nasty*', '*bad*'.

Answer: It took four years to build because the island was far away and because of bad weather.

Exercise 1

Answer the own words questions attached to the short passages below.

When Jennifer stepped from the car, she was horrified at the scene of devastation before her.

1   In your own words, explain how Jennifer felt when she stepped from the car, and the reason why she felt this way.

The rush hour traffic crawled along the road, smoke billowing from exhaust pipes.

2   In your own words, describe the rush hour traffic.

Undoubtedly, the reduction in government spending on education will lead to deterioration in literacy.

3   According to the writer, the result of the reduction in government spending on education will lead to 'a deterioration in literacy'. Explain in your own words what this means.

The creepers grew in profusion around the house, and even coiled round the window sills.

4   Explain in your own words what the writer tells us about the creepers by telling us that they 'grew in profusion' and 'coiled around the window sills'.

In the past, governments have sometimes taken strong action to preserve an environment which has been threatened. Unfortunately, these governments have often disregarded the views of the people living there.

5   Using your own words, explain what mistakes were made, according to the writer, by governments in the past which tried to preserve an environment which had been threatened.

Speed boats take tourists every day out to the coral reefs. This leads to the inevitable destruction of the reefs.

6   According to the writer, the result of tourists' speed boat trips to the coral reefs leads to their 'inevitable destruction'. Explain in your own words what this means.

With mounting astonishment, the captain saw that there was nobody in or around the lighthouse.

7   The captain reacted to the fact that there was nobody in or around the lighthouse 'with mounting astonishment'. Explain in your own words what his reaction was.

Speeding downhill on a bicycle is an experience which is both exhilarating and terrifying.

8   The writer describes the experience of speeding downhill on a bicycle as both 'exhilarating and terrifying'. Explain in your own words what this means.

Even today, coral reefs are still essential to people living in the tropics, whether used to manufacture tools or simply to adorn their houses.

9   Coral reefs are still essential to people living in the tropics as they are used to 'manufacture tools or simply to adorn their houses.' Explain in your own words the uses made of coral by people living in the tropics.

It seems likely that, in the future, schemes for the protection of coral reefs will be initiated and supervised by local people.

10 In your own words, explain the part that is likely to be played by local people in schemes for the protection of coral reefs.

Exercise 2

Read the passage below and answer the own words questions which follow.

Out of all the huts the villagers were reluctantly emerging — the children first: they were inquisitive and unfrightened.

The lieutenant barked out, 'Attention. All of you. Listen to me. Anyone who shelters him is a traitor too.' Their immobility infuriated him. He said, 'You're fools if you still believe what the priests tell you.'

Source: from *The Power and the Glory* by Graham Greene

1 The children were 'inquisitive and unfrightened'. In your own words, explain the effect the
arrival of the lieutenant had on the children. [2]

2 What had 'infuriated' the lieutenant? Answer in your own words. [1]

[3 marks]

Signposts in own words questions

Just as we saw that there are signposts in inferential questions, in the same way there are
signposts in own words questions. The obvious signpost is that the question asks you to use
your own words. However, a more subtle signpost might be a quotation from the passage.
This quotation might be a single word, an expression or even a whole sentence. (In the last
question, the quotation signpost was the word 'infuriated'.)

Quotations can be signposts which direct you to the area of text where you will find the key
words, i.e. the words which you have to select, retrieve and evaluate so that you can put them
into your own words.

> ## Remember
> If you are given quotation signposts in own words questions, use them to help you to
> find the key words, i.e. the words you will have to put into your own words.

Exercise 3

Read the passage below and answer the own words questions which follow.

> Once the newspapers got hold of the story, there was much speculation, most of it
> unconvincing. The mystery has never been conclusively solved, but for over a century many
> explanations as to what happened have been suggested. One theory is that violence broke out
> and one of the lighthouse keepers murdered his colleagues and threw them over the cliff; he
> then jumped over the cliff himself through shame at what he had done. A second, less fanciful,
> theory is that two of the men got up early to repair the devastation of a night of particularly
> inclement weather.
> Source: from *Scottish Mysteries* by Donald M. Fraser

1 According to the writer, what happened 'once the newspapers got hold of the story'?
Answer in your own words. [2]
Cambridge O Level English Language 1120 Paper 2 Q7 a, June 2005

2 The mystery 'has never been conclusively solved'. Explain in your own words what
this means. [2]

3 The second theory as to what happened is 'less fanciful'. Explain in your own words
what this means. [2]

4 According to the second theory, why did two of the men get up early? Answer in your
own words. [3]

[9 marks]

Exercise 4

Read the passage below and answer the own words questions which follow.

As communities grew and developed, the greater the variety of goods there was to inspect for bartering. So it became more and more difficult to decide what one thing was worth compared with another. Eventually, a very basic form of money appeared, often things such as knives, sword or axe-heads, made in a small size. Being fashioned out of metal, they had a special value, since it required a good deal of labour to extract them from the earth. Eventually, a currency emerged which would remain popular for a very long time and over a wide area, and that was the cowrie shell. What made cowrie shells a unique form of currency was they defied any sort of imitation. However, cowrie shells were shipped abroad in increasingly large quantities. This meant that through time their value as money was diminished.

1   According to the writer, what happened 'as communities grew and developed'?
    Answer in your own words.   [2]

2   Metal objects acquired a special value as money because 'it required a good deal of
    labour to extract them from the earth'. Explain in your own words what this means.   [2]

3   What made cowrie shells a reliable form of money? Answer in your own words.   [2]

4   'Cowrie shells were shipped abroad in increasingly large quantities'.
    Explain in your own words what this means.   [2]

5   What happened to cowrie shells 'through time'? Answer in your own words.   [2]

                                                                                              [10 marks]

Adapted from *Cambridge O Level English Language 1120 Paper 2, November 2003*

25 More exercises in own words questions

You saw in the previous chapter that some questions ask for answers which are not lifted from the text but are to be expressed in your own words. You are to evaluate the language of the passage and re-cast it in language of your own. We will use some material you have seen already.

For each of the exercises which follow:

- read the passage carefully twice

- pick out the key words which you are being asked to re-cast in own words

- find other ways of expressing the key words. You may be able to do this with a single synonym but you are allowed to use more than one word, provided you show understanding.

Sometimes these words will be given in the question. Usually in an examination you will not be required to select and retrieve these words from the text yourself, as they will be incorporated into the question you are asked. This chapter, as with the previous chapter, includes some questions where you are required to select and retrieve the key words yourself before re-casting them into your own words.

Exercise 1: Man and Animals

The hunter feared and admired the animals he pursued for their strength, speed and superior powers of sight, hearing and scent. Later this respect became a kind of worship. As man tamed and farmed certain species, however, a relationship of mutual affection developed.
Source: from *Animals on the Farm* by Judy Urquhart

1 In your own words, explain the three reasons for man's fear and admiration for the animals he pursued.   [3]
2 What happened 'as man tamed and farmed certain species'? Answer in your own words.   [3]

[6 marks]

Exercise 2: The Ruined Books

On the top shelf, the leather binding of Pappachi's set of 'The Insect Wealth Of India' had lifted off each book and buckled. Silverfish tunnelled through the pages, burrowing arbitrarily from species to species, turning organised information into yellow lace.
Source: from *The God of Small Things* by Arundhati Roy

1 In your own words, explain what had happened to the leather binding of Pappachi's books.   [2]
2 The insects were 'burrowing arbitrarily' through the pages of the books. Explain in your own words what this means.   [2]

[4 marks]

Exercise 3: Forest Destruction

For more than four hundred years settlers and farmers have been attacking Brazil's forests in one way or another. They tried to snatch land for themselves from the seemingly indestructible jungles, but their power of recovery defeated their efforts. Nowadays, modern machinery can cut down trees at an alarming speed, and the controlled burning down of the forests has meant that areas larger than some whole countries have been permanently stripped bare.

One result of this destruction is becoming alarmingly obvious. The forests contain an astonishing variety of animal and plant life which is slowly but surely disappearing.

1   The jungles were 'seemingly indestructible'. Explain in your own words what this means.   [2]

2   In your own words, explain what the burning down has done to large areas of forest.   [3]

3   The forests contain 'an astonishing variety' of animal and plant life.

    Explain in your own words what this means.   [2]

[7 marks]

Exercise 4: How Animals Became Pets

Domestic or farm animals must be able to develop a liking for man, enjoy comfort, and accept confinement and control. Not until about 10 000 years ago did man develop the idea of taking animals into captivity. There was wild game in abundance, so what prompted the idea?

It could have come naturally from his experience as a nomadic hunter. As he followed his prey on their yearly migrations he gradually began to influence their movements and behaviour in certain situations. Or perhaps the idea arose out of the keeping of young animals as pets. Predators trying to steal food from the hunters' camp were fed by the men and encouraged to become part of the community: the predator changed into the pet.

Source: from *Animals on the Farm* by Judy Urquart

1   According to the writer, domestic animals must have a liking for man and enjoy comfort.
    In your own words, explain what other features are necessary.   [3]

2   In your own words, explain what gradual effect man had on animals in certain situations
    as he 'followed their yearly migrations'.   [3]

3   'The predator changed into the pet.' Explain in your own words what this means.   [2]

[8 marks]

Exercise 5: Sharing the Earth

Today, zoologists and naturalists are alarmed by the rapid disappearance of many species of wild life due to the ruthless exploitation of the land by man for his needs, resulting in the destruction of forests and plains. These experts study animals scientifically and form societies and pressure groups to protect them and their habitats. Conflicting attitudes need to be reconciled if man is to continue sharing the earth in harmony with the animals.

1   According to the writer, what alarms zoologists and naturalists today?
    Answer in your own words.   [3]

2   Man is guilty of 'ruthless exploitation'. Explain in your own words what this means.   [2]

3   In your own words, explain what needs to happen, according to the writer, if man is to
    'continue sharing the earth in harmony with the animals'.   [3]

[8 marks]

Exercise 6: Venice

(Venice has recently been flooded and long term damage has been done to the city.)

As soon as Venice's peril was fully realised, there were endless conferences and tours of inspections. Plans have been drawn up to preserve Venice, but little action has followed. A special law was passed to save the city, but not implemented. Foreign organisations collected

and sent to Italy great sums of money for the same purpose, but this money was taxed by the Italian government.

Governments rose and fell; committees were formed and disbanded. Scientists, technicians and art specialists did experiments and made recommendations.

The government ignored them all. Those who had the power to save Venice were not prepared to take responsibility for their decisions: those who were prepared to take responsibility did not have the power.

Venice, probably in a more tragic way than anywhere else, poses a question Western society is reluctant to face: how much of its present wealth is it prepared to sacrifice to conserve the glories of the past?

Source: adapted from *The Death of Venice* by Stephen Fay and Philip Knightley

1 'Venice's peril was fully realised'. Explain in your own words what this means.   [3]

2 Explain in your own words what happened 'as soon as Venice's peril was fully realised'.   [4]

3 Although 'a special law was passed to save the city', why was it unsuccessful?
   Answer in your own words.   [1]

4 Explain in your own words what is meant by 'governments rose and fell'.   [2]

5 'Committees were formed and disbanded'. Explain in your own words what this means.   [2]

6 'Scientists, technicians and art specialists did experiments and made recommendations.'
   Explain in your own words what this means.   [2]

7 Those who 'had power to save Venice' failed to do so. Explain in your words why they failed.   [3]

8 What benefits would come about if Western society sacrificed some of it wealth?   [3]

[20 marks]

26 Combining information

When you are given comprehension questions which require you to combine information, you must follow the normal procedures for selection and retrieval of information. What makes combining questions different from other types of questions is that in a combining question you will be required to give more than one piece of information in order to answer the question properly.

Signposts of combining questions

The most obvious signpost of a question which requires you to give more than one answer is the question which asks for two reasons. We have already encountered such questions in earlier chapters.

A more subtle type of combining question is the question which asks you to answer fully. The word 'fully' often suggests that there is more than one angle to the answer. That might mean that there are two separate answers, or it might mean that, although strictly speaking there is only one answer, that answer has sufficient depth whereby there will be a more obvious answer on the surface of the text and a less accessible answer underneath the text. Or it might mean that you are required to elaborate on your basic answer in order for your answer to be considered acceptable by teachers.

Another signpost of combining questions is the number of marks allocated to any answer. It is obvious that a question which carries two or more marks is more difficult than a question which carries only one mark. If any question is allocated two marks, that is a message for you, telling you that this question might be asking for two distinct answers, or a depth or elaboration to the more basic answer.

> **Example 1**
>
> The sun beat down on the pavements of the town. It was home to three thousand or so inhabitants, with its quaint little market stalls selling hot food, its winding streets and crowded shops. Outside the town, boys played on the banks of the dried-up river.

Question: How can you tell that the weather is hot? Give two reasons for your answer.

[2 marks]

Answer 1:

1 I know it is hot because the sun beat down on the pavements.

2 I know it is hot because the river had dried up.

Answer 2:

1 I know it is hot because the sun beat down on the pavements.

2 I know it is hot because the market stalls were selling hot food.

Answer 3:

1 I know it is hot because the sun beat down on the pavements of the town. It was home to three thousand or so inhabitants.

2 Outside the town, boys played on the banks of the river. The river was dried up.

Answer 4:

1 I know it is hot because, firstly, the sun beat down on the pavements of the town and the town was home to three thousand or so inhabitants.

2 Secondly, the river was dried up.

Exercise 1

Working with a partner, decide which mark should be allocated to each of the examples above, giving reasons for the mark decided.

You should have something like the following:

Answer 1 is totally correct. Both answers are clearly stated, namely that the sun was beating down on the pavements, and that the river was dried up. Two answers were asked for, and two answers were given.

Answer 2 is only partially correct. The first answer is correct, namely that the sun beat down on the pavements, but the second answer is incorrect. The answer has merely made a wrong response to the word 'hot' in the question and automatically linked it to the word 'hot' in the text. Hot food has nothing to do with hot weather.

Answer 3 is also partially correct. Although both reasons are given for recognising that the weather is hot, this answer actually offers four reasons. In such cases, only the first answer in each limb is looked at. To offer more than two answers to a question which asks for two reasons is to offend the rubric, in other words, not to answer the question by not doing what the question asked. In this particular example, the first reason offered in the first limb is that the sun beat down on the pavements, which is correct.

The second reason offered in the first limb is that the town was home to three thousand or so inhabitants, which is incorrect, but is ignored because only the first answer in each limb is considered. In the second limb, the first answer offered is the only one to be considered and it is wrong. The fact that the correct answer is offered as a second attempt in that limb is immaterial; only one answer in each limb was invited by the question.

Answer 4 is correct and fully acceptable. We may not like the inclusion of the 'gloss' on the correct answer in the first limb, but it would be unfair to consider the whole answer to be wrong for that reason, because it nevertheless makes the point that the sun was beating down on the pavements before it makes either of the two wrong answers. Only the first limb is considered and, perhaps accidentally, it is correct.

Example 2

Samir pedalled his new bicycle along the pavement, gathering speed as he went. He suppressed the thought that his mother had told him not to go beyond the end of their street. He was proud of his new bicycle — its shiny wheels, its smart, red frame, its tinkling bell.

Perhaps if he went beyond the end of the street, he would see his school friend, Nissar. Nissar had a bicycle and might perhaps be playing with it in his own street. His mother would never find out that he had strayed into forbidden territory. Along he went, further and further.

Then he remembered his mother's anger the last time he had disobeyed her — it just wasn't worth it. He pulled on the brakes and reluctantly turned the bicycle back in the direction of his house.

Question: Explain fully why Samir decided not to go any further on his bicycle. [2 marks]

Answer 1: He decided not to go any further because his mother had told him not to go beyond the end of his street.

Answer 2: He decided not to go any further because his mother had told him not to go beyond the end of their street and because he was proud of his new bicycle.

Answer 3: He decided not to go any further because his mother had told him not to go beyond the end of their street and because he remembered her anger the last time he had disobeyed her.

Answer 4: He decided not to go any further because he suppressed the thought that his mother had told him not to go beyond the end of their street and because he remembered how angry she had been the last time he disobeyed her. It just wasn't worth it.

Exercise 2

Working with a partner, decide how correct and acceptable each of the given examples is, giving reasons for your response in each case.

You should have something like this:

Answer 1 is partially correct. It correctly mentions that Samir decided to go no further because his mother had forbidden it. However, this answer fails to take into account the word 'fully' in the question, which indicates either a two-part answer or an answer with more depth than a question which demands a single, direct answer.

Answer 2 is also partially correctly, although it responds to the word 'fully' in the question, and takes account of the fact that either a two-part answer is required or an answer with more depth, it merely gives the first two elements of the paragraph, the second of which is irrelevant to the question. The fact that Samir was proud of his new bicycle is not a reason to turn back; indeed, it would probably make him want to continue. Answer 2 does not sift through the entire paragraph to look for depth.

Answer 3 is fully correct and accceptable. This is because it gives the reason that Samir decided to turn back because his mother had forbidden him to go beyond the end of their street. But the answer also pays attention to the word 'fully' in the question, and gives the idea that Samir remembered his mother's anger the last time he had disobeyed her. Either fear of punishment, or fear of upsetting his mother, is the depth to the answer. This answer goes beyond the simple statement that his mother had forbidden him to go beyond a certain point.

Answer 4 is partially correct. This is because it is not sufficiently focused in its first section. The point is not made that Samir went no further because his mother had forbidden it. In fact, by merely copying out 'he suppressed the thought that his mother had told him not to go beyond the end of their street', the answer is actually stating the opposite of the correct answer. Samir is not remembering what his mother had told him because he is deliberately putting it out of his mind.

By adding 'it just wasn't worth it' the answer is still valid, because the final sentence doesn't make nonsense of the sentence which comes before it; it is merely an extra piece of information.

Exercise 3: The Storm

Read the passage and answer the combining question which follows.

> Huge waves pounded the stone walls built to keep the sea at bay, smashing free huge blocks of marble and flinging them aside like pebbles, until the walls cracked and then collapsed.

1   'Huge waves' pounded the sea walls. Explain fully the comparison used by the writer to show the strength of these waves.   [2 marks]

Exercise 4: After the Storm

Read the passage and answer the combining question which follows.

> Slowly at first, and then from every quarter, the flicker of tiny flames was seen as Venetians went round their stricken city by candlelight. When they met they all said the same thing: that if the wind had not dropped, and if a third high tide had entered the lake to boost the two already there, then quite likely Venice would not have survived.
>
> Because of the gradual melting of the ice at the North Pole, the level of the sea has been rising, threatening to reach the level of the streets in the city. At the same time the area around the river has been sinking, taking the city with it. Some of this sinking is natural and inevitable, but it has been accelerated by the extraction of fresh water from the ground beneath the city for use in huge industrial developments.
>
> Source: Adapted from the *Death of Venice* by Stephen Fay and Phillip Knightley

1   Venice was a 'stricken city'. From Paragraph 1, give two reasons why the disaster was no worse than it was.   [2 marks]

Exercise 5: Protection of the Environment

Read the passage and answer the combining question which follows.

> It has now become abundantly clear that, if schemes for the protection of the environment are not initiated and controlled by local people, they stand little chance of success. It is vitally important to ensure that the wealth of expertise that still remains in living memory is not lost.

1   What will be the two results, according to the writer, 'if schemes for the protection of the environment are not initiated and controlled by local people'?   [2 marks]

Exercise 6: Coral Animals

Read the passage and answer the combining question which follows.

> Coral animals, the remarkable little creatures that build coral reefs, are responsible for creating the largest structures made by life on earth, big enough, in some cases, to dwarf even the most ambitious buildings constructed by humankind.
>
> Source: Adapted from *The Greenpeace Book of Coral Reefs*

1   Explain fully why the writer describes coral animals as 'remarkable'.   [2 marks]
    Cambridge O Level English Language 1120 Page 2 Q1 c, November 2004

Exercise 7: Jasmine

Read the passage and answer the combining question which follows.

> Jasmine leant back against the seat of the train carriage, her eyes closed, trying to get her breathing back to normal. What a start to the day! Her mother had phoned as she was trying to gulp down some breakfast, with a reminder that it was her father's birthday the following week. Jasmine was irritated that her mother could not have picked a more inconvenient time to phone and, in any case, she had never forgotten her father's birthday before. The drive to the station, which should have taken ten minutes, took longer because of the accident on the motorway.

1   Give two reasons why Jasmine was late for the train.   [2]
2   Give two reasons why Jasmine was annoyed at her mother.   [2]

[4 marks]

Exercise 8: Ayesha visits a friend

Read the passage and answer the combining question which follows.

Ayesha was on her way to visit her friend Rama, who was in hospital, having just undergone major surgery. Ayesha and Rama were both teachers in the same school. They had started teaching there on the same day and, having started out as colleagues, they had become close friends. Yes, it was a matter of urgency for Ayesha to see Rama that day.

1   Give two reasons why it was 'a matter of urgency' for Ayesha to see Rama that day.   [2 marks]

Exercise 9: Joseph and Benjamin

Read the passage and answer the questions which follow.

Joseph and Benjamin were playing in a football match for the school team, while their grandparents cheered them on from the sidelines. Benjamin had already scored a goal. The fact that they were brothers meant that the bond between them led to a perfect understanding of each other's moves on the pitch. When half time came, the teams were neck and neck, but in the second half the winning goal was scored by Joseph. Could the boys' success be put down to all that training they had done over the past few months, in bad weather as well as good? And of course their parents bought them the best of sportswear, for example high quality track suits.

1   Give two reasons why Joseph and Benjamin were good players in the school team.   [2]
2   Explain two ways in which Joseph and Benjamin had been encouraged to be good football players.   [2]

[4 marks]

27 More exercises in combining questions

Exercise 1: The Great Wall of China

Read the passage and answer the combining questions which follow.

Nomadic tribes would harass and plunder agricultural areas, making farming impossible unless some ways were found to stop them. The farmers attacked them to try to force them away. Although it was expensive, they tried to bring about peaceful relations with them, but this tactic was a blow to their pride and consequently short-lived.

Finally, they built barriers to prevent invasion and to allow for military defence. Through time, the building of walls was the solution most consistently relied upon. These walls were eventually linked up to form what came to be known as the Great Wall.

In the construction of the Great Wall, the recruitment of labour was a major difficulty. In the early stages, soldiers were used to do this work, and sometimes local peasants as well as the army were forced to take part. During the reign of one emperor, over a million men were engaged in the construction of the Wall.

A special penalty existed during the reign of other emperors, under which convicted criminals were made to work on the Wall as a way of atoning for their crimes.

1   The farmers 'tried to bring about peaceful relations' with the nomadic tribes. Apart from this, what other two methods did they use to deal with them?   [2]

2   What three types of labourers built the Great Wall? Use no more than twelve words in your answer.   [3]

                                                                                                                          [5 marks]

Exercise 2: Building the Great Wall

Read the passage and answer the combining questions which follow.

Building materials could be passed from hand to hand in a human chain, which spared the builders the trouble of long walks on narrow mountain trails, thus avoiding collision. Simple tools, like the handcart and rope levers, were also used, and sure-footed animals such as goats and donkeys could be driven up the mountain carrying bricks. Donkeys were made to carry baskets filled with bricks on their backs; as for the goats, bricks were tied on to their horns.

1 If it had not been possible to pass building materials from hand to hand, what two problems would the builders have had? [2]

2 Explain fully what use was made of donkeys in the building work. [2]

[4 marks]

Exercise 3: The Destroyed Novel

Read the passage and answer the combining questions which follow.

Having spent some time working, I had just written and counted my first five hundred words when I remembered baby Octavia; I could hear her making small, happy noises somewhere along the corridor, but felt it time I should go and see if she was doing something destructive, like unravelling the end of the hall carpet. She was remarkably persistent in destruction for her age.

I was rather dismayed when I realised she was in Lydia's room and that I must have left the door open, for Lydia's room was always full of nasty objects like aspirins and bottles of ink.

I rushed along to rescue her and the sight that met my eyes when I opened the door was enough to make anyone quake. She had her back to the door and was sitting in the middle of the floor surrounded by a sea of torn, strewed, chewed paper. I stood there transfixed, watching the neat small back of her head and her thin, stalk-like neck and flowering curls; suddenly she gave a great screech of delight and ripped another sheet of paper. 'Octavia,' I said in horror, and she started guiltily, and looked round at me with a charming and deprecating smile; her mouth, I could see, was wedged full of wads of Lydia's new novel.

Source: from *The Millstone* by Margaret Drabble

1 Give three reasons why the writer feels she should check up on the baby. [3]

2 Give two reasons why the writer was upset when she realised where the baby was. [2]

3 Explain fully what the baby had been doing. [3]

[8 marks]

Exercise 4: Fatima's Favourite Subject

Read the passage and answer the combining questions which follow.

'Bye, Mum!' shouted Fatima as she rushed to get the school bus. She was looking forward to her day; a double lesson of her favourite subject. If anyone had asked her for the reason for this devouring interest, she would have said she didn't really know. However, her passion for literature had begun when her grandfather, himself a keen reader, had given her a copy of a famous novel when she was only eleven years old; she had found the story so fascinating she had finished reading it within the week.

Her grandfather's favourite subject at school had been literature and, like her, he had read this novel over and over again. In Fatima's school, there was a limited number of spaces for the literature class, and Fatima was more than a little anxious she might not be accepted. When one of the teachers of the subject retired at the start of the holidays, that had made her even more anxious. However, she was one of the lucky few, and loved every minute of the classes. She acted out — in her head at least — the key events in the novels she read, and pretended — again in her head — to be the central character.

As she sat on the school bus, Fatima thought of her notebook hidden in her cupboard, where she had begun to write her own novel, in order to be famous herself one day.

1 Give three reasons why it was appropriate that Fatima's grandfather gave her a copy of a famous novel.   [3]

2 Explain fully how we can tell that Fatima found the novel her grandfather gave her 'fascinating'.   [2]

3 Give two reasons why Fatima was anxious that she might not be accepted for the literature class.   [2]

4 How can we tell that Fatima 'loved every minute of the classes'? Give two reasons for your answer.   [2]

5 Explain fully the purpose of Fatima's notebook.   [2]

[11 marks]

Quotation Questions

Another type of question which tests your ability both to appreciate ways in which writers make use of language and to evaluate information is the quotation question. In a quotation question, you are asked to find a word or expression in the text which means the same as another word or expression which comes either from the text or which is a synonym provided by the writer of the question.

Example 1: The Beauty of Animals

Read the short passage and answer the question which follows.

Whenever we see pictures of animals or look at them in a zoo, we are often amazed by their beauty. The tiger, with black and yellow stripes, is a truly magnificent creature, while the leopard is equally eye-catching, with its richly spotted fur.

Question: Write down one word which emphasises the writer's admiration of animals' beauty.

The key word in the question is the word 'admiration', which means wonder and delight. We must therefore scrutinise the text carefully to find a link with wonder and delight, linked to 'beauty', another important word in the question.

Reading the text with 'wonder' and 'beauty' at the front of our minds enables us to home in on 'amazed' and 'magnificent' and 'eye-catching'. Any of these words, in fact, is sufficient to answer the question.

Another important factor in giving a correct answer here is to look at the rubric carefully for what we are being asked to give as an answer. In this particular question, the rubric asks for one word.

Consequently, the answers 'amazed by their beauty' or 'equally eye-catching' are incorrect, because they infringe the rubric, i.e. they do not give the answer asked for. It is a pity that such answers would fail to impress the teachers even when there is clearly understanding behind them.

Exercise 1: The Rain Forests

Read the short passage and answer the questions which follow.

> Scientists, now keenly aware of dangers to the earth's environment, see the destruction of the rain forests as a major peril for Brazil and also for the rest of the world.
>
> Politicians have joined scientists to try to stop the foolish waste of the precious resources of these forests.

1   What two consecutive words in the passage tell us that scientists are not lacking in knowledge about what is happening to the rain forests?   [1]

2   Pick out and write down the single word in the passage which tells us that the writer thinks that the destruction of the rain forests is silly.   [1]

[2 marks]

Exercise 2: Climate Change

Read the short passage and answer the questions which follow.

> Even more alarming is the threat to the world's climate. The burning of the trees accelerates the warming up of the earth's atmosphere, which scientists say will bring dramatic changes to our climate.
>
> Moreover, the blazing torches of the jungle will add to the harmful gases that cars and modern industries are pouring into the air we breathe.

1   What single word in the passage tells us that the earth's atmosphere is getting warmer and warmer?   [1]

2   Pick out and write down an expression from the passage which tells us that the burning forests are both bright and hot.   [2]

[3 marks]

Exercise 3: Amy

Read the short passage and answer the questions which follow.

The next moment, though, she saw something more reassuring. In the far corner of the cave a large white cloth screen was being erected, musicians were gathering and people were taking their places for some sort of show.

An old man made his entrance by the side of the screen, dressed in a tattered, grimy cloak. But it was his intense expression that startled Amy. Her feelings of uneasiness returned as she watched him gaze round the audience.

1 Amy saw something 'reassuring'. What single word used later in the passage shows that later she was no longer feeling reassured?   [1]

2 Pick out and write down the single word which shows that the old man's clothes were dirty.   [1]

[2 marks]

Exercise 4: After the Show

Read the short passage and answer the questions which follow.

The audience broke into a stuttering applause, clearly moved by the realism of the contest. The old man appeared by the side of the screen, holding up the two puppets, the fighters in the grim contest. One of the puppets bore a fearful resemblance to the old man's assistant, the little boy with his large, sad eyes.

Amy panicked wildly. She ran outside, stumbling down the steps, blundering past the crowd, desperate to get away from the ghastly presence in the cave.

1 Write down one word which shows us that the audience did not start to clap at once after the show.   [1]

2 Amy 'ran outside'. Write down two separate words which show that she was frightened as she ran.   [2]

[3 marks]

Vocabulary Questions

In this type of question, you will be asked to think about a word or phrase in the fiction passage you have read and work out its meaning. You will have four possible answers to consider before choosing which of these has the same meaning that the word or phrase has in the passage.

You may be absolutely certain which is the correct answer, and you are fortunate if that is so. However, you may be uncertain and, if that is the case, there are several useful steps to use to approach this question. It may be useful to use these steps to confirm your choice even if you feel sure your choice is correct.

Step 1: check the context of the word or phrase. The context is the area around the word or phrase, and the key to understanding may lie in the passage before rather than after the word or phrase in the question.

Step 2: read carefully the passage in the area of the word or phrase, substituting each of the four options to decide which of these gives a synonym for the sense of the original passage.

Step 3: think of another part of speech linked to the word in the question. For example, you may be unsure what the noun 'drama' means, but moving on the adjective linked to the word, namely 'dramatic' may help to clarify the meaning of the noun.

Exercise 5: Keeping Pets

Read the passage, the question and the commentary below.

It is a curious thing, but when you keep animals as pets you imagine they will behave exactly as you would like them to.

Question

For the word below, tick the option (A, B, C or D) which has the same meaning that the word has in the passage.

Curious

| A | fascinating | B | inquisitive | C | strange | D | obvious |

Step 1 suggests we look at the context, both before and after the word tested. There is no text before the word 'curious' and so we are able to look only at the passage after the word 'curious'. The word' but' suggests an element of surprise in the fact that pet owners would expect animals to behave as humans do.

When we try Step 2, and substitute 'inquisitive' into the passage, it doesn't seem to make much sense; although we may know that curious can mean the same as 'inquisitive', it is difficult to see that 'inquisitive' is a synonym here. When we substitute 'obvious' it doesn't seem to fit with the element of surprise we have identified. That leaves us with 'fascinating'; perhaps this is too strong a term to describe how we might expect animals to behave. Therefore it seems that the correct answer is 'strange'.

Exercise 6: Benjamin

Read the passage and for each of the words or phrases below, tick the option (A, B, C or D) which has the same meaning that the word has in the passage.

It was hardly surprising that Benjamin did so well in the examination, as he did four, and occasionally five, hours homework every night. He studied at weekends and was a delight to his teachers because he never declined to take on extra homework tasks.

i   Occasionally

| A | always | B | sometimes | C | slowly | D | especially |

ii   Declined

| A | stopped | B | stooped | C | refused | D | slowed |

[2 marks]

Exercise 7: Sophie

Read the passage and for each of the words or phrases below, tick the option (A, B, C or D) which has the same meaning that the word or phrase has in the passage.

Sophie stood on the edge of the pavement waiting for the traffic lights to change, so that she could cross the road. The city was teeming with people, some in cars, some, like her, on foot.

She had been apprehensive about coming to Chittagong, but, now that she was here, she found it a thrilling place to live.

i   Teeming with

| A | short of | B | shared with | C | overrun by | D | full of |

ii   Apprehensive

| A | appalled | B | afraid | C | amazed | D | attentive |

iii   Thrilling

| A | exciting | B | fulfilling | C | frightening | D | welcoming |

[3 marks]

Exercise 8: World Food Shortage

Read the passage and for each of the words below, tick the option (A, B, C or D) which has the same meaning that the word has in the passage.

The world's population is increasing at an astonishing rate and in some countries there is a shortage of food, although this is often caused by natural disasters rather than as a direct consequence of the population explosion.

i   Astonishing

    A amazing   **B** absolute   **C** alarming   **D** appalling

ii   Shortage

    A reduction   **B** little   **C** lack   **D** decrease

iii   Consequence

    A link   **B** reaction   **C** connection   **D** result

iv   Explosion

    A burst   **B** increase   **C** destruction   **D** discovery

[4 marks]

29 Appreciating the ways writers make use of language

We have already considered a number of questions which you might ask yourself before answering a question in a comprehension exercise or task. The final two questions in the list were the following.

- Is the question asking only about the story or argument of the text?

- Is the question asking only about particular features of language, e.g. figures of speech?

These questions test the extent to which you are able to understand nuances of language and are able to evaluate why writers uses particular words or expressions. Questions based on your reading are often questions which test your ability to respond to the skill of the writer of the comprehension passage.

Questions about the writer's craft go beyond literal and inferential comprehension. They assume that the reader understands the meaning of what has been written, but draw the reader into responding to writing skills which are the signs of a good piece of writing. The answers to literal and inferential questions really answer the questions 'What?' or 'Who?', whereas answers to questions about the writer's craft really answer the question 'How?'

Example 1: The accident

The police car sirens sounded; people stood aside and cars stopped to let them past. It was clear that an emergency had occurred up ahead. Ambulances sped along the road and screeched to a halt at the spot where the collision had taken place. As the ambulance crew stepped out of the vehicle to examine the injured drivers, it seemed that a real-life drama was about to begin.

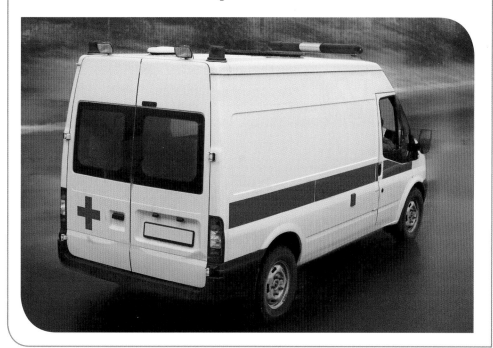

Question: Why does the writer say that the ambulances 'sped' along the road?   [1 mark]

Answer 1: The writer says that the ambulances sped along the road because they were going to the scene of an accident.

Answer 2: The writer says that the ambulances sped along the road because he wants to emphasise that they were going very fast.

Answer 3: The ambulances sped along the road because the drivers were racing one another.

Exercise 1

Working with a partner, decide how correct and acceptable each of the given answers is, giving reasons for your response in each case.

You should have something like this:

Answer 1 is wholly incorrect. It is true that the ambulances were going to the scene of the accident, but that is not what the question is asking. This answer is an answer to a different question, such as 'Where were the ambulances going?' This particular question is drawing your attention to the use of the word 'sped'.

Answer 2 is correct, because it does, in fact, answer the question by focusing on the word 'sped'. This answer appreciates that the writer could have used, for example, the words 'went' or 'drove' or 'travelled'. The meaning would not have been affected in that we would still have known that what is being described is the scene of an accident and the ambulances going there to help the injured. But the word 'sped' has been carefully chosen by the writer to give the impression of a great dash, of the greatest possible speed, because this is a serious emergency.

Answer 3 is also wholly incorrect, because, although it recognises the fact that the word 'sped' has connotations of speed, it makes the wrong connection, and the wrong inference that the drivers were speeding because they were in some sort of competition with one another.

> ### Example 2: Visiting Easter Island
> Easter Island is the most remote inhabited place in the entire world. Until an airport was made in the 1960's, it was all but impossible to get to, because the only connection with the rest of the world was a ship which visited the island once a year. There is now something called a hotel on the island, so at least now visitors can stay there.

Question: 'There is now something called a hotel on the island'.
Why does the writer not simply say 'There is a hotel on the island'? [1 mark]

Answer 1: The writer thinks the reader might not know what a hotel is and so he gives an explanation.

Answer 2: The writer wants to emphasise that visitors can stay on the island whereas in the past this wasn't possible.

Answer 3: The writer wants to tell us that by our own standards it is a very basic hotel. It would hardly be described as a hotel by most people.

Exercise 2

Working with a partner, decide how acceptable and correct each of the given answers is, giving reasons for your response in each case.

You should have something like this:
Answer 1 is wholly incorrect, because it is not reasonable to assume that someone capable of understanding a passage at this level would not know the meaning of a common and international word like 'hotel'.

Answer 2 is also wholly incorrect, because it is a literal comprehension of the question, explaining only the advantage of now having a hotel on the island. However, it does not answer the question, which was asking for an explanation of why the writer says 'there is something called a hotel' and not 'there is a hotel'. This answer merely answers the first possible question, i.e. 'why does the writer tell us there is now a hotel?' rather than the real question, which is 'why does the writer tell us there is something called a hotel?'

Answer 3 is correct, because it responds to the key difference between the obvious question of why the writer tells us there is a hotel and the more subtle question of why the writer tells us there is something of a hotel. The word 'something' is used unusually and this answer focuses on that. There is a clear difference between a 'hotel' and 'something of a hotel', and the thrust of the use of the word 'something' is that it isn't much of a hotel, it's of poor standard, it isn't what we would expect a hotel to be.

> ### *Example 3: The Streets of Dhaka*
>
> As Hemu walked through the streets of Dhaka, he marvelled at the vastness of the city, so different from the little village he had left behind. He loved the feel of the city — the crowds making their way through the evening darkness, the roar of the traffic and the illuminated buildings like stars by which people navigated their way home.

Question: Explain fully why the writer says that the buildings were 'like stars'?   [2 marks]

Answer 1:   The writer says that the buildings were like stars because they were lit up.

Answer 2:   The writer says that the buildings were like stars because they were beautiful.

Answer 3:   The writer says that the buildings were like stars because they were bright and people used them to work out their whereabouts.

Exercise 3

Working with a partner, decide how correct and acceptable each of the given answers is, giving reasons for your response in each case.

You should have something like this:

Answer 1 is partially correct, because it makes one comparison between stars and the buildings. The buildings were bright and twinkling with light, just as the stars in the sky are bright and twinkling. However, if the mark allocation had been taken into consideration, and the word 'fully' in the question, it should have been seen that there are two parts to the answer.

Answer 2 is wholly incorrect, because, although most people would consider the stars to be beautiful, there is nothing in the passage to link stars to beauty. The answer is not based on the passage but rather comes from the opinion of the person answering the question.

Answer 3 is correct and fully acceptable, because it has responded both to the allocation of two marks for the question and to the presence of the word 'fully' in the question. It focuses on the word 'illuminated' in the text and makes that link between the brightness of the stars and the lights in the buildings.

It has then gone on to focus on the word 'navigated' and make the further connection that sailors use the stars to navigate their way through the sea, in the same way as people in the city use the light from buildings to find their way through the city.

Exercise 4: The Flood

Read the passage and answer the writer's craft questions which follow.

> People came down from the safety of the upper floors of their houses to inspect the ruin caused by the flood: oil stains, debris, filth and drowned animals were everywhere.
>
> Slowly at first, and then from every part of the city, the flicker of tiny flames was seen as the people went round their stricken city by candlelight. The candle flames danced in the soft breeze and their gentle movements seemed to mock the occasion.
>
> Source: from *The Death of Venice* by Stephen Fay and Phillip Knightley

1   People 'went round their stricken city'. What effect is gained by the word 'stricken' that would not have been achieved by the word 'flooded'?   [1]

2   Why is it appropriate to say that the candle flames 'danced'?   [1]

3   Explain fully what the writer means when he tells us that the candle flames 'seemed to mock the occasion'.   [2]

                                        [4 marks]

Exercise 5: The Kitchen Table

Read the passage and answer the writer's craft questions which follow.

We sat down to table in the cramped kitchen. The table was left from the shop's bakery days, a massive piece of rough-cut pine cross-hatched with knife scars into which veins of ancient dough, dried to the consistency of cement, had worked to produce a smooth marbly finish.

Source: from *Chocolat* by Joanne Harris

1   What effect is produced by the writer's use of 'scars' instead of, for example, 'marks'?   [1]

2   The marks on the kitchen table have 'veins of ancient dough'. Explain exactly what is being described here.   [2]

3   Why does the writer describe the surface of the table in places as 'marbly'?   [1]

[4 marks]

Exercise 6: The Market in Mumbai

Read the passage and answer the writer's craft questions which follow.

Rohit meandered through the market in Mumbai. He was on holiday after all, and the day was stretched out before him like a century.

1   Explain fully what effect the writer gains by her use of the word 'meandered'.   [2]

2   Rohit was on holiday for the day. Why, therefore, does the writer compare the day to a century?   [1]

[3 marks]

Exercise 7: Spring

Read the passage and answer the writer's craft questions which follow.

Spring has come with little prelude, like turning a rocky corner into a sheltered valley, and gardens and their borders have blossomed suddenly, lush with daffodils, irises, tulips.

Even the derelict houses of Les Maurads are touched with colour, but here the ordered gardens have run to rampant eccentricity: a roof carpeted with dandelions; violets poking out of a crumbling facade.

Source: from *Chocolat* by Joanne Harris

1   Explain fully why the writer describes the arrival of spring as 'like turning a rocky corner into a sheltered valley'.   [2]

2   What effect does the word 'lush' have on our picture of spring?   [1]

3   What does the writer mean when she describes the roof as being 'carpeted' with dandelions?   [1]

[4 marks]

Exercise 8: The New School

Read the passage and answer the writer's craft questions which follow.

Padma and Rita approached the gates of their new school with some dread and trepidation. Girls in uniforms identical to theirs snaked in front of them; Padma and Rita envied their assurance, their composure—this was familiar territory to them, whereas Padma and Rita were explorers in new territory.

'There are millions of them!' whispered Rita. 'Absolutely millions!'

1   Explain fully what effect is achieved by the word 'snaked'.   [2]

2   In what way were Padma and Rita 'explorers in new territory'?   [2]

3   There could not have been 'millions' of girls in the school. Why, then does the writer have Rita say that there were?   [1]

[5 marks]

Exercise 1: The Gardener

Read the passage and answer the writer's craft questions which follow.

There is a look of desperation about him nowadays as he works, digging and hoeing furiously — sometimes bringing out great clumps of shrubs and flowers along with the weeds — the sweat running down his back.

He does not enjoy the exercise. I see his face as he works, features crunching with the effort. He seems to hate the soil he digs, to hate the plants with which he struggles. He looks like a miser forced to shovel banknotes into a furnace: hunger, disgust and reluctant fascination.

And yet he never gives up. Watching him I feel a familiar pang of fear, though for what I am not sure. He is like a machine this man, my enemy.

Source: from *Chocolat* by Joanne Harris

1   Why does the writer describe the man's face as 'crunching with effort'?   [1]

2   The writer describes the man as being 'like a miser, forced to shovel banknotes into a furnace'. Explain fully what the writer is saying here.   [2]

3   When the writer says that the man was 'like a miser' she is using a simile.

    Pick out and write down another simile from the passage and explain why it is effective.   [3]

                                                                                [6 marks]

Exercise 2: The Well-dressed Lady

Read the passage and answer the writer's craft questions which follow.

'Well, if it's no trouble … ' Her manner was different today. There was a kind of crispness in her voice, a studied casualness which masked a high level of tension. She was wearing a black straw hat trimmed with a ribbon and a coat — also black—which looked new.

'You're very chic today,' I observed.

She gave a sharp crack of laughter. 'No one's said that to me for a while, I'll tell you,' she said.

Source: from *Chocolat* by Joanne Harris

1   Explain fully what the writer means by describing the woman's behaviour as 'studied casualness'. [2]

2   The woman gave 'a sharp crack of laughter'. Explain fully what effect is achieved here that would not be achieved merely by 'she laughed'. [2]

[4 marks]

Exercise 3: The Traveller

Read the passage and answer the writer's craft questions which follow.

> Jungle once more shrouded the path I was following. I plunged into the undergrowth, grateful that the path was still visible, but instead of simply having to put one foot in front of the other in order to go forward, I had to keep on climbing.

1   The writer says that he 'plunged' into the undergrowth. What effect is created by the word 'plunged' that would not be achieved by the word 'went'? [1]

2   What effect is achieved by the writer's use of the word 'shrouded' that would not have been achieved by the word 'hid'? [1]

3   The writer says 'instead of simply having to put one foot in front of the other'. What does his use of this expression tell you about the nature of his progress so far? [1]

[3 marks]

Exercise 4: Cell Phones

> For many people, cell phones are a lifeline, a connection to family and friends, a way of keeping in touch with the work place in a fast moving world where we never seem to have enough time to complete all the jobs we have planned. They provide an oasis of calm into which we can step from the desert of modern living.
>
> But for others, cell phones are the scourge of modern society. You only have to watch people who are, supposedly, on an afternoon in each other's company. What are they doing? They are engrossed in conversation with someone other than their companion, their cell phone pressed to their ear as if their life depended on this little rectangular jewel.

1   Why does the writer describe the cell phone as a 'lifeline'? [1]

2   Explain fully what the writer means when she says that cell phones 'provide an oasis of calm'. [2]

3   Pick out and write down the single word in the passage which links to this idea of 'oasis'. [1]

4   Why does the writer describe cell phones as sometimes being a 'scourge'? [1]

5   Explain fully what is meant by 'this little rectangular jewel'. [2]

[7 marks]

Exercise 5: Nizam and Hemu

> It was easy to see that Nizam and Hemu were excellent English teachers. Their students were clay in their hands, as they moulded them through gentle correction of their grammatical errors and the praising of their achievements. They loved English literature and lit a flame in many of their students which would never be extinguished.
>
> When the bell rang to signal the end of one lesson and the beginning of the next, their students flew down the corridor to their classrooms. They were obviously passionate about teaching and this showed in the excellent results they achieved and the high regard in which they were clearly held by the Principal of the school as well as by their students.

1 Explain fully why the writer describes the students of Nizam and Hemu as 'clay in their hands'. [2]
2 Pick out and write down the single word in the passage which adds to the idea of 'clay'. [1]
3 What is the 'flame' referred to by the writer? [1]
4 What effect is produced by the use of the word 'flew' which would not be produced by 'went'? [1]

[5 marks]

Exercise 6: Calling the Doctor

After I had made up my mind to see the doctor, I consulted my friend Lydia, who suggested that I should ring up the doctor and ask him to come and see me at home, instead of going to him; I immediately thought how nice it would be if only I dare. 'Of course you dare,' said Lydia. 'You can't take a sick baby out in weather like this.' Then, with sudden illumination, she said, 'Anyway, look how flushed she is! Why don't you take her temperature?'

Astounded, I stared at her, for truly the thought of doing such a thing had never crossed my mind. Looking back, after months with the thermometer as necessary as a spoon or a saucepan, I can hardly believe this to be possible, but so it was; my life had not yet changed for ever. I took Octavia's temperature and it was high enough to justify ringing for the doctor. To my surprise, the doctor's secretary did not sound at all annoyed when I asked if he could call: I think I had half expected a lecture.

When the doctor arrived, he took Octavia's pulse and temperature, and told me it was nothing serious, in fact nothing at all. Then he said he ought to listen to her chest; I pulled up her vest and she smiled and wriggled with delight as he put the stethoscope on her fat ribs. He listened for a long time and I, who was beginning to think that perhaps I should not have bothered him after all, sat there absently aware of how innocent she was, how sweet she looked and that her vest could do with a wash. Had I known, I would have enjoyed that moment more, or perhaps I mean that I did enjoy that moment but have enjoyed none since. For he said, 'Well, I don't think there's anything very much to worry about there.' I could see that he had not finished, and did not mean what he said. 'Just the same,' he added, 'perhaps I ought to book you an appointment to take her along to the hospital.'

I suppose most people would have asked him what was wrong. I think that the truth was the last thing I wanted to hear. When I heard his voice coming at me, saying that the hospital appointment would probably be for the next Thursday, I was relieved a little; he could not be expecting her to die before next Thursday. I even mustered the strength to ask what I should do about her cold, and he said, 'Nothing, nothing at all.'

Explain (i) what each of the following phrases tells us about the personality of the mother and (ii) the effect of the words used.

1 'I immediately thought how nice it would be if only I dare' (paragraph 1)
   i _____
   ii _____ [2]
2 'I could see that he had not finished, and did not mean what he said' (paragraph 3)
   i _____
   ii _____ [2]
3 'I suppose some people would have asked him what was wrong' (paragraph 4)
   i _____
   ii _____ [2]

Practice in Reading

Section 1: Reading for Ideas

Passage 1 Time for Tea

After water, tea is the most widely consumed beverage in the world and, by the time you have read this passage, hundreds of thousands of cups of tea will have been drunk globally. But how many of us ever stop to consider the origins of tea or the reasons for its continuing popularity down through the ages?

There is plenty of evidence to show that tea was popular thousands of years ago in China because it was drunk for its medicinal properties. There were many myths surrounding the origins of tea and, as these myths spread, the popularity of tea increased. For example, one influential myth concerns Emperor Shennong: taking a sip from a bowl of boiling water into which some leaves from a nearby bush were blown, he was pleasantly surprised by its flavour. This delicious drink began to be drunk as a stimulant because of its restorative powers; there's no better pick-me-up than a good cup of tea. Use of tea for this purpose was supported by another myth about a prince who developed the habit of chewing leaves from the tea shrub in order to keep himself awake for prayer. Tea drinking spread when tea leaves were formed into the shape of bricks because they were easy to trade and transport; they were even used as a form of currency instead of metal coins. A book entitled 'The Tea Classic', written by scholar Lu Yu, was the single greatest influence in developing the popularity of tea in China. 'The Tea Classic' is fascinating to read, describing the weather conditions in which tea should be picked and even the best water to be used to make it.

By the 6th century AD, tea had spread to Japan, where at first it was the drink of the aristocracy, before becoming widely accessible to ordinary people when production grew. Tea in Japan took on religious significance with The Tea Ceremony, in which the making of tea expresses the quest for greatness in the smallest details of life. Thus, the link in Japan between tea and religious observance increased the importance and popularity of tea. Through time, tea drinking extended to other Asian countries, for example Vietnam, Korea and Taiwan.

It was not until the 17th century that tea reached the West, when Dutch traders imported it from China. In addition, British merchants had been exporting goods to the East, but their ships returned empty; thus began a vigorous campaign in Britain to popularise tea among the ordinary people there to develop it as a profitable return cargo.

There are many reasons for the continuing popularity of tea. The ability of tea plants to replenish their leaves every week during the growing season means that there is always plenty available, which helps keep down the cost to the consumer. In addition, tea is highly receptive to absorbing the aromas of other plants. This may cause problems with transportation and storage, with the true flavour of the tea being adversely affected by other goods, but the advantage of the ability of tea leaves to absorb other aromas allows for an almost endless range of scented and flavoured teas, such as vanilla and caramel.

Moreover, the development of mixing different types of tea, called blending, makes it possible to obtain better-tasting tea at lower prices. Then came the invention of tea bags, which led to the 'quick cuppa'. Although connoisseurs of tea complain that tea bags contain merely the waste products of high quality tea, and that their small size does not allow the leaves to diffuse properly, it cannot be denied that tea bags have made tea accessible and cheap.

As well as being a stimulant because of its caffeine content, a cup of tea is considered by millions to be wonderfully relaxing. Perhaps the best explanation of this paradox is that the very act of making tea has a soothing effect on us. In modern times, there is various scientific data about tea, which of course was beyond the knowledge of Emperor Shennong, but it seems that he was right to have been impressed by what he stumbled upon all those centuries ago.

Read **Passage** 1 and answer **all** the questions below in the order set.

1 a **Notes** [15 marks]

Identify and write down the reasons for the initial popularity of tea and the spread of tea drinking, and the reasons for the continuing popularity of tea.

Use only the material from paragraph 2 to paragraph 6 inclusive.
At this stage, you need NOT use your own words. To help you get started, the first point in each section of notes is done for you. You will be awarded up to 15 marks for **content** points.

Main Points
Reasons for the initial popularity of tea and the spread of tea drinking.
• It was used as a medicine.

Reasons for the continuing popularity of tea.
• Tea plants' ability to replenish themselves makes it plentiful/keeps the cost down.

1 b Summary [5 marks]

Now use your notes to write a summary of the reasons for the initial popularity of tea and the spread of tea drinking, and the reasons for the continuing popularity of tea. Try to use your own words as far as possible.

This time, you will be awarded marks for **using your own words wherever possible and for accurate use of language**.

Your summary, which must be in continuous writing (not note form), must be no longer than **160** words, including the 10 words given below.

Thousands of years ago in China, tea became popular because

_____

_____

_____

_____

_____

_____

_____

_____

_____

_____

_____

_____

_____

_____

_____

_____

_____

_____

_____

_____

_____

_____

No of words   [10]

2 From paragraph 2, select and write down **three** opinions.

One opinion is

_____

_____

[1]

Another opinion is

_____

_____

[1]

Another opinion is

_____

_____

[1]

Cambridge O Level English Language 1123 Paper 22 Q1 a & b, Q2, June 2011

Section 2: Reading for Meaning

Passage 2 The Chinese Money-Lender

Peter stood on the balcony of his son's apartment and sighed contentedly. Peter and his wife had been concerned when their son, Christopher, had announced his intention to emigrate but, Peter reflected, it had been the right decision after all, despite his parents' original misgivings. This country offered unsurpassed employment opportunities. Christopher's apartment was situated in a lively and increasingly popular location, where accommodation was relatively inexpensive, there was an excellent public transport service and new restaurants and cafes were springing up all around.

Soon Peter and his wife, Marian, were on the bus for yet another trip to the market recommended by the guide books as a priority for tourists. Stalls selling fabrics in a plethora of sizes and colours were interspersed with food stalls, their tantalising aromas wafting in all directions. Peter bought an impressive warrior carved out of dark wood from a stallholder who assured him that the purchase was an opportunity not to be missed. At another stall, he purchased a tiny green tortoise which, the stallholder claimed, was made of genuine jade. Marian hid her impatience; she did not share her husband's love of shopping and, besides, she was less inclined to be swept away by smooth sales talk.

As they strolled on, Peter's attention was suddenly drawn by an antiques shop, crowded in amongst hardware stalls and food outlets. A glint of metal caught his eye and he quickly entered the shop, discovering that the source of his curiosity was a somewhat mysterious-looking ornament, the figure of a man, no more than three inches high, seated at a solid-looking desk. Peter peered intently at it. 'It's a Chinese money-lender,' said the young shop assistant who, it seemed, had appeared out of nowhere. Closer inspection showed the money-lender's desk to be stamped on the front and the base with indecipherable inscriptions. There was an over-laden moneybag at one end, its contents spilling over the desk, and an abacus balanced on the money-lender's knee. The gilded figure, hunched over the desk, with palms upturned as if beseeching yet more money, glittered in the shop lights. One look at his face — spectacles shining on his nose, mouth agape, trembling beard – revealed the satisfaction of a deal well concluded, and the desire for more money. The Chinese money-lender cried out to Peter to become another purchase.

The shop assistant turned his full attention towards the bewitched Peter. Simultaneously he positioned himself so that Peter could not see Marian's furrowed brow, her silent rebuke for Peter that enough money had already been spent that day. 'I will charge you a fair price for this money-lender,' promised the shop assistant. 'Peter, it's time we were heading back for lunch,' warned Marian. 'Whoever buys him will never have ill-fortune,' promised the shop assistant. The money-lender had cast his spell, and within minutes Peter left the shop carrying his purchase, as the smiling shop assistant waved a cheerful farewell.

On the way back, Marian eventually saw the humour in the situation. Her awkward silence was short-lived and she soon linked her arm affectionately through her husband's, her free hand holding the jade tortoise and the wooden warrior, while Peter clutched the Chinese money-lender. 'You were really talked into that!' she laughed. 'Ah, but it's a unique work of art,' replied Peter, 'and who knows what it will bring?'

A few days later, their holiday over, it was their own house they were entering, dropping their bulging suitcases gratefully to the floor. Peter quickly unpacked the tortoise, the wooden warrior and, of course, the Chinese money-lender, while Marian took up the more mundane task of opening the pile of mail which had accumulated since their departure. In the living room, Peter, with the utmost care, was tenderly positioning the Chinese money-lender on a shelf. Now what was the best angle at which to display him for maximum aesthetic effect? He heard the rustling of paper and the ripping open of envelopes. Reluctantly he dragged his attention away from his new friend as he heard Marian's voice from the hallway: 'Peter, I can hardly believe this. I've won the top cash prize in that competition I entered before we went away … I can hardly believe it!' Smiling, Peter adjusted the position of the Chinese money-lender yet again by a fraction of an inch. 'Oh, but I can believe it,' he said.

Read Passage 2 and answer **all** the questions below in the order set.

From paragraph 1

3 a   How did Christopher's parents react to his announcement that he intended to emigrate? [1]

   b   The country to which Christopher had emigrated offered 'unsurpassed employment opportunities'. Explain in your own words what this means. [2]

   c   What evidence is given to suggest that the location of Christopher's apartment was 'lively'? [1]

   Cambridge O Level English Language 1123 paper 22 Q4 a and c

From paragraph 2

4 a   Peter and Marian went on 'yet another' trip to the market. What effect does the writer achieve by the use of the word 'yet'? [1]

   b   The stallholder 'claimed' that the tortoise was made of genuine jade. What effect does the word 'claimed' have that would not be achieved by 'said'? [1]

   Cambridge O Level English Language 1123 paper 22 Q5 a and b

From paragraph 3

5 a   The Chinese money-lender was 'somewhat mysterious'. What **single** feature of the ornament was most mysterious? [1]

   Cambridge O Level English Language 1123 paper 22 Q6 a

   b   Why did the Chinese money-lender glitter in the shop lights? [1]

   Cambridge O Level English Language 1123 paper 22 Q6 c

From paragraph 4

6 a   Peter was 'bewitched'. Pick out and write down the **single** word which continues the idea of 'bewitched'? [1]

   b   In what **two** ways did Marian try to indicate to Peter that he had already spent enough money that day? Number your answers (i) and (ii). [2]

   c   Peter was persuaded by the shop assistant to buy the Chinese money-lender because he was giving a good price and because whoever bought the Chinese money-lender would never have ill-fortune. Explain **in your own words** what these **two** reasons were. [2]

   Cambridge O Level English Language 1123 paper 22 Q7 a, b and c (adapted)

From paragraph 6

7 a   Peter quickly unpacked the Chinese money-lender. Explain fully the other ways in which his behaviour indicated the importance to him of the Chinese money-lender. [2]

   b   'But I can believe it'. What exactly did Peter believe? [1]

   Cambridge O Level English Language 1123 paper 22 Q9 a and b

From the whole passage

8 For each of the words below, tick the option (A, B, C or D) which has the same meaning that the word has in the passage

   i   plethora (paragraph 2): A variety B excess C range D multitude
   ii   wafting (paragraph 2): A flying B drifting C emerging D sailing
   iii intently (paragraph 3): A curiously B carefully C closely D cautiously
   iv   unique (paragraph 5): A single B special C solitary D exclusive
   v   mundane (paragraph 6): A ordinary B worldly C boring D daily [5]

Re-read the passage

9 Explain (i) what the following phrases tell us about what is happening and (ii) why it is happening.

   a   The young shop assistant, who, it seemed, had appeared out of nowhere [2]

   b   The Chinese money-lender cried out to Peter to become another purchase [2]

Answer key

All answers are written by the authors.

All answers are worth 1 mark unless otherwise stated

Chapter 11: Reading a variety of texts

Exercise 3

Fiction: 2, 4, 5, 6, 7, 9

Non-fiction: 1, 3, 8, 10

Chapter 12: Selecting content points in summary question

Exercise 4: Cafe India

She liked Cafe India because:

1 the coffee was perfect

2 the service was excellent

3 the familiarity was comforting

4 she could sit on the balcony and watch people in the street

5 she could meet friends

6 she could read novels

7 she could listen in to other people's conversations

Exercise 5: A Frightening Experience

The reasons why Salman was terrified:

1 the street lights had gone out/it was dark

2 the wind was howling

3 he was alone/the streets were deserted

4 he remembered a newspaper story about a robber on a nearby street

5 it might be later than he thought/his watch might have stopped and he would get a row at home

6 he heard footsteps behind him

7 which got louder and louder

Exercise 6: Anna

The reasons why Anna was troubled:

1   her relationship with Chris/her boyfriend had come to an end

2   Chris was going to Australia to study/she wouldn't see him for three years

3   his parents did not approve of Anna

4   her parents complained about him

5   and she avoided seeing her parents

6   her father had to have an operation

7   she had failed her driving test

Chapter 13: More exercises in summary content points

Exercise 2: The Lonely Lighthouse

The problems which alerted the crew to the fact that something was wrong:

1   There was no welcoming flag.

2   There was no reply to the ship's whistle.

3   There was no movement in or around the lighthouse.

4   There was no response to the rocket.

5   There was no response when the sailor called out their names.

6   The gate to the yard was closed.

7   And the door (of the lighthouse) was open.

8   There was no reply to the sailor's (further) shouts.

9   A chair toppled over (in the kitchen).

10 The ashes in the fireplace were cold/there had been no fire was a while.

11 The clock had stopped.

12 The beds were unmade/they had got up (and left) in a hurry.

13 There was dust on the lamp.

14 The record was incomplete/not done for several days.

15 There was still no trace of the keepers.

Exercise 3: School Uniform

The advantages of school uniform:

1   Uniform encourages a sense of belonging/makes students seem like a family.

2   No student is better than another.

3   All students look the same, which levels social groups.

4   Students concentrate on studies without worrying about fashion.

5   Fashion items are kept in good condition.

6   There are no worries about who is the most fashionable.

7   Students can be identified outside school.

8   Students won't misbehave/will behave well, otherwise they might be in trouble with the school, and/or with their parents.

9   Good behaviour advertises the school to parents.

10 Pupils want to go there/provides role models.

The disadvantages of school uniform:
11 But uniform suppresses individuality.

12 Uniforms gives more expense to families, especially poor families.

Exercise 4: Titanic
Contributing factors in the sinking of Titanic:
1   Not all reports of icebergs reached the control room

2   The captain took the risk of maintaining Titanic's speed

3   The captain did not wish to appear timid

4   The captain wanted to protect his (good) reputation

5   The lookouts weren't worried about icebergs

6   There were no extra lookouts

7   The engineers hadn't been told to stand by for emergency manoeuvres

8   The captain didn't think it was important to slow down (only if P2 is not made)

Exercise 5: Rickshaw Cyclists in Dhaka
Six ways in which rickshaw cyclists put themselves and others in danger:
1   they weave in and out of traffic

2   they cycle against the oncoming traffic

3   the bicycle tyres get dented

4   the wheels get scraped

5   cyclists don't wear helmets

6   passengers are not strapped in/have no safety belts

Exercise 6: Tourists in Sri Lanka
Six reasons why tourists come to Sri Lanka
1   the wonderful climate

2   the beauty of the island

3   the high standard of the hotels

4   the variety of shops

5   the variety of prices/everyone can shop there

6   the good food/the variety of food

Chapter 14: Writing summary content points: relevance and cohesion

Exercise 1: Punctuation

The moment had arrived. All those weeks of preparation had been moving them towards this day. It was a difficult syllabus but the class had had a good teacher. How happy they were about that! All the students filed into the examination hall with butterflies in their stomachs. Was there anyone who was not really nervous? What would the comprehension passage be about this year? Would it be narrative or discursive? Would it suit everyone? Everyone was silent. The papers were give out. They were thinking about what they had been taught about literal comprehension and inferential comprehension, not to forget, of course, the summary question, which carried half of the marks. Everyone started to read the passage but they could not believe their eyes. It was impossible to understand. There was no punctuation whatsoever!

Chapter 15: Writing summaries which are relevant and coherent

Exercise 2: Conjunction

1   Lucky was very tired because she had been studying sentence structure all day.

2   When Lucky got home, her mother was there to greet her.

3   Lucky ate her lunch and went straight to her room to study.

4   After Lucky revised that day's lesson on sentence structure, she felt very cheerful because she felt she understood how to use conjunctions.

Exercise 3: Relative Pronouns

1   Tulen was an English teacher who worked in a high school in Bangladesh.

2   Tulen taught English in a high school which had almost five hundred students.

3   Tulen met one of his former students whom had taught for three years of high school.

4   Tulen lived next door to Nath, whose son he had taught for two years of high school.

Exercise 4: Present Participles

Combine the following sentences by using present participles

1   Walking to school, Indrani met an old friend from high school.

2   Chatting together, they walked along the street.

3   Hearing that her friend was a teacher, she told her friend that she was a teacher too.

4   Smiling, her friend told Indrani that she had heard from many colleagues that Indrani was a wonderful teacher.

Chapter 16: More practice in writing coherent English

Exercise 1: The Lighthouse 1

The ship's crew noticed immediately that something was wrong because there were no welcoming flag flying from the lighthouse when the ship was near. A whistle and a rocket were used, but still there was no response from those lighthouse keepers. The gates that should have been open was closed and the door of the lighthouse was wide open. The fire had not being lit for some time. The last entry of the lighthouse record book was the fifteenth of December. This puzzled the searchers. The lamp was covered with dust, showing that it also had not been lit for some time, and the beds was unmade. Two of the three sets of waterproof clothing were missing from the cupboard. The grass along the edge of the cliff was torn away when they investigated outside the lighthouse. The railings around the platform where the crane stood were broken. A huge boulder which was part of the cliff had been moved a great distance down the staircase and was blocking it.

Exercise 2: The Lighthouse 2
The ship's crew noticed immediately that something was wrong because the welcoming flag should have been waving for their welcome. They thought that the keepers might be busy working out of sight. The whistle was blown to call the keepers but there was no response. The ship's captain ordered his crew to fire a rocket but it didn't make the keepers notice them. A small group of sailors was ordered to check the area. They found out that the warning lamp was in working order and, when they checked the record book, it haven't been filled in for eleven days. The sailors told their captain that they didn't find the keepers. The next day they searched the lighthouse and found out that two of the three sets of waterproof clothing were missing. The railing around the platform was broken and a huge boulder was moved down the stairway. There was no trace of the three keepers. All the crew of the ship thought there was a mystery.

Exercise 3: The Lighthouse 3
The ship's crew noticed immediately that something was wrong because there was no welcoming flag flying from the shore. The captain asked them to send a rocket over the island but still nothing was seen of the keepers. Some sailors were ordered to find out what had happened ashore. They started calling the keepers' names and there was no answer. The entrance gate were closed, but it should have been opened by the keepers as they were coming there. The main door was open and again they called the names of the keepers.

In the kitchen too, chairs stood next to the table and one of them was knocked over and lying on its side. The beds were unmade and it seemed that the occupants had just risen from them and left hurriedly. There was dust over the warning lamp. They found that two sets of waterproof clothing were missing and one still hung there. They also found that the grass had been torn away along the top edge of the cliff.

Exercise 4: The Threat to Coral Reefs 1
When hotel developers near coral reefs compete for land, they raise its price and as a result force local people to leave their homes. In fact, in some places, hotels have been built on burial sites on the coast. Little by little the construction of golf courses for tourists has proved fatal to coral reefs as the golf courses are treated by large amounts of water and also by fertilisers and pesticides, which contain deadly loads of waste materials and chemicals. Airport runways are built and their construction produces too much waste, which is sufficient to kill coral. Local people lack food, caused by the destruction of coral. The increase of pollution, noise, roads and the destruction of natural habitats of animals have been caused by the arrival of tourists. Sailing ships create severe damage on coral reefs with their heavy anchors. Coral continues to be damaged by submarines and diver also damage coral reefs considerably.

Exercise 5: The Threat to Coral Reefs 2
When hotel developers near coral reefs compete for land they force local people out of their homes. It is easy to understand the location of hotels in these magnificent areas but the way of life of the country is exploited to a great extent. Tourist attractions like golf courses deprive the local people of shorelines which are necessary for their way of life. Pollution is an important factor in the destruction of wonderful coastal areas. Pollutants are dumped on the coral reefs, which destroys life in the reefs. The rock from coral reefs has been used on a small scale to build houses but the rocks are now being excavated in large quantities for hotel development, yet again depriving the local people of their own houses. Lagoons are being dug deeper, affecting the area where fish breed, and the prices of popular fish has been raised so high that the people cannot afford them. Boats that carry people cause severe damage to reefs.

Exercise 6: The Threat to Coral Reefs 3

When hotel developers compete for land they force local people out of their homes. The country is frequently exploited for tourist entertainment. The construction of golf courses for tourists deprives local people of coastal areas. The water used by golf courses drains out on the coral reefs and carries a deadly load of chemicals. Airports are built along the coast on coral reefs. Their construction produces large quantities of waste. Rock from coral reef is taken in uncontrolled quantities to built tourist hotels, thus depriving local people of building material. Pleasure boats destroy the areas where fish breed, depriving local people of food. Some fish are too expensive because they can only be afforded by tourists. Villages are destroyed by pollution created by tourists. Huge jetties and docks are built over coral reefs. Hotels often lack proper sewage facilities. Boats carry people to dive. These boats increase the destruction of coral. Everyday boats send their anchors crashing down on reefs.

Chapter 18: Analysing, evaluating and developing facts, ideas and opinion

Exercise 2: Facts and Opinions

1 Fact	4 Fact	7 Fact	10 Opinion
2 Fact	5 Opinion	8 Fact	
3 Opinion	6 Opinion	9 Opinion	

Exercise 3: More Facts and Opinions

Facts

There are no security checks on trains.

From a train you can see rural scenes/villagers tending animals/villagers gathering crops. More trains have air conditioning.

Opinions

Everybody likes travelling by train. Security checks are stressful.

There is nothing nicer than zipping through the countryside on a train. Air conditioning makes train travel comfortable.

Exercise 4: More Facts and Opinions

Facts

Some people think that television was the best invention of the twentieth century.

Too much lounging in front of 'the box' as it is called, takes people away from other pursuits.

Opinions

Watching television is a great way to relax.

People who watch too much television are boring individuals.

Exercise 6: Sport and Study

2   The writer thinks that sport is just as important as studying.

Exercise 7: Pakistan

3   The writer prefers the bazaars of Pakistan.

Chapter 19: Exercises in fact gathering from short texts

Exercise 1: Joseph and Rohit

1   Joseph intimidated him and got better marks than he did

2   pleased

3   he liked him

4   he was good company/had quirky sense of humour/was thoughtful/kindhearted

5   he was clever

Exercise 2: Anna

1   the bus was crowded when it arrived

2   the market

3   the stall selling clothing material

4   dress for herself or shirt for father

5   the caves (near the market)

6   no, she was not allowed

Exercise 3: Modern Travel

1   ordinary people can travel more

2   shorter working week

3   they can travel further

4   they cut back on extra services

5   affluence/money

6   travel

Exercise 4: A Bad Day

1   his alarm didn't ring/the battery in his alarm needed replaced

2   pack his bag the night before/leave an organised bag at the front door

3   school bus

4   he missed the bus

5   he was hungry

6   it was not appropriate for a boy of his age

Exercise 5: The Intruder

1   break into/rob a house

2   so that he wouldn't later be identified

3   dressed in a nondescript way/wore a baseball cap over his eyes

4   it was a deserted part of town

5   four

6   the owner/husband/father

7   Tuesday

8   a bag of tools

Chapter 20: More about fact gathering questions

Exercise 1: Literal and Inferential Questions

Literal: 1, 2, 4, 7, 9

Inferential: 3, 5, 6, 8, 10

Exercise 2: City Life

1   Advantages: access to work/services/education/entertainment/friends (any for 1 mark)

    Disadvantages: traffic/cost of living/crime (any for 1 mark)

2   difference in property values/deterioration in public services

Exercise 3: Classroom Computers

1   deterioration in educational standards

2   computers

3   computers will become a substitute for teachers

4   it brings together the best work of teachers and students

Exercise 4: Inferential Questions

1   there would be fewer people to pay for services

2   kids: young people having fun (round a computer) [1]

    students: young people taking education seriously/receiving good education [1]

Exercise 6: Exploring a Cave

1   the damp/dusty smell

2   (light casts) eerie/frightening shadows on the wall

3   he wouldn't see the roof [1] and he would bang his head [1]

4   pain in the knees

5   getting to the end [1] and getting back [1]

6   he would be tired

7   rocks could hurt his feet [1] and he could walk into pools of water [1]

Chapter 21: More exercises in literal and inferential comprehension

Exercise 1: Julia

1   late childbirth [1]/trying to please her husband [1]

2   fifteen

3   he tried to make her departure unpleasant

4   she had a scholarship

5   she could never face living with another man

6   she had taken her for granted [1]/she had not treated her as well as she might [1]

7   without thinking things through

8   because she had learned to love someone else

9   you don't know you're lonely

10 the stress Julia's loneliness

Exercise 2: Selling the Flat

1   sell her flat

2   he invited her in [1]/gestured hospitably [1]/made her teas [1]

3   garden looks seedy

4   the turf was parched

5   the ducks were bedraggled

6   the sum Mr Akbar was offering was low

7   ask for more/tell him he wasn't offering enough

8   Mr Akbar's eyes were pleading

9   she had bought the flat for a good price

10 it had been Mr Akbar's suggestion to buy the flat [1]/Mr Akbar didn't look wealthy [1]

Exercise 3: Anna's Journey

1   weep/cry/burst into tears

2   i   she was in a state of great anxiety/she was nervous/anxious/in a panic

     ii   her bag was overloaded/she had too much in her bag

3   i   kind/understanding/patient/helpful

     ii   disdainful/disapproving

4   she had come straight from the airport/she had not been delayed and so there had not been enough time for her bag to have been delivered

5   i   people are always in a hurry

     ii   people don't care/look out for one another

6   cars/they were inching along the road/traffic was slow moving

7   her bag might be stolen/there might be thieves

8   i   her luggage has arrived

     ii   she was beginning to settle down

Chapter 22: Selecting and retrieving information by lifting

Exercise 1: Coral Reefs

1   It is beautiful/teeming with life/set among a rich and random pattern of colours.

2   Coral reefs are second only to rain forests in the huge number of plants and animals they support.

3   Just as forest plants have been used for hundreds of years for medicinal purposes by people living in the rain forests, so some reef plants and animal have been used by people in coastal communities to help cure diseases like malaria.

Exercise 2: Grandfather

1 he read her stories

2 his voice was gruff

3 his skin was wrinkly (and she liked to trace with her eye particular lines as they meandered from one side of his face to the other)

4 she had to sit very still as his clothes were scratchy and made her legs red if she move too much

Exercise 3: Friendship with Jennifer

1 spending a day with an old friend

2 first day at primary school

3 local youth club/walked/talked/went shopping

4 it made her reflect on the nature of real friendship – having someone value you for what you are.

Exercise 4: Chris

1 his friend was a doctor

2 his build was neither slim nor athletic

3 he had committed himself to raising money for charity

4 running on the pavements around his home [1]/he sweated on the treadmill in his local gym [1]

5 he had had a great tour of London

Chapter 23: More exercises in lifting

Exercise 1: Grandfather's Study

1 In Grandfather's study, mounted butterflies and moths had disintegrated into small heaps of iridescent dust that powdered the bottom of their glass display cases)

2 glass display cases

3 the room was rank with fungus and disease/dirty glass panes/dust on the floor

4 the floor

5 dragged to the bookshelf

6 dragged to the table and lifted on to it

7 the leather binding had lifted off each book and buckled (like corrugated asbestos) [1]

   insects tunnelled through the pages (burrowing arbitrarily from species to species, turning organised information into yellow lace) [1]

8 Rahel groped behind the row of books

9 (they were) behind the books

10 (they were) wrapped in clear plastic and stuck with sellotape

Exercise 2: The Brazilian Rain Forest

1 The skies of Western Brazil grow dark by day (as well as by night).

2 To clear land for crop growing and cattle rearing.

3 They burn down vast areas.

4 Scientists see this great annual destruction as a major peril for Brazil [1] and also for the rest of the world [1].

5 Politicians have joined scientists to try to stop the foolish waste of the precious resources of the planet.

6 No, because for more than four hundred years settlers and farmers have been attacking Brazil's forests.

7 The feature is that the jungles are seemingly indestructible, and the evidence he gives is that their power of recovery defeated their efforts.

8 Areas larger than some whole countries have been permanently stripped bare.

9 They cut down trees.

10 The forests contain an astonishing variety of animal and plant life which is slowly, but surely disappearing.

Exercise 3: Estha and Rahel

1 to hospital (in Shillong)

2 they flagged down a (crowded State Transport) bus

3 the passengers were poor and the parents were rich

4 they saw how hugely pregnant Ammu was

5 to prevent it from wobbling

6 they'd have got free bus rides for the rest of their lives.

7 it wasn't clear where he's got this information from

8 for having diddled them out of a lifetime of free bus rides.

9 the Government would pay for their funerals

10 there were no zebra crossings to get killed on in Ayamenem

Exercise 4: The Domestication of Animals

1 they have been domesticated

2 so that her milk can be used for human consumption.

3 they must be able to find food for themselves

4 they must breed freely in captivity

5 i food

 ii clothing

 iii transport

6 (It could have come) naturally from Man's experience as a nomadic hunter

7 i low-growing plants appeared then

  ii grass

8 there was wild game in abundance

9 as he followed his prey on their yearly migrations he gradually began to influence their movements and behaviour

10 they could more easily be rounded up and some of them slaughtered

11 they were encouraged to become part of the community/pets

Chapter 24: Answering in your own words
Exercise 1
1 HORRIFIED: shocked DEVASTATION: destruction

2 CRAWLED: moved slowly (smoke) BILLOWED: blew

3 DETERIORATION: worsening LITERACY: reading and writing

4 IN PROFUSION: plentifully COILED: wound

5 DISREGARDED: ignored VIEWS: opinions

6 INEVITABLE: unavoidable DESTRUCTION: wasting

7 MOUNTING: increasing ASTONISHMENT: surprise

8 EXHILERATING: exciting TERRIFYING: very frightening

9 MANUFACTURE (tool): make ADORN: decorate

10 INITIATED: begun SUPERVISED: guided

Exercise 2
1 INQUISITIVE: curious (not) UNFRIGHTENED: not afraid

2 IMMOBILITY: (they did) not move

Exercise 3
1 UNCONVINCING: difficult to believe SPECULATION: guessing

2 CONCLUSIVELY: finally SOLVED: worked out

3 LESS FANCIFUL: not so [1] imaginative [1]

4 REPAIR: put right DEVASTATION: destruction INCLEMENT: bad

Exercise 4
1 GREATER: more VARIETY: different types

2 LABOUR: work EXTRACT: get out

3 DEFIED IMITATION: could not be [1] copied [1]

4 INCREASINGLY (large): growing QUANTITIES: amounts

5 VALUE: worth DIMINISHED: grew smaller

Chapter 25: More exercises in own words questions

Exercise 1: Man and Animals

1 STRENGTH: power SPEED: swiftness SUPERIOR: better (than others)

2 RELATIONSHIP: involvement MUTUAL: with each other AFFECTION: love

Exercise 2: The Ruined Books

1 LIFTED: separated BUCKLED: twisted

2 BURROWING: going underneath ARBITRARILY: without a plan

Exercise 3: Forest Destruction

1 SEEMINGLY: appears to be INDESTRUCTIBLE: unbreakable

2 PERMANENTLY: for ever STRIPPED: deprived BARE: of everything

3 ASTONISHING: amazing VARIETY: different types of

Exercise 4: How Animals Became Pets

1 ACCEPT: tolerate CONFINEMENT: restriction CONTROL: not having freedom

2 INFLUENCE: affect MOVEMENTS: where they could go BEHAVIOUR: what they did

3 PREDATOR: hunter PET: domestic animal

Exercise 5: Sharing the Earth

1 RAPID: quick DISAPPEARANCE: removal SPECIES: types

2 RUTHLESS: cruel EXPLOITATION: taking advantage of

3 CONFLICTING: opposing ATTITUDES: outlooks

Exercise 6: Venice

1 PERIL: danger FULLY: completely REALISED: known

2 ENDLESS: (seemed to be) for ever CONFERENCES: meetings TOURS: rounds INSPECTIONS: viewings

3 (not) IMPLEMENTED: (not) put into effect

4 (governments) ROSE: were appointed (and) FELL: were voted out

5 FORMED: made (and) DISBANDED: separated

6 MADE: put forward RECOMMENDATIONS: suggestions

7 NOT PREPARED: unwilling RESPONSIBILITY: to be the leader DECISIONS: plans of action

8 CONSERVE: keep GLORIES: treasures/wonders PAST: former times

Chapter 26: Combining Information

Exercise 3: The Storm

1 i   they smashed free blocks of marble and

   ii   flung them aside like pebbles

Exercise 4: After the Storm

1 (i) the wind (had) dropped; (ii) no third high tide (had) entered the lake

Exercise 5: Protection of the Environment

1 i they will not succeed

   ii wealth of expertise (in living memory) will be lost

Exercise 6: Coral Animals

1 i they are responsible for creating the largest structures made by life on earth

   ii (and yet) they are small

Exercise 7: Jasmine

1 i her mother phoned

   ii an accident on the motorway

2 i her mother picked an inconvenient time to phone

   ii she never forgot her father's birthday

Exercise 8: Ayesha visits a friend

1 i Rama has just had major surgery

   ii Rama and Ayesha were close friends

Exercise 9: Joseph and Benjamin

1 i The bond between them led to a perfect understanding of each other's moves

   ii They had done a lot of training

2 i Their grandparents came to matches to cheer them on

   ii Their parents bought them the best of sportswear

Chapter 27: More exercises in combining questions

Exercise 1: The Great Wall of China

1 i attacked them

   ii built barriers

2 i soldiers

   ii ocal peasants

   iii convicted criminals

Exercise 2: Building the Great Wall

1 i long walks on narrow mountain trails

   ii colliding with one another

2 i they carried bricks or stones up the mountain

   ii in baskets on their backs

Exercise 3: The Destroyed Novel

1 i she had been working for some time

   ii she couldn't see Octavia

   iii Octavia was destructive

2 i she must have left the door open

   ii Lydia's room was always full of nasty objects

3   i   she tore out the pages

     ii   and threw them around

    iii and chewed them

Exercise 4 : Fatima's Favourite Subject

1   i   she was a keen reader

     ii   her favourite subject at school was literature

    iii she had read this novel over and over again

2   i   she finished reading it within a week

     ii   she read it several times

3   i   there was a limited number of spaces (in the class)

     ii   one of the teachers retired

4   i   she acted out key scenes

     ii   she pretended to be the central character

Chapter 28: Quotation questions and vocabulary questions

Exercise 1: The Rain Forests

1   keenly aware

2   foolish

Exercise 2: Climate Change

1   accelerates

2   blazing torches

Exercise 3: Amy

1   uneasiness

2   grimy

Exercise 4: After the Show

1   stuttering

2   i   stumbling

     ii   blundering

Exercise 6: Benjamin

i   sometimes

ii   refused

Exercise 7: Sophie

i   full

ii   afraid

iii exciting

Exercise 8: World Food Shortage

i   surprising

ii   lack

iii result

iv increase

Chapter 29: Appreciating the way writers make use of language

Exercise 4: The Flood

1 to give the idea of devastation/destruction

2 the movement of the flames

3 candles are pretty/gentle/attractive [1] but the situation is serious/ugly/sad/bad [1]

Exercise 5: The Kitchen Table

1 it was like an injury/deep/destructive

2 the shape (veins)/long and thin [1] continues the 'scar' idea/table like a person/ personification

3 different colours/patterns

Exercise 6: The Market in Mumbai

1 he wandered/had no fixed aim/was relaxed [any two for 1 mark each]

2 he was relaxed/felt he had plenty of time

Exercise 7: Spring

1 change from the unpleasant winter [1] to pleasant spring [1] (is like going from unpleasant, difficult terrain to pleasant, fertile land

2 fertility/plenty of growth/new life

3 a covering (as a carpet covers a floor)

Exercise 8: The New School

1 long queues (of girls) not a straight line/curved line

2 it was strange to them [1] they were going to find out about it [1]

3 to show how many there seemed to be/to show how crowded it was/how over whelmed she felt

Chapter 30: More exercises in appreciating writers' craft

Exercise 1: The Gardener

1 he was straining/it took a lot of effort/he didn't want to do it

2 he doesn't want to do the work/he grudges the effort [1] in the same way as a miser doesn't want to part with his money

3 he seems programmed to do the work/he does it automatically [1] he is not like a human being [1]

Exercise 2: The Well-dressed Lady

1 she looks as if she hasn't thought about how she looks/looks as though she is dressed casually/looks relaxed [1] but she has worked hard to create the look/it didn't come naturally/easily [1]

2 the sound is short/artificial/she doesn't really find it funny she is cynical/it isn't really humour (Any two for 1 mark each)

Exercise 3: The Traveller

1 as if the jungle was wrapped around the path/connotations of death

2 it had been easy/he had not been climbing

Exercise 4: Cell Phones

1 (they seem to) keep people alive/save them (from burdens/troubles)

2 we can be restored/refreshed/relax/take time out [1] by getting into a different/better place/situation (with our cell phone) [1]

3 desert

4 (cell phones) hurt/destroy/hip (society) [1]

5 cell phones [1] are precious/valuable [1]

Exercise 5: Nizam and Hemu

1 they shaped them (through their teaching) [1] students did not resist/were anxious to learn/it was not hard to influence them [1]

2 moulded

3 love/skill/knowledge (of English/literature)

4 they rushed/were eager/anxious to get to class

Exercise 6: Calling the doctor

1 i The mother is timid/shy/doesn't like to push herself forward [1]

 ii *'if only'* suggests she has never been daring/never pushed herself forward/suggests <u>how much she wants to assert herself</u> [1]

2 i The mother is clever/perceptive/sensitive. [1]

 ii The reader wonders what information the doctor is hiding/expects something bad to happen. [1]

3 i The mother finds it hard to cope with bad news/avoids difficult problems. [1]

 ii The reader wants to know what is wrong with the baby. [1]

Practice in Reading

Passage 1: Time for Tea

1 a *Reasons for the initial popularity of tea and the spread of tea drinking.*
 1 It was used as a medicine.

 2 Myths about origins of tea (increased its popularity).

 3 Drunk as a stimulant/restorative.

 4 Tea bricks made it easier to trade/transport.

 5 Lu Yu's book *'The Tea Classic'*.

 6 Tea spread to Japan/became accessible to people in Japan/was drunk by aristocracy in Japan.

 7 Religious significance of tea in Japan (increased popularity).

 8 Spread to other Eastern/Asian countries/Vietnam/Korea/Taiwan.

 9 Dutch brought tea to the West/Dutch imported tea.

 10 In Britain, trade was encouraged (so that ships didn't return empty)/campaign in Britain.

Reasons for the continuing popularity of tea

11 Tea plants' ability to replenish themselves makes it plentiful/easily available/cheaper.

12 Variety of tea/tea such as vanilla and caramel achieved through absorption of flavours/aromas.

13 Blending produced better taste/lower prices.

14 Tea bags reduce time.

15 Tea bags reduce cost/are cheaper.

16 Tea is a stimulant (but only award if P3 is not scored).

17 Tea/making tea calms/soothes/relaxes (people) (link to caffeine spoils).

2 One opinion is tea is delicious. [1]

Another opinion is there's no better pick-me-up than a good cup of tea. [1]

Another opinion is 'The Tea Classic' is fascinating. [1]

Passage 2: The Chinese Money-Lender

3 a (they had been) worried/concerned/upset/anxious [1]

Lift, in whole or in part, of 'Peter and his wife…his intention to emigrate' [1]

b unsurpassed = unbeaten/unrivalled; couldn't be bettered/beaten/improved; better than anywhere else [1]

No marks for: good/amazing

Employment opportunities = chances of (getting) work/a job [1]

c (there were) new cafes/restaurants/eating places [1]

Lift: 'new cafes and restaurants were springing up all around' [1]

No marks for: any reference to accommodation/public transport

4 a They had already done <u>a lot</u> of shopping there; they had visited the market/it <u>many times</u> before. [1]

b Answer can focus on either the tortoise or the stallholder.

The tortoise wasn't made of jade; was a fake/phoney/a trick/con [1]

OR the stallholder was lying/exaggerating/saying anything that would get a sale/a conman/trickster [1]

5 a The inscriptions on: it/the front/the base/him were: indecipherable/couldn't be read/worked out/fathomed [1]

No marks for: blurred/unclear/difficult/strange

Lift, in whole or in part of 'Closer inspection… inscriptions' [1]

No marks for reference to: glint of metal/three inches high/being seated/moneybag/abacus.

b it/he was made of gold/was gilt/gilded/golden [1]

No marks for mere synonyms for 'glitter' e.g. shiny/sparkling/twinkling

6 a   spell   [1]

    b   i   she furrowed her brow/frowned   [1]

                Lift of line 'her furrowed brow'   [1]

                No marks for: Grimaced/pulled a face

        ii   she <u>told/warned</u> him it was time (to go) for lunch   [1]

                Lift of 'Peter, it's time… warned Marian'   [1]

    c   Fair = reasonable/just/not excessive/good (sic)/without exploitation   [1]

         Ill-Fortune = bad luck/be unlucky; would have good luck/be lucky   [1]

         No marks for: rich/poor

7 a   A. he <u>tenderly/carefully</u> positioned him/it on a shelf   [1]

         Lift of 'Peter, with the utmost care… on a shelf'   [1]

         B. he adjusted: the position/him/it <u>many/several</u> times/kept adjusting the
         position/him/it   [1]

         No marks for: lift of 'Peter adjusted…by a fraction of an inch.' The answer must be
         distilled.

    b   The (Chinese) money- lender had brought Marian/them good luck; had caused
         Marian/her to win the competition   [1]

8   i   multitude

    ii   drifting

   iii   closely

   iv   exclusive

    v   ordinary   [5]

9 a   The shop assistant/he came quickly/immediately   [1]

         So that he could make a sale   [1]

    b   Peter wants to/will buy the Chinese money- lender   [1]

         Because it is very attractive (to him)   [1]

Index